Smack

POLITICS AND CULTURE IN MODERN
AMERICA

SERIES EDITORS

Glenda Gilmore, Michael Kazin, and Thomas J.
Sugrue

Volumes in the series narrate and analyze political and
social change in the broadest dimensions from 1865 to
the present, including ideas about the ways people have
sought and wielded power in the public sphere and the
language and institutions of politics at all levels—local,
national, and transnational. The series is motivated by
a desire to reverse the fragmentation of modern U.S.
history and to encourage synthetic perspectives on
social movements and the state, on gender, race, and
labor, and on intellectual history and popular culture.

Smack

Heroin and the
American City

Eric C. Schneider

PENN

UNIVERSITY OF PENNSYLVANIA PRESS

PHILADELPHIA

Published by
University of Pennsylvania Press
Philadelphia, Pennsylvania 19104-4112

Printed in the United States of America on acid-free paper
10 9 8 7 6 5 4 3 2 1

Library of Congress Cataloging-in-Publication Data

Schneider, Eric C.
   Smack: heroin and the American city / Eric C. Schneider.
      p. cm. — (Politics and culture in modern America)
   Includes bibliographical references and index.
   ISBN 978-0-8122-4116-7 (alk. paper)
1. Heroin abuse—United States—History. 2. Minorities—Substance use—United States—History.   3. Drug traffic—United States—History.   4. Drug control—United States—History. I. Title.
   HV5822.H4S36 2008
   362.29'320973—dc22   2008007790

For Janet Golden

CONTENTS

INTRODUCTION: REQUIEM FOR THE CITY

HEROIN WAS A city-killing drug, and in the early 1970s the American city appeared to be on its way to the morgue. Abandoned and burned-out buildings, which addicts had converted into places to sell and shoot heroin, scarred some urban neighborhoods. Urban residents worried about burglaries and muggings as crime rates soared. In New York City, addicts stole an estimated $1.5 billion each year, and street crime threatened to make life there untenable. Stewart Alsop, a *Newsweek* columnist and long-time New York journalist, believed he felt the dying pulse of a once-great city, arguing that New York was becoming a place inhabited only by the desperate and the well guarded as others packed their bags to leave.[1]

New York City did have more addicts, more crime, and more disorder than any other major American city, but it shared its death struggle with all of them. They too suffered from declining population, job loss, and a rising crime rate. The urban crisis of the late twentieth century was rooted in numerous decisions made over the previous twenty-five years: by residents choosing to abandon old neighborhoods in the face of new migrants, by bankers deciding to withdraw capital from the urban core and invest it in the periphery, by politicians and government officials inaugurating federal programs that created a white, suburban middle class while reinforcing urban apartheid, and by businessmen moving jobs out of the city, to the South and to the West, and eventually out of the country altogether. Urban decline was visible in its effects, however, not its causes, and the most visible form of decline, its human face and literal embodiment, was found in the stereotypically grim features of the heroin addict.

Stewart Alsop described those features as African American. He recounted a visit to a heroin selling spot on the West Side of Manhattan where everyone from the pusher in a limousine to the doorkeeper at the front of the building and the addicts inside were black. Only the building manager and the policeman accompanying Alsop were white. Alsop conflated addiction, crime, and color, as did many other Americans, and he invited his readers to ascribe the city's death knell to them.

Although Alsop's writing was sensationalistic, what he reported was plainly visible in any number of urban neighborhoods, and his columns contained more than a kernel of truth. The majority of known heroin users were African American and Latino, with proportions varying in different parts of the United States. According to federal authorities, approximately half of the nation's heroin addicts lived in New York City, and African Americans and Puerto Ricans comprised about three-quarters of the city's users. A tidal wave of heroin addiction had swept through the inner city in the late 1960s, and those heroin users engaged in an inordinate amount of street crime that threatened the life of the city.

President Richard Nixon also pointed to heroin users when he declared the first war on drugs. Drug abuse, he asserted, had grown from a local police matter to "a serious national threat to the personal health and safety of millions of Americans."[2] The President returned again and again to this theme when reviewing the state of the union over the next several years, calling drug abuse "America's public enemy number one" against which the government and its citizens had to wage an "all-out offensive." While Nixon rarely distinguished among drugs, he was most adamant about heroin because of its widespread use and its relationship to crime. Nixon concluded, "if we cannot destroy the drug menace in America, then it will surely in time destroy us." Nothing less than a "total war" would do.[3]

From our perspective, President Nixon's rhetoric appears overblown, the concern for the death of the city exaggerated, and the conflation of addiction, race, and crime, verging dangerously close to racism and at best offering only a partial explanation for urban decline. But considering the climate of the 1970s, the claims are more understandable. American cities seemed to have reached their nadir, with declining tax revenues, collapsing school systems, and the steady increase in the sort of street crime—muggings especially—that eroded public confidence and undermined the possibility of civic life. The existence of open-air drug markets and increasing narcotics experimentation, even among middle-class youth, easily justified declaring heroin "public enemy number one."

Even though our perceptions of cities have changed, both the war on drugs and our understanding of heroin are rooted in the urban crisis of the 1970s. We have an intuitive sense of the destructiveness of heroin use, but little understanding of how cities controlled the heroin trade and how urban environments shaped the experience of becoming a heroin user. Instead of focusing on those urban environments—the "social setting" (a concept I will define more carefully below)—that continuously produced heroin use, public policy has focused on the individual drug user and has increasingly emphasized arrests and incarceration. Not surprisingly, this policy has failed. I would like to reverse the cause and effect that has located urban decline in the rise of heroin addiction and has seen the solution in arresting drug users. I will instead analyze the interaction between social setting and heroin use, show how they evolved over time, and argue for an urban-centered approach to the heroin problem.

I began this book because I was astounded at the toll heroin took on inner-city communities. While interviewing former street gang members for a previous book, I was told repeatedly that a third or more of their acquaintances had died or had been imprisoned as young men, not because of gang conflict, but on account of heroin. It became clear to me that heroin use was highly "spatialized"—concentrated within specific populations and located in specific areas of the city. Understanding who used heroin, who became addicted to it, how it affected their lives and the life of the city around them, what changed over time and what did not, seemed important—indeed essential—for understanding both heroin and the American city in the second half of the twentieth century.

The book is thus driven by four interrelated questions. First, what was "urban" about heroin use? With the concentration of heroin users in New York and a number of other major cities, especially in the two decades after World War II, the problem of heroin use seems obviously urban. What is the relationship between the urban environment and heroin use? How did the city "produce" heroin users? Second, what was the impact on the city, especially New York, of having such a large number of heroin users residing there? Clearly there was a relationship between heroin and the crime rate, but both heroin use and crime were concentrated within specific communities. How did those communities respond to the waves of heroin use that engulfed them? Third, how do we understand the shifting ethnic dimensions of heroin use? Before World War II, the average heroin user was an aging, white, working-class male but immediately after the war, this changed completely. How did heroin become primarily an African American and Latino drug in the postwar years and what were the sources of this change? And why did young whites begin to use the drug again in larger numbers in the 1960s and 1970s?

Fourth, how did heroin—a product made from morphine that was itself manufactured from opium poppies grown outside the United States—move from international into national, regional, and local marketplaces? In other words, how do we understand the narcotics market? How did the market work and how was it regulated?

In order to answer these questions, I employ geographic concepts of concentration, centralization, and marginality. Social and economic marginalization linked the less developed with the developed world, and those who grew opium poppies with those who consumed them in the form of heroin. While my focus is on the consumers, it is impossible to write about heroin consumption without analyzing the shifting sources of supply. Curtailing the cultivation of opium poppies in one part of the globe led to the rapid emergence of new suppliers in other, equally marginal, areas ready to satisfy the demand in the United States. That demand concentrated in cities, especially New York, but including Chicago, Detroit, Philadelphia, and Los Angeles, which organized the international trade in heroin through the size of their heroin-using populations. The migration of African Americans and Latinos to these cities after the war provided spatially concentrated, centralized, and marginalized people—the perfect market for heroin entrepreneurs because of their spatial and social location. In turn, the concentrated population of users demarcated certain areas in inner-city neighborhoods as specialized drug retailing areas that served as "central places"—sites to purchase and consume heroin—for drug users from the entire metropolitan area. Just as readily identifiable districts for services such as entertainment, wholesaling, and banking evolved over time, so too did specialized heroin marketplaces.

The emergence of heroin marketplaces contributed to the persistence of drug use and to its concentration in specific urban neighborhoods. Individuals, usually adolescents, who wanted to start using narcotics had to acquire "drug knowledge," learning where and how to purchase the drug, how to prepare it for use, what amount to ingest, and how to interpret the body's reaction to heroin (which for some first-time users included intense bouts of vomiting) as pleasurable.[4] Adolescents living in or near heroin retailing sites did not have to search for knowledge about drugs; rather the experience of heroin use was immediately available to them—indeed it was unavoidable— thus facilitating the creation of a new cohort of users and sellers.

Heroin use depended upon social setting, which usually is interpreted in sociological terms and includes the rituals surrounding drug use and the immediate physical setting in which drugs are used.[5] I would like to broaden the concept of social setting to include spatial location. Specific social groups, such as jazz musicians, punk rockers, and inner city hustlers were identified with heroin and inhabited subcultures that supported its use. I argue that these subcultures were spatial as well as sociological entities and that these groups depended on the development not only of spaces, such as clubs, bars, or pool halls that fostered heroin use, but also of a larger urban environment in which these spaces existed. The combination of the social and the spatial is essential to understanding what is urban about heroin use, and it is what I mean when I use the term "social setting."

This book reflects my belief in the power of the spatial to shape human actions. The neighborhoods in which city residents live are the physical expressions of social relations, the reflection of economic decisions made about the investment or withdrawal of capital, social decisions made about the clustering of racial and income groups, and political decisions made about the provision of social services. This combination of physical environment and social effects has a profound influence over the decisions and actions of area residents, including the decision to use heroin.

It is this emphasis on and exploration of the spatial dimension of heroin use—the marketing of heroin through a hierarchy of cities, the location of retail markets in inner-city neighborhoods, the concentration of heroin users in these neighborhoods, the creation of landscapes that supported the heroin trade, the interaction between economic and social disadvantage that occurred in these areas—that is the unique contribution of this book. Other works have examined the rise of regulatory regimes and the development of policy on a national and international level.[6] Still others have emphasized the medical context of drug use, the rise and fall of "medical addiction," and the scientific research done on opiate and other addictions.[7] There are accounts of treatment and recovery, federal policing, the political uses to which addicts have been put, and general histories of drug use.[8] Social scientists, generally in the 1950s and 1960s, analyzed the relationship between social disadvantage and heroin, but they did not examine how heroin users and their social settings changed over time.[9] I am indebted to this scholarship, which has influenced my work throughout, but I am interested in other questions, and my focus differs in a significant way. To the degree that others have considered the city, it is generally only a backdrop against which events occurred, rather than a primary shaper of those events. Mine is an urban history of heroin in which I see cities as the organizers of the world opiate market, I find the origins of heroin use in the interaction between the individual and the urban environment, and I trace the evolution of both of those phenomena over time.

I focus on the years between 1940 and 1985 since that is when heroin became a major social problem in the United States and it is a period that has been neglected by other historians. Three separate waves of heroin use emerged during this period, with reverberations that are still being felt in the American city. The first wave arose immediately after World War II. The war had disrupted international trafficking and the military had absorbed potential heroin users into service, with the result that heroin use hit an all-time low during the 1940s. The prewar generation of heroin users was declining in number and, taken together with the disruption of supply and the absence of new initiators, a reasonable observer might well have predicted that the opiate problem was about to disappear from the national scene. However, the expansion of opium-growing in Mexico, the reconstitution of trading routes following the war, and the migration of African Americans and Latinos to a segregated city reestablished both supply and potential demand. African American and Latino adolescents, who began using heroin between the end of the war and the early 1950s, formed what I refer to as the first wave of heroin use. Although white, middle-class youngsters were the least likely to experiment with the drug, they became the focus of the moral panic of the 1950s, and this moral panic resulted in stiffer penalties for heroin trading and greater power for the Federal Bureau of Narcotics, the principal antidrug trafficking agency. The consequences of enlarged federal authority and tougher sentencing were borne by African American and Latino users.[10]

The second wave of heroin use began among African Americans and Latinos in the early to mid-1960s as the baby boom began reaching its teenaged years, only this surge included a number of young whites as well. The explosion in the crime rate that accompanied the increase in heroin use provoked two contradictory responses. On the state level, New York initiated a trend soon followed by others toward longer jail sentences and harsher treatment of users, while at the national level, the federal government dramatically increased funding for treatment. The use of heroin by American soldiers in Vietnam was especially troubling to the Nixon administration, since it threatened not only the war effort but also attempts to curb crime and drug abuse domestically as addicted veterans returned home. In response, the President proclaimed a war on drugs, instituted drug testing for returning servicemen, persuaded Turkey to curb poppy cultivation, and most importantly, expanded treatment options, including federal support for the methadone program. Although these measures seemed to solve the heroin crisis in the early 1970s, drug trading was firmly entrenched in city neighborhoods, and by mid-decade a third wave of heroin use began to swell as other sources for heroin emerged. I end my study in 1985 because there was a decline in the number of heroin initiators in the early 1980s as new drugs—cocaine and crack—gained in popularity, as other cities challenged New York's dominance of the drug trade, and as the criminal justice approach to drug use became firmly entrenched in public policy.

A word about terminology is in order. I have tried to avoid using the term "addict" unless a person self-identified as one or I am reporting someone else's words or position, as with Stewart Alsop. This is not to deny the reality of addiction, to downplay the dangers of heroin use, or to denigrate the struggles of the addicted to become and remain "clean." Rather it reflects more accurately variations in heroin use. Many regular users of heroin distinguished between themselves and "addicts" or "junkies," a status that implied a loss of control over drug taking. In addition, weekend users, occasional experimenters, and people who gave up use of the drug for some period of time before returning to it, all had a status other than "addict." Therefore the term "heroin user" is a more accurate characterization of the population. Many users (including the vast majority of U.S. servicemen who ingested very potent heroin in Southeast Asia) were able to give up the drug with a change in their social setting. Addiction was a risk—in fact, it was part of heroin's allure—but, despite popular opinion, addiction was not inevitable.

The language of war and disease has dominated the discussion of drug use in our society, with unfortunate consequences. A "war on drugs" may allow a political leader to mobilize scarce resources in response to a national emergency, but it leads eventually to their misapplication. Metaphors of war demand the identification of enemies, encourage the search for foreign threats, and lead to a self-perpetuating militarization of domestic and foreign policy. Crop eradication, military interdiction, and ever-growing levels of domestic incarceration have all followed logically from a war on drugs, but one can question if they have brought us any closer to ending drug abuse. With only vaguely identified enemies and unclear goals, is it ever possible to declare victory in a metaphorical war? We have become the unfortunate prisoners of our rhetoric, unable to signal a change of course without conceding defeat in a war that successive administrations have declared central to the national interest.

If military metaphors are problematical, so too are medical ones. The term "heroin epidemic" that dominates the literature obscures as much as it reveals. It describes a level of crisis that, like the "war on drugs," is useful for mobilizing attention and resources, and it suggests that nonmilitary measures need to be undertaken in order to prevent the further spread of the "disease." And to be sure, drug knowledge spread from person to person and heroin use was concentrated both spatially and socially in specific populations, as epidemics frequently are. But to discuss heroin use as a disease still focuses on symptoms and leads to the search for a medical solution, a magic bullet or a physical "cure," for what I believe is a more complex and ultimately social and political problem. Finally, historians believe in human agency, and a metaphor of epidemics obscures the actions of those who chose to use heroin, and of those who chose to sell it, turning them into the hapless victims of larger forces. As I make clear, heroin users' choices were heavily mediated by their social setting and, once consumption had begun, by the drug itself, but they were choices nonetheless.

It is, perhaps, too much to hope that an urban history of heroin can reorient our discussion of drug use. It should, however, turn our focus away from individual addicts and the foreign sources of our drug problem and toward the issue of demand and the social setting in which drug use is produced. It is here that the only solutions to drug abuse may be found because, as any student of introductory economics can attest, it is demand that organizes the market.

CHAPTER ONE

New York and the Global Market

AMERICAN HEROIN USERS had their own nation, and New York City was its capital. Not only has New York organized the heroin trade both nationally and internationally since the 1920s, it has also hosted the nation's largest population of heroin users. Heroin passed from an international trading system into a national one in New York, which then redistributed heroin to other cities throughout the country. New York served as the central place that established the hierarchical structure of the market, with virtually the entire country as its hinterland and other cities serving as its regional or local distribution centers.[1] However, the world trade in heroin is based on a raw material, opium, which is not native to the United States, so it is reasonable to ask how New York City came to play a central role in the world market. The answer to that question lies in the politics of opium and its conversion into an illegal commodity.

Opium poppies are relatively easy to grow, which has always made controlling their supply difficult. Many regions of the globe now produce poppies in a process of proliferation that has accelerated over time. In the ancient world, poppy growing occurred first in Egypt, and then spread into Persia (Iran), India, Pakistan, Afghanistan, and Turkey, the so-called "Golden Crescent." The poppy followed Arab traders into Asia, and the "Golden Triangle" of Burma (Myanmar), Laos, and Thailand became a major source for the global market in the mid-twentieth century. China began growing poppies in the nineteenth century to serve its population of opium smokers, while Mexico and Latin America began to export opiates in the twentieth century to supply the U.S. market. European countries—including Greece, Bulgaria,

Russia, the Balkan states, and even Britain—all produced opium poppies at one time or another. As different states attempted to regulate the cultivation of opium, entrepreneurs drew new regions into the opium trade. Again and again, the opium poppy escaped like a wisp of smoke from the grasp of those who sought to control it.

Not all poppies are created equal, however. The opiate content of poppies grown in different regions of the world varies considerably, as does the desirability of the opium they produce. The richest opium poppies are from Southwest and Southeast Asia, while European and Latin American poppies have lesser opiate value. Nonetheless, even the less desirable poppies find a market, especially in times of shortages elsewhere. The supply of opium poppies may not be infinite, but it is nearly so, which indicates the problem faced by international control efforts. Poppy cultivation has spread across the globe in response to the demand for opiates and in reaction to opium controls, and opium poppies have become an unbeatable cash crop in poor regions that cannot otherwise enter the market.

Poppy cultivation requires a small investment in technology and capital, which makes it an appealing crop in poor areas. Opium poppies are hardy and need plentiful sun, not too much rainfall, and modestly rich soil, but little irrigation and few pesticides or fertilizers. Poppies spread naturally into the furrows left by the cultivation of staple crops, and thus allow farmers to use their fields intensively. While cultivation is not difficult, harvesting is a laborious process that is difficult to mechanize and requires an abundance of inexpensive labor, which is usually readily available in less developed regions of the world. The opium poppy typically produces white, pink, or purple flowers, and a small bluish-green pod that laborers cut by hand. A sticky, milky-white substance oozes out of the pod and is hand-scraped with a small blade and collected into balls that, when dried, boiled, and strained, becomes morphine base, the source of manufactured opiates.[2]

Although opium has important medical uses, its conversion into a commodity of mass consumption in the nineteenth century dominates its modern history. European traders introduced tobacco, the tobacco pipe, and opium into China, and the practice of smoking a mix of tobacco and opium developed as a malaria preventative in China's coastal regions. Eventually the Chinese converted this into a recreational practice, discarding the tobacco and smoking opium in opium houses while consuming tea and delicacies in the company of friends. The population of opium smokers exploded in the mid-nineteenth century after Britain defeated China in the opium wars and forced it to legalize the opium trade. By 1900, China consumed 95 percent of the world's opium crop, and over sixteen million Chinese smoked regularly.[3]

The practice of smoking opium followed the Chinese throughout the world, including to the United States. Opium smoking occurred in opium houses in American Chinatowns, and initially the Chinese were the drug's primary consumers. However, opium smoking gradually leaked into the urban underworld. In many cities, the police tolerated vice, such as prostitution and gambling, as long as it took place within specifically designated districts, and often these vice districts overlapped with Chinatowns. As these communities mingled, the practice of smoking opium spread, and by the end of the nineteenth century, it had become popular among prostitutes, criminals, entertainers, and other habitués of the "sporting life."[4]

Concerns about the alleged goings-on in "opium dens" inspired the first domestic attempts to control opium. The association of whites, particularly white women, and Chinese men in opium smoking parties led municipalities to impose fines and authorize imprisonment for operating or patronizing an opium den. Scenes such as one described by a San Francisco physician of "young white girls from sixteen to twenty years of age" lying around "half-undressed on the floor or couches" in mixed-sex and mixed-race smoking parties fed the public outcry.[5] Congress first imposed increasingly high duties on opium, then forbade Chinese merchants from importing it. Finally, in 1909, Congress acceded to racialized fears about opium smoking and passed a ban (the Smoking Opium Exclusion Act) on opium imports for nonmedicinal purposes, as part of a worldwide movement to restrict the opium trade.[6]

Smoking opium was the most vilified, but not the most common, form of opium consumption in the United States in the nineteenth century. The oral ingestion of opium was central both to medical practice and to commercial and home remedies for common ailments, and this led to more abuse than smoking opium did. Laudanum—as well as widely available patent medicines, syrups, and tonics—contained opium as the principal ingredient, and opium was one of the few effective forms of pain control. Physicians used opium pills to relieve a wide variety of symptoms, such as diarrhea and coughs, and women frequently resorted to opium-based medications to ease menstrual cramps. While morphine became an effective pain reliever after the introduction of the hypodermic syringe (1853), its use was limited largely to those able to afford medical care, and so opium remained a mainstay of the nineteenth-century home medicine cabinet. With the notable exception of Civil War veterans and Chinese and underworld opium smokers, the

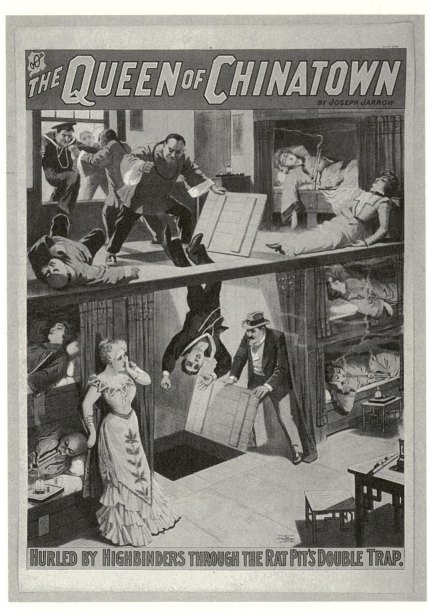

A poster for the play *The Queen of Chinatown,* c. 1899, with its images of white women in languid, opium-induced repose, Chinese opium smokers, sailors being dropped into a rat pit, and menacing gangsters illustrates the anti-Chinese themes that motivated opium-control efforts. Theater Poster Collection, Library of Congress, LC-USZC4-583.

typical American opium user was a middle-aged white woman of middle-class background who had become habituated to opium through self-medication.[7]

By the early twentieth century, the use of oral opiates was declining. The commercialization of aspirin by the German pharmaceutical company Bayer in 1899 established an effective substitute for many common medicinal uses of opium. Then, following the passage of the Pure Food and Drug Act (1906), companies changed the ingredients in their over-the-counter nostrums as consumers became more aware of the dangers of the drugs they took. Finally, physicians became more careful about dispensing narcotics so that fewer patients were likely to become addicted to opiates following medicinal use. As per-capita opium consumption fell in the United States, a shift occurred in the profile of the average opium user that made the passage of prohibitory legislation—aimed at "deviant" users—easier.[8]

With fewer middle-class women using opium, the average user became a white male member of the urban working class, who took opiates for recreational purposes. These young men lived on the margins of respectable society and enjoyed little public sympathy for their drug use. Charlie, born in Greenwich Village to Italian parents, left school at fifteen and learned to snort heroin from fellow workers in a chandelier factory. Similarly, Jerry, who grew up in Williamsburg in Brooklyn, began using heroin at a young age, claiming "I was a youngster when I took the first shot in the arm [at age fifteen]." He had started snorting heroin with other young workers from the candy factory where he was employed, but he did not like the effect. Soon after he started taking a "joy shot" once in a while, and reacted more favorably, becoming a life-long heroin user.[9]

Controlling the drug use of working-class men such as these became an argument in favor of federal control over domestic narcotics consumption. The Harrison Act (1914) became the basis for prohibiting the nonmedicinal use of any narcotic drugs, and its passage culminated decades of effort, both nationally and internationally, to limit access to the opiates and cocaine.[10] By the early twentieth century, the outlines of both the international and the domestic narcotics prohibition policies that dominated the rest of the century were largely in place.

The passage of the Opium Exclusion and the Harrison Acts certainly had an impact on opiate users, but not the ones legislators intended. Restrictions on smoking opium forced users to switch drugs, either to morphine or heroin, which also became the drugs of choice for new opiate users.[11] Both of these drugs were more dangerous for users than opium smoking. While the practice of smoking opium was not benign, it was a relatively inefficient means of transmitting a small dose of opiates to the lungs and brain. Some opium smokers became addicted, but many others limited the number of times and the number of pipes that they smoked because of the elaborate, time-consuming preparations and rituals involved in using the drug.[12] Because morphine and especially heroin were so powerful, sniffing or injecting the drugs delivered a far higher dose of opiates to the body, which increased the possibility of addiction. Since retail dealers cut heroin heavily with quinine, mannitol (a children's laxative), milk sugar, or any other white powder that was handy in order to increase their profit, users did not know the purity of the drug or the cutting agents with which it had been mixed. This increased the possibility of an overdose if the drug were unusually strong or an allergic reaction to the combination of ingredients in the cut. Adding to the danger, morphine and heroin use, while not necessarily solitary, were less ritualized than opium smoking, and less adaptable to the social controls established by fellow users. Therefore users were more prone to overindulge and increase their consumption over time.[13]

Prohibitory legislation, except for a short period when narcotics clinics dispensed opiates legally, forced these users underground and led to the creation of a thriving black market that became centered in New York.[14] While white opium users in most parts of the country changed to morphine, those in New York switched to heroin, which was first introduced commercially as a pain reliever and cough suppressant by Bayer in 1898, and eventually took over the national market for opiates.

Heroin use clustered in New York because it was home to the nation's major pharmaceutical companies. These companies produced heroin legally for the medical market until 1924, when additional federal legislation prohibited the practice. Like their European counterparts, American companies manufactured more heroin than the legitimate market could absorb, with much of the excess being sold illicitly.[15] New Yorkers therefore led the switch from opium to heroin, which became entrenched among the city's opiate users by the 1920s. As the legal production of heroin was eliminated in the United States and as legal manufacturing of heroin abroad became more closely regulated, underground factories, first in Europe and then in China, began producing heroin for export to the New York market.[16] These international sources supplied heroin to illicit wholesalers, and as a result heroin use spread outward from New York and gradually replaced morphine in the illegal markets in the rest of the country.[17]

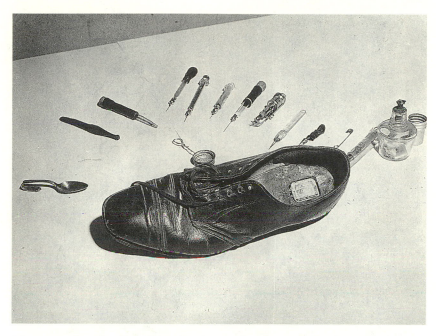

A bent spoon, used to "cook" heroin, along with various syringes, drug paraphernalia, and a heroin tin, hidden in a shoe, were all confiscated from patients entering the Federal Narcotics Hospital in Lexington, Kentucky. *New York World Telegraph and the Sun.* Photograph Collection, Library of Congress.

As an illegal commodity, heroin had distinct advantages over both opium and morphine, which explain its market dominance. It was more powerful than either drug, and it offered a ready solution to the basic problem of smuggling, namely reducing the ratio of volume to value. Smugglers found that it was easiest and most efficient to smuggle the item with the highest value and lowest volume, which in this case was heroin. Because opium was simply too bulky and smelly to smuggle easily, opium traders wanted to convert crude opium into morphine base, which reduced its volume by about 90 percent, at the earliest possible stage in the smuggling process. As the conversion process was relatively simple, it usually occurred near the site of agricultural production. Morphine base withstood the rigors of smuggling, but it was a "semi-finished" product that required additional and more complicated chemical processing in order to be transformed into morphine and then into heroin. Skilled underground chemists handled the tricky manufacturing process in well-equipped and well-ventilated labs at a point close to

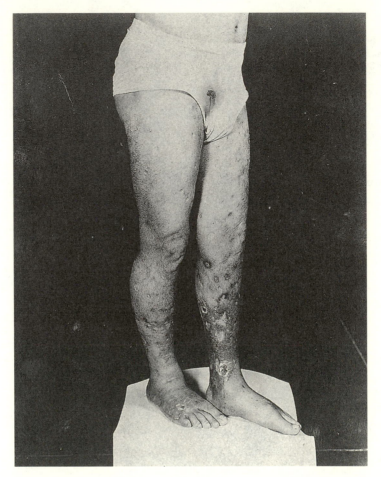

Using dirty needles and impure drugs resulted in abscesses on this man's legs. *New York World Telegraph and the Sun* Photograph Collection, Library of Congress.

final shipment. Since heroin was several times more powerful than morphine, it was the preferred product for smuggling: it had high value but low volume that could be expanded with adulterants once it had crossed through the bottleneck created by international controls.[18]

Once heroin took over the illicit opiate trade, New York's fate was sealed. Geography and a history of underground entrepreneurship predestined New York to become the key site for the importation and distribution of heroin in the United States. With one of the world's greatest harbors, rail and highway connections to the rest of the nation, and criminals with experience in the delivery of illicit services, the city possessed both the natural and the human resources needed to import and distribute heroin. Beginning in the 1920s, Jewish and Italian traffickers, bankrolled by the underworld financier Arnold Rothstein, made heroin purchases in China and Europe and smuggled them back to New York. Bootlegger Waxy Gordon, seeing the end of Prohibition looming, switched his product line to heroin, while mobster Louis "Lepke" Buchalter added heroin smuggling to his repertoire of homicide for hire (so-called Murder, Inc.) and labor racketeering.

World War II disrupted this international traffic temporarily. Importers eventually acquired inferior-grade Mexican heroin to supply the city's and nation's heroin users, but once trade connections were reestablished after the war, New Yorkers capitalized on their ties to heroin distributors abroad and reasserted the city's role as both the most important market and the most important distributor of heroin in the nation. Italian crime families from New York established links first to legitimate Italian drug manufacturers and then, when this supply was cut off, to Corsican gangsters in Marseilles, who supervised the smuggling of Turkish opium and its manufacture into heroin. The city's underground entrepreneurs ensured that most of the heroin imported into the United States in the postwar period made its way through the city of New York.[19]

New York's role as a transportation hub provided its illegal entrepreneurs with a major advantage in the heroin trade. The size and volume of merchandise shipped on a daily basis through the port of New York made smuggling contraband easier than it might have been in a smaller port. Although the Bureau of Customs and the Federal Bureau of Narcotics made large seizures of imported heroin, authorities knew that the thousands of shippers, workers, and passengers who streamed through New York's wharfs and airports presented an insurmountable problem of traffic control. The early 1960s provide an interesting moment to examine the scope of the problem: the port of New York remained a prime mover of freight, passenger ships still docked weekly at the city's piers, and airline traffic, though picking up, was still a novelty. More than 30,000 longshoremen were employed daily in the port of New York, approximately 25,000 people visited the New York piers each week, and as many as 4,000 might visit a ship on sailing day. Any one of these individuals might pick up a small package of heroin and carry it off a ship. The growth of air travel also increased opportunities for smugglers. In August 1962, 187,000 passengers disembarked from airlines in New York airports with more than 600,000 pieces of luggage, making careful searches nearly impossible. The Bureau of Customs admitted that without advance intelligence, finding smuggled narcotics was a matter of luck. And of course the problem would only become worse over time.[20]

Much of the heroin smuggled into New York was destined to remain there. Estimates of the number of heroin users varied wildly, with the Federal Bureau of Narcotics reporting that in 1963, 48 percent of the nation's 48,535 "active addicts" listed in the federal narcotics registry resided there. Two years later the city estimated that it housed between 25,000 and 60,000 heroin "addicts" and between 50 and 60 percent of the nation's total, while by the end of the decade some estimated that the number of addicted New Yorkers approached an improbable 300,000. Regardless of the actual number, it is clear that the nation's largest and most concentrated market was in New York City.[21]

The size of New York's market and its role in the international heroin economy were apparent to individuals at all levels of the trade. Major traffickers, small-time hoods, and groups of heroin users pooling resources to make a score all turned to the New York marketplace. Arrest records and information from the Federal Bureau of Narcotics provide evidence about professional drug trafficking while interviews with heroin users in a number of cities show how they bypassed the local drug market to obtain cheaper and purer drugs if they lived close to New York. New York's centrality went unchallenged in the postwar decades.

Major dealers from the East Coast, Chicago, and even Los Angeles received their supplies from international traffickers through the New York City hub. In the system that evolved after World War II, heroin was shipped from Marseilles to New York (the "French Connection"), smuggled in false-bottomed suitcases carried by passengers, secreted in specially made side panels of automobiles, or hidden in a cargo container full of legitimate items. The New York crime families of Gaetano (Tommy "Three Fingers Brown") Lucchese and Vito Genovese both arranged to have heroin imported into New York, where it was redistributed to other cities around the country. Lucchese worked with a Corsican exporter named Joseph Orsini, who shipped heroin from Marseilles to New York in automobiles, while Genovese was convicted for organizing a ring that smuggled 160 kilos of French-made heroin from Cuba into New York between 1954 and 1958, when the group was broken up. In both cases, regional dealers from Chicago, Cleveland, Washington, D.C., Las Vegas, and Los Angeles purchased their heroin from these New York importers.[22]

Regional dealers wanted to enter the distribution network near the top, which meant gaining entry to the New York wholesale marketplace. Once a heroin shipment entered the United States, its volume was expanded repeatedly by adding adulterants as it traveled down the urban hierarchy and came closer to the consumer. By dealing directly with New York wholesalers, regional dealers ensured themselves a steady supply of relatively pure heroin at a good price while also controlling the amount their heroin would be cut. At the same time, dealers on every level wished to keep their client list short and selective in order to minimize the risk of arrest, and this desire for secrecy reinforced the tendency toward a hierarchical structure of the market. Regional dealers jealously guarded their New York connections, who had little incentive to seek out new distributors.[23]

Once heroin left New York, it moved into secondary markets. Authorities identified Chicago as the most important secondary center in the United States and it served as a distribution point for other cities in the Midwest and Southwest. The Chicagoans obtained heroin in New York, cut it, and then resold it to representatives from other lower-order urban centers that lacked New York connections. FBN agent George Belk testified before Congress that "traffickers operating out of Chicago . . . [furnish] cities such as Detroit, Cleveland, St. Louis, Kansas City, Dallas, Houston [and] New Orleans."[24] A specific example illustrates this larger pattern. In the early 1950s, Jack Roy Clayton, who owned a plane and a private landing strip near Kansas City, entered into a partnership with a Kansas City narcotics entrepreneur. Clayton, who had occasionally ferried stolen goods from Chicago to Kansas City, now agreed to carry a kilo of heroin each month along with his other items. The heroin he picked up in Chicago originated in New York and was transmitted to Kansas City. There dealers from Tulsa, Oklahoma, Omaha, Nebraska, Council Bluffs, Iowa—as well as from Arkansas, Texas, Tennessee, and Florida—purchased the drug. These dealers in turn supplied their local retailers much in the way cities have always supplied their regional and local hinterlands with legal goods and services. Underground entrepreneurs were simply agents of the market.[25]

Of course there were exceptions to this model, as dealers with the right contacts and a sufficiently large market share could negotiate directly with New York wholesalers. According to the Federal Bureau of Narcotics, Joseph "Cockeyed Joe" Catalanotte, an important organizer of illegal enterprises in Detroit, sidestepped his regional center in Chicago and enjoyed direct access to New York. Catalanotte avoided having the Chicagoans take a cut of his profit while he sought to limit his own risk by not touching the heroin himself and not keeping a supply on hand in Detroit. James Galici, Catalanotte's trusted associate, traveled back and forth between Detroit and New York, ferrying cash one way and heroin the other, usually in response to a specific order. "In a great many cases," a Bureau agent noted, "they did not maintain a cache of drugs at Detroit. They would see the customers' money, ascertain that he was ready to buy . . . and then Galici would make the trip and return with the drugs."[26] In the language of modern management, they engaged in "just in time" delivery, which in this case lowered their financial and legal risk. The organization of the Detroit operation suggests that it rivaled Chicago both in the amount of narcotics distributed and in the geographic range of markets to which it sold. While dealers in other cities might have wished for the same level of access enjoyed by Catalanotte, not all of them handled the volume or had his connections to New York.

The underworld, like the world of legitimate business, had a color line, and African Americans did not have access to the top international sources of heroin until the 1970s. However, African American entrepreneurs organized their regional networks of sellers in the same hierarchical fashion that whites did, and for the same reasons. African American trading operations revolved around Harlem, which formed the apex in the system. For example, John Freeman was the intermediary between New York's largely Italian and Jewish heroin dealers and African American dealers from the city and elsewhere in the country. According to the FBN, Freeman "has been engaged in so many illegal operations it is impossible to list them all," so the agency simply referred to him as the "king-pin of colored Harlem." Yet, for all of his prominence, Freeman had access only to middle-range Italian dealers. Freeman, who owned two flower shops in New York that provided legitimate cover for his narcotics sales, purchased heroin from Joseph Valachi, a middle-ranking member of the Genovese crime family, among other suppliers. Once he had his heroin, Freeman did not simply sell in a local market. He also sold to dealers from the South Side of Chicago, Detroit, and Los Angeles, becoming, in the words of the FBI, "one of the most active Negro interstate traffickers of heroin in the United States."[27] Race dictated the entry point into the market and therefore affected the quality of the product, but it did not have an effect on the market's organization.

The closer one got to New York, the more difficult it was for a group of entrepreneurs to establish primacy in the marketplace. Heroin users and small-scale dealers living near New York could buy drugs in New York's retail marketplaces, where the heroin, although heavily cut, was still cheaper and purer than it was at home. Charles Ward of the FBN argued that there was little organized drug selling in New Jersey and Philadelphia because they were so close to New York. "It is cheaper for the addicts," he testified, "to jump on a Greyhound bus or the Pennsylvania Railroad and ride to New York and purchase narcotics from the lower echelon traffickers in that area [Harlem]." "Baltimore and Washington," he concluded, "more or less fall in the same category because of their proximity to New York City."[28]

Ward described a marketplace that was open to many entrepreneurs. Individuals, called "ounce men," traveled to New York and purchased any- where from five to ten ounces of heroin, paying between $200 and $500 an ounce, depending on its purity. These small-scale entrepreneurs were the type of dealers who purchased from John Freeman's Harlem operation and then adulterated, bagged, and resold their product in their local markets through a network of street dealers, who probably were heroin users.

Smaller-scale operators, so-called "addict peddlers," also entered the New York marketplace and arranged deals unavailable to their counterparts elsewhere in the country. Users from Baltimore or Philadelphia traveled to Harlem to make purchases, and local police knew enough to stake out the train stations for returning addicts. Dusty, for example, went from Philadel- phia to Harlem on the train three or four times a week, leaving at night "because if you left during the day, somebody [a narcotics officer] would be waiting at 30th Street or North Philadelphia Station." Dusty sometimes disembarked in the suburbs and made his way into the city via the trolley in order to avoid detection by the narcotics squad. Such dealers purchased even smaller amounts of adulterated heroin called "loads"—usually consisting of twenty-five small packets, selling for about $75 to $100—that were then further cut ("stepped on") before getting bagged and sold on the streets in the home market. Even at the load level a substantial profit could be made. While a five-dollar packet in New York might contain 150 to 200 milligrams of heroin, a five-dollar packet in Philadelphia averaged only 30 milligrams of heroin, accounting for about a fivefold gain for the dealer prior to expenses.[29] The proximity of New York, the relative purity of the heroin that could be purchased there, and the dramatic markup in price once that heroin was adulterated again and resold, enticed medium- and small-scale entrepreneurs alike to enter the New York marketplace and hindered the creation of a hierarchical market in nearby cities.[30]

Heroin users were well aware of the structure of national and local markets for heroin. Testifying before a Congressional committee in 1951, a Baltimore user named Woodrow commented that he would pay $3 in Baltimore or Chicago for a package of heroin that would sell for a dollar in New York or a dollar and a quarter in Philadelphia. Another witness, Jeanne, told Senators that heroin cost $4 a cap in her hometown of Cincinnati as compared to $2.50 in Detroit and Chicago and $1 in New York. "I think New York is cheaper than any place I have ever been," she declared. "I mean, there are a lot more peddlers in New York City than any place I have been." (Both Woodrow and Jeanne were in position to compare prices: Woodrow was a musician who traveled across the country as part of his work, and Jeanne ran con games in different cities.) Heroin users knew that New York was the center, the capital of the heroin homeland, and that the farther they traveled from it, the more expensive and the less pure the drug became.

Of course, not all heroin users were able to take advantage of this knowledge. Several heroin users from Baltimore testified that they went to Washington, D.C., to purchase heroin. While the heroin was not as cheap as in New York, Washington was closer and less expensive to get to, and the heroin was still cheaper than that purchased on Baltimore's Pennsylvania Avenue. As a way of maximizing their investment, users traveled to Washington for heroin binges that lasted several days. Clearly consumers had to weigh transportation costs in their market choices more carefully than dealers did, but for consumers as well, the marketplace had a geographic logic. Heroin in regional centers such as Washington was less expensive than in local markets, but for the real deals, one had to turn to New York. Some users, such as Rocky, did just that and added to the growing population of heroin users in the city: "He eventually moved to New York, just like everybody else, where the dope is better, cheaper, and easier to cop."[31]

The heroin marketplace was subject to pressures not found in a legitimate market, and as a result, factors other than geographic organization affected heroin distribution. While New York may have been the logical entrepot for narcotics smuggled from European heroin laboratories, smugglers in the mid-1950s began shipping through the port of Montreal and, later, through Havana, Montevideo, and Mexico City, even though New York remained the final destination. Heroin markets had a collection problem typical of illegal marketplaces with no courts or regulatory agencies to mediate commercial transactions, and smugglers constantly switched partners and travel routes in response to these problems. As Martin Pena of the Office of Naval Intelligence testified, "The traffickers in Montreal have established a considerably better record [compared to Mafiosi in New York] as to financial responsibility and are, therefore, more trusted by the French sources of supply." Evidence for Pena's point came in the same hearings, when Joseph Valachi attested to the untrustworthiness of all the parties involved in a heroin deal. Valachi, after borrowing eight thousand dollars as a down payment for a fifteen-kilo heroin shipment, was told after the fact that not only did he have nine equal partners in the deal, but also that a debt owed by Vito Genovese was going to be taken off the top of the proceeds. Valachi eventually received two kilos of heroin as his share, which he gave to two associates to sell. However, they only paid him $1,000 of the $5,000 they promised. Valachi in turn never repaid his $8,000 loan, nor did he pay his French supplier for the heroin. As the result of such experiences, Corsican exiles, making use of their ties to the Marseilles underworld, acted as intermediaries and shipped heroin to New York from Latin American cities, while other French suppliers shipped through Montreal and sent trusted confederates to supervise delivery and payment.[32]

Despite the collections problems with New York gangsters, heroin smuggling did not shift permanently from New York to other cities. The illegal marketplace was inherently unstable, and problems with collections and disputes over market share or the quality of a shipment happened regardless of place. New York remained the prime destination for heroin in the postwar period simply because of its market. Smugglers sometimes used other cities, and traffic shifted from one site to another depending on the regulatory environment and the changing coalitions of importers.[33] But the size of New York's internal market and its traditional role as the heroin distributor to the nation kept the city central to the heroin trade.

From the end of World War II until the 1970s, New York shaped the international trade in heroin. From the first plantings of poppy seeds to the harvesting of opium gum to the processing and smuggling of morphine base to the manufacturing and selling of heroin, all activity stirred in response to New York's market. It was the largest market in the world (Hong Kong had a higher per capita distribution of heroin users but a smaller overall number),[34] and the city resold heroin in a large and wealthy hinterland. To the degree that order existed in this marketplace, it was supplied by an invisible hand operating through a network of central places organized by New York.

But a geographic analysis of the heroin market only takes us so far. It explains New York's rise to prominence as the import center of the opiate trade in the twentieth century and why New York became home to the largest concentration of heroin users in the nation, but it begs important questions: What motivated people to begin using heroin in the first place? And why did African Americans replace whites as the primary consumers of heroin in the years after World War II?

CHAPTER TWO

Jazz Joints and Junk

On the eve of World War II, the Federal Bureau of Narcotics (FBN) maintained that the problem of drug abuse was well in hand, and the data seemed to confirm this. There were a few, mostly elderly, Chinese opium smokers, and a stable, if aging, population of largely white heroin and morphine users. There was a large population of marijuana smokers, but recent legislation had granted the FBN new enforcement powers to handle them. Within a few years, however, that portrait changed and confidence about the declining use of illicit drugs disappeared. Heroin use surged after the war, dominating the illegal marketplace, especially among African American and Latino youth. Where did this wave of heroin use come from?

Social setting is key to understanding the increase in heroin use. A drug subculture is rooted in physical spaces that sustain it and allow it to flourish and continue over time. In other words, there was a spatiality to drug use and to the transmission of "drug knowledge" that occurred in places where interested novices could interact with experienced users. In the immediate postwar years, these were fairly few—specific jazz and after-hours clubs, bars, and cafeterias that catered to a crowd of pimps, hookers, drug dealers, jazz musicians, and their hangers-on. A transformation in drug culture occurred in these social spaces, which initially sustained a marijuana-smoking subculture that after the war turned into a heroin-using one.

New York sported a lively marijuana-using subculture, and in 1938, New York City Mayor Fiorello LaGuardia asked the New York Academy of Medicine to study it. LaGuardia knew marijuana use was increasing, but he was unsure how seriously to take the problem. He had heard that marijuana was not addictive and that those who became habitual users could stop without experiencing withdrawal symptoms. But there were also disturbing reports that marijuana smokers were prone to acts of violence and that teenagers in New York were experimenting with the drug. An investigative feature in the *New Yorker* highlighted the existence of hundreds of "tea pads" in Harlem, places with dimmed lights and hot jazz, where couples danced sinuously and indulged in elaborate marijuana-smoking rituals. (The article also warned "an overdose of marijuana generates savage and sadistic traits likely to reach a climax in axe and icepick murders.")[1] In addition, the federal government had recently used its commerce and revenue-raising powers to control marijuana, much as it had regulated opiates with the Harrison Act. The Marijuana Tax Act, which took effect in October 1937, placed a tax on all marijuana transactions, and failure to pay the tax was a federal violation. On the other hand, payment of the tax alerted local authorities to make arrests in those jurisdictions where marijuana sales were illegal, such as New York, which had prohibited the drug in 1934. In order to examine the problems posed by marijuana and to investigate the extent of marijuana use in the city, Mayor LaGuardia decided to assemble an impartial team of experts.[2]

Marijuana had migrated north along with jazz musicians from New Orleans (although it was also popular among Mexican Americans in the Southwest). By the 1930s its use had spread across the nation and was celebrated in popular songs such as "If You're a Viper," "The Stuff Is Here and It's Mellow," "Light Up," and "Sweet Marijuana Brown."[3] In New York marijuana sales centered around two locations: "the Corner," 131st Street and Seventh Avenue—the site of several Harlem after-hours clubs frequented by entertainers and hustlers—and in the Times Square entertainment district, along 42nd Street and up Broadway, especially near "Swing Street" (West 52nd Street) with its collection of speakeasies-turned-jazz clubs.[4]

Jazz infused the lingo of marijuana users, and many jazz musicians and fans believed that smoking marijuana enhanced the experience of hearing and performing music. Marijuana united entertainer and audience in a transcendent moment that challenged the normal limits of space, time, gender, and race. According to jazz musician and Harlem's leading marijuana dealer, Mezz Mezzrow, marijuana use created a charged environment for performer and audience. He recalled returning to the bandstand after smoking some reefer and having the audience go "crazy" over the change in their play: "some kind of electricity was crackling in the air and it made them all glow and jump." While most jazz musicians and fans accepted marijuana (when he was on the road, Louis Armstrong even sent veiled greetings across the radio airwaves to Mezzrow back in New York), it was not clear how far beyond the world of musicians, fans, and hustlers marijuana smoking had penetrated.[5]

In response to the mayor's request, the New York Academy of Medicine's Committee on Public Health launched a two-part investigation, one analyzing the pharmacological effects of marijuana and the other examining the marijuana-using subculture that so troubled authorities. To test the powers of marijuana, physicians solicited volunteers from the prison population on Riker's and Hart Islands and the Women's House of Detention. Physicians administered controlled doses of "marijuana concentrate" to seventy-two subjects, including forty-eight marijuana users and twenty-four nonusers. Investigators asked subjects to perform various psychomotor tests, as well as tests to measure their visual acuity, memory, and perception of time. Generally the nonusers proved more sensitive to the higher doses, with all subjects experiencing difficulty in concentrating and in undertaking more complex psychomotor tasks. However, the clinical study concluded that marijuana was of little medical concern; it was nonaddictive and, contrary to popular belief and official claims, it did not promote aggressive behavior. The most common physical reactions included an increased pulse rate, sometimes drowsiness or a feeling of nausea, and a mixture of both apprehension and euphoria.[6]

While the published report dwelled largely on the physiological effects of the drug, the sociological study was equally significant. A team of six plainclothes police officers observed street corner drug sales, gained admission to parties at tea pads, interviewed high school principals, attended high school dances, and went to famous night spots to investigate reports of marijuana sales. They focused on Harlem and East Harlem, areas that were identified as the geographic centers of marijuana use, and they sought to document the extent of marijuana smoking among teenagers.

Here the news was as unalarming as that found in the scientific section of the report. Investigators concluded that smokers tended to be unemployed adults between the ages of twenty and thirty, and they found no evidence of aggressive or antisocial behavior. They also concluded that marijuana smoking among adolescents occurred only in "isolated instances."[7]

The notes of one of the investigators provide a "thick description" of the sites where marijuana was smoked and some sense of the rituals that accompanied its use.[8] Olive J. Cregan traveled through the marijuana-using underground along with two other plainclothes police officers, one African American and one white.

Cregan compared tea pads to social clubs, informal settings where patrons knew each other, conversed casually, and, instead of having drinks together, passed around reefers. Cregan gained admittance to one tea pad in the Sugar Hill section of Harlem because Patrolman Hughes, an African American police officer, had been there before and his presence dispelled suspicion about his two white guests. After being allowed into the building, they entered the apartment. "We passed the kitchen door and sat down on a sofa in the foyer which was dimly lighted with an orange-bulbed lamp. A doorway led from the foyer into a living-room in which I could discern by the light of a very dim blue lamp the figure of a woman lying on another sofa." The dim off-color lighting contributed to a languid atmosphere in which guests could smoke, talk, and idle away the evening. The investigators asked for a "trey," or three marijuana cigarettes, which the proprietor fetched for them. He also informed them that as it was a Saturday night, he and his girlfriend would cook a waffle and sausage breakfast for their guests before they left. Because it was still early in the evening, other guests had not yet arrived and the trio, after pretending to smoke their reefers, headed for another pad.

Their next stop was seedier, in an apartment building in a poorer neighborhood under the elevated train tracks. Here two women in a blue-lit bedroom danced a jitterbug together to tunes on a record player, four or five men and women talked in the kitchen, and the sounds of laughter and conversation emerged from another bedroom. The proprietor admitted them to the apartment, but refused to sell them any marijuana. He told Hughes that it would be okay to sell to him, but not to his white friends ("he wouldn't have anything to do with white folks since he had recently done a stretch"). Then he left the apartment. Cregan did not see any marijuana smoking there, just drinking and dancing, as in any other house party. Marijuana smoking would occur later, she thought, when the tea pad really got going, around two or three in the morning. While people smoked reefers in preparation for an evening out, they arrived at a tea pad at the conclusion of the evening, for a final bout of conviviality before heading home. She apparently did not think that her presence inhibited anyone even though it clearly bothered her host.[9]

Both well-off and poor African Americans patronized the tea pads, and Cregan's reception suggests that, at least on the more middle-class Sugar Hill, mixed parties of blacks and whites were accepted. But not just anyone could get in. In both places proprietors recognized Patrolman Hughes from previous visits and then admitted them. Tea pads were not for whites out for a casual night of slumming after going to a jazz club; only those with a guide could attend, and even then they faced suspicion. The tea pads may have seemed exotic and the rituals bizarre, but nothing Cregan and her colleagues uncovered seemed threatening, and marijuana smokers did not appear particularly hostile or dangerous. But if tea pads were part of a little-known underground subculture, marijuana sales in more central locations were somewhat more accessible to investigators and therefore to a wider public as well.

Cregan bought reefers in various midtown bars on the West Side, though mostly through intermediaries. Waitresses and bartenders proved to be valuable connections who could arrange for a sale to a known customer. Cregan visited one club, the International Artists' League, in the Times Square area. It consisted of "one smoky, filthy room with a long bar stretching along one side. It is usually crowded with people of every sort—from top hat and white tie down to the next level above a bum. It is the worst dive I have ever seen." After visiting several times, she asked if a bartender could get some reefers. He readily agreed and said he would send a "kid" to pick some up. Here again Cregan was admitted to an inner circle, an after-hours club patronized by white "vipers." Outsiders still seemed suspicious, however, and she was able to buy marijuana only through a third party. In the final report, the authors concluded that porters at railroad terminals provided one of the few examples of truly "public" guides who could be approached by a complete stranger and who might establish contact for a marijuana purchase. Generally transactions occurred only in specific locales among individuals with at least nodding acquaintanceships under carefully controlled circumstances.[10]

Cregan and her fellow investigators also wanted to see if rumors of adolescent marijuana use, particularly among African American teenagers, were true. Cregan attended Wadleigh High School, where adolescents reportedly smoked marijuana in the bathrooms. After finding no evidence of marijuana use in the day session, Cregan began attending at night. She slipped into the girls' bathroom, observed the students, and even engaged some in conversation. "Each evening out of the twenty to thirty girls who entered the room, no more than two or three would light a tobacco cigarette in order to get a few quick puffs. No one at all even took out a reefer or marijuana cigarette." She found that most knew nothing about marijuana but a couple claimed "some high school students did smoke it, but then mostly at dances or parties." (What the African American students thought of some unknown white woman loitering in their bathroom went unrecorded.)

In order to investigate marijuana smoking at dances, Cregan and an escort attended a session at the Renaissance Ballroom hosted by the Harlem Evening High School. If Cregan hoped to find marijuana-smoking youths at the dance, she was disappointed. She and her partner were two of seven whites in attendance at the dance with around two hundred total participants. Cregan believed she was able to observe the actions of the other guests, and she remained until the end of the dance at three in the morning. She found "the dancers were conservative and well-behaved. Such jitterbug dancing as there was went on at the corners of the ballroom and was neither excessive or violent. . . . There was no excessive drinking, and to my knowledge there wasn't a reefer in sight. Even the musicians in the band smoked regular cigarettes between numbers."[11]

Cregan followed up her observations with a survey of high school principals. She interviewed thirteen high school and junior high school principals; only one, the principal of Fenimore Cooper High School, at 116th Street, west of Fifth Avenue, admitted that his students smoked marijuana. Several boys had been caught with reefers in their possession, but the principal did not seem to think it was a big problem: "Since there is a great use of marijuana in the neighborhood, it is only natural that it should crop up as a school problem every so often."[12] If New York's African American teenagers were part of a widespread marijuana-smoking subculture, school authorities were not aware of it, and police investigators could not supply evidence to the contrary.

While Cregan was not an ethnographer and did not reflect on being a participant-observer or probe into the meaning of her observations, she possessed a policewoman's careful eye for detail that makes her account believable. She described a relatively contained subculture that supported good-natured social exchange, threatened no one, and appeared to pose no danger of attracting adolescents, most of whom were ignorant of its outlines.

Neither the scientific nor the sociological data supported the FBN's contentions about the dangers of marijuana use. Dreamy marijuana smokers, content to lie on sofas listening to music or dancing languidly in dimly lit apartments, seemed unlikely to turn suddenly into ax murderers. Mayor LaGuardia's committee concluded that alarmism about marijuana was unfounded.

But was it? The issue was not marijuana itself but rather the social setting in which marijuana smoking occurred. Prohibitory legislation turned marijuana smokers into lawbreakers and drove them underground, where they created social settings to protect themselves from the intervention of public authorities. The secretive nature of these spots, with passwords and barred doors, and with participants sharing secret language, distinctive clothing, and nods of recognition, resembled speakeasies during Prohibition. The marijuana subculture depended on jazz clubs, bars, and after-hours spots—themselves frequently holdovers from Prohibition—that provided users with places to meet, exchange information, make sales, enjoy each other's company, and be entertained. Marijuana smoking was relatively benign, but its users were primed to disregard official and media-generated alarms about drugs, which, according to their experience, had little basis in reality. And, most important, they traveled in an underground social setting in which one drug fad could easily give way to another.

That was not going to happen during World War II; few drugs other than marijuana were available in underground social settings. The opium dens that had been part of urban tenderloins at the end of the nineteenth century had long disappeared. Interviews with opium smokers confirm that occasional connections could be made with Chinese opium users, but even the latter faced difficulties in obtaining the drug, which was very expensive on the rare occasions it could be found. Cocaine use had declined since its peak at the turn of the century, and the numbers of morphine and heroin users were declining. Hardcore opiate addicts went to pharmacies and stocked up on paregoric, which they boiled down and injected for its narcotic content. Others took to the road in the hope that country or small-town doctors might be more gullible or more sympathetic to tales of woe and write prescriptions for morphine. (In fact, the FBN warned physicians to look out for such ruses or risk losing their licenses.) Some heroin from Mexico eventually made its way to New York, but opiate use was so rare that voluntary commitments to hospitals for heroin detoxification nearly disappeared in New York by 1943 and federal authorities considered closing the narcotics hospital in Lexington, Kentucky.[13] Although the problem of drug use was not solved, it certainly appeared to be held at bay.

It came as some surprise, then, that heroin seized the nation's headlines after World War II. Narcotics arrests rose dramatically in the postwar period for all groups, with the most phenomenal increases coming among adolescents. Court appearances by New York teenagers charged with heroin possession increased more than tenfold between 1946 and 1950.[14] This was not just a problem in New York. Surveys of the patients at the Lexington narcotics hospital showed that adolescents—specifically African Americans and Latinos—formed a new and distinct patient population arriving from the nation's cities.[15] Suddenly heroin use was no longer confined to the urban underworld and an aging population of hustlers, but was spreading among American teenagers and young persons in their twenties.

The same jazz clubs, bars, dance halls, hotels, and streets (sometimes literally the same addresses) identified in the prewar marijuana study were the vectors for the surge in heroin use in New York. That is to say, a spatial logic dictated the transmission of information about drugs and the practices that were associated with their sale and use, and this logic transcended the particular drug being consumed. Drug knowledge was conveyed in those social settings where novices and experienced users mingled, and these places incubated a jazz musician and a hipster subculture that became inexorably intertwined with heroin use in the immediate postwar years.

The association between jazz musicians and heroin is well known, almost a cliché, in popular culture. A list of narcotics-using musicians reads like a litany of jazz greats: Charlie Parker, Miles Davis, Billie Holiday, Dexter Gordon, Art Pepper, and John Coltrane to name but a few. Many of the artists who transformed jazz in the postwar period from big band music into bebop also led the way into using heroin. Musician Red Rodney called heroin use a badge of distinction, the trademark of a unique jazz generation. "It was the thing that made us different from the rest of the world," Rodney proclaimed. "It was the thing that said 'We know, you don't know.' It was the thing that gave us membership in a unique club." Admission to the club was not limited to the well known. Over half of 350 New York jazz musicians reported in a survey that they had tried heroin at least once, and a quarter used it at least occasionally.[16] As a population, musicians were dramatically overrepresented among heroin users, but the problem was not jazz musicians per se. Rather the social setting of the jazz joints and after-hours clubs mixed jazz musicians, dealers, music fans, and hipsters, which fostered the postwar upsurge in heroin use.

The Times Square area was not the only marketplace for heroin in postwar New York, but it was the most important one. The Times Square entertainment district hosted many bars, clubs, inexpensive hotels, cafeterias, and cheap eateries where experienced users and novices could meet. More important, it was truly central, geographically accessible to all, especially whites who were intimidated by Harlem, which had grown less hospitable to them since the end of the war. It was a nexus for public transit, with subway and city bus lines depositing and picking up thousands of riders daily. The nearby Port Authority Bus Station (which opened in 1950) and Grand Central Station, just a few blocks away on the east side, made Times Square easily reached by thousands of suburbanites as well. And it was crowded: people gathered in Times Square, the "crossroads of the world," with squares, soldiers, workers, hustlers, and hipsters shouldering their way through the crowd. Heroin users melted inconspicuously into the scene, visible to each other and perhaps to the police who patrolled the area, but made invisible too by the sheer number of passersby and seedy, down-on-their-luck pedestrians. Times Square's centrality and anonymity were essential in the spread of heroin from a small circle of users to a broader population.[17]

Times Square was preeminent among the nation's tenderloins and had long been home to all sorts of vice, including drug distribution.[18] Jack Kerouac captured the feel of Times Square in his description of Ritzy's Bar in *On the Road*. Ritzy's served as the "hustler's bar" for the Times Square area, where young men in zoot suits and other "hoodlum cloth" gathered. "There were Negro queers, sullen guys with guns, shiv-packing seamen, thin, noncommittal junkies, and an occasional well-dressed middle-aged detective, posing as a bookie and hanging around half for interest and half for duty."[19]

Out-of-towners were equally aware of Times Square's notorious reputation. Herbert Huncke, an acquaintance of William Burroughs and Allen Ginsberg who became a minor Beat writer, arrived in New York from Chicago just prior to World War II as a penniless, addicted drifter. He headed directly for Times Square, where he knew he could exchange sex for lodging and drugs. There at the Bucket of Blood bar he met the man who became his "running partner" and together they went out to get some heroin. Huncke spent the war years "making croakers" (getting physicians to write prescriptions for morphine) and selling the drugs he acquired to local prostitutes. Like other Times Square hustlers, he rolled drunks, broke into cars, or stole luggage from unsuspecting tourists in the absence of other opportunities.[20]

While heroin had been around the jazz scene before World War II (Charlie Parker had begun using heroin in the 1930s back in Kansas City), the drug took on new salience in the postwar years. Jazz critic Leonard Feather commented that marijuana use seemed suddenly to give way to heroin. "The whole situation changed around 1945," Feather noted, "when one became aware of the existence of heroin and heroin peddlers. Suddenly you knew about a large number of hooked musicians."[21] Opiate-using entertainers in the past had favored opium smoking, which was considered more elegant than heroin or morphine ("Opium smokers always considered themselves above any other kind of drug user," as Ann put it in an interview). But with opium unavailable even to celebrities, smokers such as Billie Holiday switched to heroin, which also became the drug of choice for newly initiated narcotics users. And Times Square brought jazz musicians, narcotics users, and interested novices together.[22]

New York's Times Square area was the center of postwar jazz. The Depression had concentrated jazz making in New York, with its many clubs, recording studios, and media outlets, and the city popularized bebop, the jazz movement of the 1940s that swept big band music from the stage. When music critic and bassist Bill Crow arrived in Times Square in 1945, he discovered a "carnival of entertainment" with big-name bands appearing at most of the movie theaters in the area and, like other jazz musicians, he moved to New York to be part of this jazz scene.[23]

Jazz clubs had concentrated on West 52nd Street, known as "Swing Alley" or simply "The Street," when the former speakeasies added music to attract audiences after the repeal of Prohibition. As many as a dozen clubs dotted the two blocks between Fifth Avenue and Broadway, as well as nearby streets. While the clubs had initially been segregated—black performers such as Billie Holiday were not allowed to mingle with the white audience at the Famous Door and had to wait outside in the alley between sets—at some point during the war segregation broke down. In fact, southern soldiers passing through New York found the interracial mixing on 52nd Street outrageous, and they attacked mixed couples, especially, in streets nearby. Dizzy Gillespie recalled that 52nd Street was one of the few places in New York where there was "very little racist feeling," "but once you left Fifty-second Street, look out."[24]

The jazz clubs provided an intimate setting for musicians. Often the clubs occupied the converted basements of brownstones, with narrow ("shaped like shoeboxes"), dingy, smoke-filled rooms with a few small tables, chairs, a bar, perhaps an upright piano, and a small bandstand. The tiny clubs depended on turnover for profit and usually cleared the audience after a thirty-minute set. Fans went from club to club while musicians on break wandered in to hear the featured stars at other spots. In the 52nd Street clubs, unlike in concert or dance halls, the usual distinctions between audience and performers faded. The sheer concentration of brilliant musicians—each club featured two or three different combos each evening—and eager fans in a few square blocks created a unique, exciting social setting that fostered the exchange of ideas and provided an exhilarating musical experience for fans and musicians alike. But the concentration of musicians and their followers inevitably attracted hustlers and dealers as well.[25]

Nightclubs in New York were reputed to be affiliated with organized crime. The 52nd Street jazz clubs' origins as speakeasies make the connection obvious, but burlesque houses, strip joints, and other entertainment sites had mobster backers. (These associations were often hidden since the licensing and fingerprinting system inaugurated by Mayor LaGuardia restricted liquor and cabaret licenses to persons without criminal records; often a bartender or manager would hold a club's license rather than the partners backing the club.) The widely held belief that the clubs were part of underworld empires created an aura of illegality that appealed to thrill-seekers and added to the allure of jazz played in one of postwar New York's few integrated social settings.[26]

Although some musicians and critics have argued that underworld figures deliberately addicted musicians since more money could be made from their heroin use than from either alcohol or marijuana consumption, a less conspiratorial explanation is more logical.[27] Certainly there is evidence that managers sometimes used access to drugs in an attempt to control their artists, and even profited from their addiction, and many times theater owners and recording studios did little to prevent drug dealers from having access to musicians. But much of this came after the fact, once musicians had already begun using narcotics, and in the numerous autobiographies and interviews with jazz musicians, the heroin users themselves provide a different explanation. A combination of factors explains the initiation of heroin use: a Times Square social setting that mixed musicians, hustlers, dealers, and fans; a hipster subculture based in this social setting that valorized heroin as part of its rejection of square America; and the music itself (with the related influence of Charlie Parker) together account for the spread of heroin among bebop-playing musicians.

The social setting of the jazz clubs, bars, and restaurants supported constant interaction among hustlers, musicians, and fans. As Miles Davis recalled, the clubs were full of "fast-living pimps with plenty of whores, hipsters and drug dealers. I mean, these kinds of people—both black and white—were a dime a dozen on The Street." And according to jazz pianist Hampton Hawes, they did not come just for the music. Rather, they looked for "a steady clientele for their dope and access to the fine chicks who hung around the musicians." Hustlers, and sometimes fans, were all too eager to press gifts of drugs on favored musicians, hoping to share a moment or acquire a loyal customer. The location of the clubs in a small geographic area also contributed to heroin's spread. Pianist Billy Taylor concluded that "one thing that may have made narcotics traffic easier in New York then was that everyone was concentrated in one area"—the Times Square entertainment district.[28]

Musicians, isolated from the more mundane work world, developed their own subculture. Playing jazz, particularly avant-garde jazz, fostered a sense of social unity among players. Working until the clubs closed at 4 A.M., sometimes following that with jam sessions at after-hours clubs or gatherings at local eateries that catered to musicians, hookers, and other late-night workers, sleeping until late in the day, and practicing for long hours all limited the jazz musician's contact with the workday world and the people who inhabited it. Structurally a jazz musician's life reinforced a sense of belonging to a select circle, one with different habits and values than those of the square world. It encouraged participation in an oppositional subculture that posed the hip, jazz world against that of the squares.[29]

Bebop more than other jazz encouraged the expression of an oppositional, hipster subculture. Dizzy Gillespie thought that for the generation that came of age after World War II, bebop represented "a rebellion against the rigidities of the old order, an outcry for change in almost every field." Bebop rejected big band jazz and the no longer innovative sounds of swing, and it prized an individualistic virtuosity. Nurtured in Harlem's after-hours clubs, such as Minton's, Small's Paradise, and Monroe's Uptown House, and then brought downtown, bebop was designed, in the words of one critic, "to slap its audience awake." While appearance on 52nd Street in itself represented a desire for commercial success, bebop like other avant-garde art forms demanded a lot from audiences. Bebop conveyed the excitement of being on the edge, at the very frontier of musical expression where listeners followed if they dared. Bop musicians shared jive talk, berets, and rumpled suits, and created a style that connected music, politics, and heroin.[30]

Heroin too was on the edge, part of a rejection of the square world. Miles Davis recalled upon returning to New York from Paris in 1949 that he found a lot of musicians who were "deep into drugs, especially heroin. People—musicians—were considered hip in some circles if they shot smack." Heroin became the "in-drug," according to journalist Nat Hentoff, "because it was so defiantly anti-square."[31]

Bebop even became part of a shared code signaling one's hipness to drugs. Hampton Hawes recalled that when he lived in Los Angeles the distinctive triad of Charlie Parker's "Parker's Mood" was a kind of hipster's Morse code that someone whistled. "It signified that you were using but cool, and when you went to buy dope late at night . . . if the bell wasn't working or you didn't want to jar the Man out of a sound sleep or there might be someone uncool on the premises, you went B♭-G-D in that fast, secret way and the cat would pop his head out the window."[32] Bebop was part of the code, the heroin user's secret language that spread across the country.

The music itself also played a role in the use of narcotics. Some musicians used heroin to help them play, while others used it to come down from playing. Trombonist Bob Brookmeyer explained that heroin helped musicians relax. Playing jazz was an ecstatic, almost orgiastic, experience, and heroin allowed them to unwind after a night of hard work. Other musicians found heroin essential to the creative process. Hampton Hawes believed bebop's intensity and demand for creativity led its players to experiment with heroin. Red Rodney, Dexter Gordon, and Gerry Mulligan have all argued that heroin was integral to their music making or writing. Unlike booze, which made a player sloppy, heroin heightened their playing ability, they believed. They all recalled being able to concentrate, to focus on the intellectual aspects of the music, to experiment while under heroin's influence, and to work intensely for hours at a time. "When a guy is loaded and at peace," said Rodney, "he shuts everything else out except what he's interested in." Arranger Marty Paich concluded that "most of the players that I knew" felt that heroin was necessary to achieve artistic perfection. Charlie Rouse put it simply: "You had to get high to play."[33]

Charlie Parker also influenced a generation of jazz musicians, not always beneficially. No one ever accused Parker of encouraging drug use; by all accounts, the opposite was true, but Parker's example spoke more loudly than his words. The arranger Walter Gilbert Fuller remembered Bird on stage, going into a heroin nod, while "the younger musicians in there were looking up to him." Hampton Hawes argued, "some were turned on by Bird—not by him directly, but by reasoning that if they went out and got fucked up like him they might get closer to the source of his fire." Red Rodney, among many others, freely admitted that this was the case, wondering "could I play like that?" if he used heroin.[34]

Bird did not just influence well-known musicians. West Indian Tom, who worked principally as a hustler, was a trumpet player as a youth and wanted to emulate Charlie Parker. "To be a real solid jazz musician, you had to be into something," he explained. "Everybody wanted to be Charlie Parker." Whiskey wasn't the way and reefers were for kids. "The heavy guys that really knew their music, they didn't mess with no reefer. They messed with coke, heroin, and . . . morphine." Certainly, the youthfulness of many jazz musicians also made them more susceptible to such influence. Gerry Mulligan stated "you've got to remember that some of us were *very*, very young . . . and you've cut out a life for yourself which is more than you can handle." These young musicians wanted to establish as close a connection as possible with each other, and in the words of musician George Freeman, "it was almost expected for any new man to show his sense of brotherhood by sticking that needle into his arm." The combination of the social setting, the music, and the desire to emulate greatness fostered the spread of heroin among the bebop generation.[35]

If heroin had remained isolated among a few hustlers and bebop-playing musicians, it might not have attracted much attention. But in the social setting of Times Square's music scene, heroin did not remain confined. A youthful audience, fascinated by bebop and anxious to appear hip, mimicked the style of their musical idols, and in the jazz clubs and late-night establishments catering to musicians had the opportunity to acquire the drug knowledge they needed in order to move from wish to reality. Susan Miller, in her memoir of growing up with an addicted father, asked how a smart young Jewish boy from Brighton Beach, who became a window dresser in Manhattan stores, got to be a junkie in the 1940s. "It was partly the crowd he hung out with: white musicians deeply under the influence of Charlie Parker—and Charlie Parker's drug, heroin."[36]

The people who hung out with musicians, their friends, lovers, and acquaintances, all became susceptible to heroin use, sometimes with disastrous results. When Florrie Fisher began using heroin, she did not find it in her Bensonhurst, Brooklyn, neighborhood. Fisher grew up the daughter of middle-class Jewish parents. The man she married, David, worked as a musician, wore a zoot suit, smoked marijuana, and epitomized the cool style of the jazz musician. Fisher learned to smoke marijuana from her husband, but neither of them had any experience with heroin or other drugs. One night at a party of jazz musicians in an after-hours club near Times Square, a musician friend asked her if she wanted to try something new. She agreed and the next thing she knew, "he bent over me and I felt a quick, stinging jab in my leg."

Unlike many first-time users, Fisher did not become nauseated, but experienced an incredible exhilaration, as if an electric current had flashed through her body, that left her feeling detached and yet connected to the music and to everyone in the room.[37] Fisher gradually entered a nether world of hookers and heroin, and her husband became her pimp. Heroin connections for whites at this time were limited enough that David was able to control his wife by controlling her access to heroin as well as handling her money.

Youths like Miller and Fisher flocked to the jazz scene and some became drug users because they wanted to emulate the style of and gain admission to the charmed circle around famous musicians. Bebop's position as a genuinely popular music that attracted many followers in the 1940s is sometimes overlooked because of the tremendous popularity of rhythm and blues and rock and roll that came later.[38] Gilbert Sorrentino recalled that as a sixteen-year-old, "I moved in a group which thought that music began and ended with be-bop: anyone who thought differently was a square." Nat Hentoff argued that prior to the rise of rock and roll, modern jazz was the music for adolescents in the know. "It was something like belonging to a secret society." The problem was that members of this secret society came to share the language, the clothing, and the hipster style of cool heroin users. Drug users depended on a language of furtive signs, a shared style of dress, bearing and movement, and the assurance, often repeated, that one junkie could always tell another. Bebop fans, hanging around the overcrowded clubs and late-night scene, mingling with musicians, dealers, and hustlers, cracked the code.[39]

The police, club owners, and band leaders claimed they tried to control the heroin trading associated with the jazz scene. Police patrolled 52nd Street in increasing numbers in the late 1940s and made arrests of dealers and musicians. In addition, four clubs—the Onyx, the Downbeat, the Three Deuces, and the Spotlight—all lost their cabaret licenses for a time in 1945 because of narcotics trafficking on the premises.[40] But the problems posed by drugs persisted into 1950s. Ralph Watkins, the owner of Kelly's Stables on 51st Street, agreed that "in jazz today [mid-1950s] the great danger is in drug addicts and drug peddlers." Industry journals, such as *Downbeat* and *Metronome*, constantly warned against narcotics use, and orchestra leaders like Dizzy Gillespie, Jay McShann, and Woody Herman tried to keep pushers away from the backstage dressing rooms of their bands. Some club owners tried to limit the activity of drug sellers on their premises without involving the police. They feared losing their cabaret licenses, and they did not want the bad publicity of a raid that would inevitably ensnare musicians and audience members alike. One owner claimed that he "hired hard guys who knew almost all the pushers. One night we took seven pushers into the office and, one by one, busted open their heads. The word soon got around."[41]

It is difficult to know how seriously to take these claims; certainly they did little to curtail the heroin scene. Pianist Billy Taylor commented that the dealers eventually became more interested in the fans than in the musicians: They found a "lucrative market" in the Times Square area, and "were preying on the school kids and others who came down." A former addict, Whitehead, explained in an interview that when he was eighteen he started going to 52nd Street to be with the musicians. "I was a hanger-on, . . . [I] liked to be with them and then, when I got involved with narcotics, I started selling a little bit too." Saxophonist Jackie Maclean was another one of those school kids. He recalled that as a teenager, hanging around the jazz clubs, traveling with street gangs, he saw a lot of heroin being used. "I can't say that I really knew what was involved in it when I started using it. I just thought it was something else that adults didn't want high school kids to do."[42]

And there were plenty of high school kids in the Times Square district. Bebop was sufficiently popular that when new clubs opened in the late 1940s—Bop City, Birdland (named for Charlie "Yardbird" Parker), and the Royal Roost—they added inexpensive bleacher seats and soda fountains to cater to an underage crowd ("it wasn't a whiskey-drinking audience"). Besides the jazz clubs, Times Square's arcades were designed to draw a young audience, and its movie theaters, which routinely out-grossed those in the rest of the city, were another major attraction. Young people were everywhere, including the places frequented by hustlers and dealers.[43]

The spread of heroin among young New Yorkers sparked an investigation by New York State Attorney General Nathaniel Goldstein in 1951. Although dealing had spread beyond the Times Square area by this time, a number of Times Square businesses remained central to the heroin trade. One witness interviewed by investigators was a young woman who worked as a composer and arranger (and who had turned to prostitution to support her $200 a week heroin habit). She reported that she knew of three dealers who used the jazz club the China Doll to peddle drugs: "I guess it's a respected night club and you can't be too open about it there, and they [dealers] usually sit in there and buy drinks and do sort of an under the table business." Birdland was more important with its bleachers for teens and its live radio broadcasts with Symphony Sid, which made it the jazz spot of the 1950s. One nineteen-year-old witness claimed that dealers came to Birdland to make contact with users: "usually the connection comes down without any stuff on him; he has it stashed in the street somewhere." At another club, she reported, users would "take off [inject] in the ladies room and the men's room upstairs. . . . You have a lot of junkies taking off in the bathrooms up there." The Roseland Building, home of the Roseland Ballroom, a popular dance hall, had a bathroom accessible from the first floor where junkies could also be found "taking off." Herbert Huncke remembered that for a time the doorman at the Royal Roost was an important connection. You gave him money at the door, he wrote down the number of capsules you wanted, and then you went downstairs to the men's room. There the attendant prepared the amount you had paid for and you went into one of the stalls to shoot up. If there was too much police pressure and the dealers feared a raid, they moved at least temporarily to other sites. Sometimes they retreated to 1690 Broadway, a music publishing building next to Bop City and just a couple of blocks from Birdland, where they stood around in the hallway in order to catch the musicians and songwriters, if not the fans.[44] Police Captain Thomas McVeigh stationed policemen to patrol Seventh Avenue between 49th and 52nd Streets, and he testified to numerous arrests, but to little effect. Heroin permeated the entertainment district.[45]

Habitués of the urban underworld also used the other quasi-public institutions in Times Square to buy and sell drugs and drug paraphernalia. Charlie's Tavern, a musicians' bar on 50th Street, where a decade earlier Olive Cregan went to purchase marijuana, became known as a good place to score heroin. Users thought that the police did not look for junkies in a bar because of the widespread belief that heroin users did not drink alcohol. Users would come in and sit at the bar, order a coke, and wait for the connection. "And the pusher came in, and, of course, he would order a drink and go right straight back to the men's room" where he transacted business. Stella mentioned in an interview that she purchased her "works" at the Whelan's Drug Store in Times Square. "After 12 [midnight], they had this particular man working there and he used to sell you the whole outfit—you know, the needle and the rest of it in a bag." "It was only fifty cents for the needle and the dropper and whatever you needed."[46]

Cafeterias were particularly notorious as drug-selling locales. These have all disappeared from the city, but in the postwar period they were the epitome of modernity and attracted crowds at all times of the day or night. Equally important, they featured large plate-glass windows that offered a view of the streets. Both customers and police could be spotted coming down the block, and plans adjusted accordingly. The La Salle Cafeteria was one such place frequented by musicians, club owners, and theater people. After the bars closed at 4 A.M. musicians and their hangers-on, as well as hookers and their pimps, met there for cheap food and the possibility of a score. "All you have to do is just go in, purchase a cup of coffee, glass of milk, and sit around and naturally one addict would always recognize another one and if you come up to the peddler, if you talk right, he'll sell you some right in there." The B and G coffee shop, one block farther downtown, was a haven for upscale cocaine users, while Hanson's Drug Store, right next door, was a gathering place for musicians and theater people as well as a place where dealers sat in booths for "two or three hours" waiting for customers. Hector's Cafeteria, the Garden Cafeteria, and Bickford's Cafeteria, all within blocks of each other around 50th Street and Broadway, were open marketplaces. At Hector's you didn't even have to buy food—"just come in, put your money down in front of the peddler, pick up the drugs and leave." At other places dealers loitered over a cup of coffee or a piece of pie, watching for their usual customers. "Connections usually sit near the window," recalled an informant, and "they can see you coming, you just go in, they got the drugs ready, they say 'How much you want?' "[47]

The social settings that catered to jazz musicians and their followers supported a subculture that linked music, a sense of alienation, style, and heroin use. Heroin became the signature drug for many among a generation of musicians, hustlers, and admirers. Using heroin reinforced a sense of being part of a hip elite that was culturally superior to working squares and possessed a different, "higher" sensibility. The Times Square entertainment district nurtured the transformation of the drug subculture, hosted meetings between users and novices, and facilitated the transmission of drug knowledge. Once planted in the social setting of jazz clubs, dance halls, cafeterias, and other venues that catered to a late-night crowd, heroin spread more freely into neighborhoods and other social settings beyond those that had to do with jazz or nightlife. Most disturbing was the continued spread of heroin among adolescents, which became a national crisis by the early 1950s.

CHAPTER THREE

The Plague

HEROIN AFFLICTED INNER-CITY neighborhoods from New York to Los Angeles in the late 1940s and early 1950s. The author Claude Brown recalled from his own youth, "I didn't know of one family in Harlem with three or more kids between the ages of fourteen and nineteen in which at least one of them wasn't on drugs." Neighborhood boys hustled money for heroin, while girls took their place in the hooker's lineup on 125th Street.[1] If jazz musicians, hustlers, and white hipsters formed a cultural elite of sorts, the same cannot be said of the largely poor adolescents who made up the vast majority of new heroin users in the years after 1945. They were socially and economically marginal, limited by a color line to the oldest neighborhoods, shabbiest schools, and worst jobs. Heroin offered a way to identify with the hipsters, the "cool cats" in the neighborhood, rather than the working squares—their parents whose dreams of a promised land had soured. News of heroin's magical power to transform their consciousness circulated like wildfire as small groups of users, sometimes classmates in a particular high school or young men who hung out together on a street corner, proclaimed the wonders of the new drug. Candy stores, pool halls, rooftops, parks, basement clubs—the institutions of an urban adolescence—were the social settings in which youngsters learned about heroin.[2]

Tommy Gordon, Jr., a Chicago adolescent, was one of these youths. In September 1947, near the beginning of the postwar heroin wave, fifteen-year-old Tommy took a fatal overdose of heroin; his distraught father wrote to the Federal Bureau of Narcotics to demand an explanation. The father admitted to federal agents that he thought his son had been taking heroin for about a year, although he had confirmed this only recently. Tommy had been a good student and obedient at home, but around the beginning of eighth grade his parents noticed that his behavior changed. First Tommy began to skip school and lie to his parents regarding his whereabouts. Then his clothing began to disappear; when questioned, he said that he had pawned it and claimed he had given the pawn tickets to some boys. Next, in the summer of 1947 Tommy and another boy were arrested for larceny and brought before the juvenile court. The judge was sympathetic to a first-time offender whose father was partially disabled, had worked steadily for fifteen years as a butcher in Chicago's Union Stockyards, and was clearly trying to do his best for his family. The court agreed to have Tommy placed on probation with the condition that he be sent out of Chicago before the opening of a new school year.

Even after his court appearance, Tommy revealed few clues about his change of behavior. His parents, with Tommy's probation officer assisting, questioned the boy—"trying to get a truthful statement from my son," as Thomas Gordon put it—but Tommy denied that he was having any problems. Several weeks later, Thomas Gordon was going through his son's clothes when he found an eyedropper and a hypodermic needle. "I showed these articles to him and questioned him about them, but he would not admit that he even knew what they were." Gordon was unsure what to do, and so continued with the plan to send Tommy to Pittsburgh to live with relatives. Tommy was scheduled to leave right after Labor Day, in time for the new school year, and Thomas Gordon therefore thought nothing of giving his son five dollars to take his girlfriend out to the amusement park for a little Labor Day fun.[3]

Apparently Tommy really did intend to go out with his girl. He met Hugh Dabney and Ulysses "Bunky" Gougis and told them he was on his way to Riverview Park but would come over to their house if he did not see his girlfriend. Around three or four in the afternoon a neighbor knocked and told them that Tommy was downstairs. Dabney recalled, "Bunky and I went downstairs and found him sitting on the concrete steps as you enter our building and he was slumped over and out." He and Bunky carried Tommy upstairs, put him on the bed, and tried force-feeding him milk and placed ice on his groin and temples to revive him. These were standard measures for handling overdoses, but neither worked. Hugh and Bunky were not particularly concerned, however: Bunky had found Tommy on the street unconscious from an overdose before. On that occasion Bunky carried him upstairs, gave him milk, kept him upright, and slapped him in the face a few times, until Tommy began to protest the slapping. The boys thought that Tommy would come around this time as well, and they left him to sleep it off on the bed while they went downstairs. They returned after half an hour, but Tommy was still unconscious. Worried, the boys called a cab to take him home; they "told his mother and father that Tommy had been out for a couple of hours and they better get a doctor."[4] But by then it was too late; Tommy died at 2 A.M. on the day he was supposed to leave for Pittsburgh.

If Tommy Gordon's parents were shocked at his senseless death, so too was the senior FBN agent in Chicago. R. W. Artis, the Chicago supervisor, wrote to Harry Anslinger, the Commissioner of Narcotics, "This is the only territory in which I have worked where young boys from fourteen years old to the very early twenties are addicted to the use of narcotic drugs." Although Artis did not realize it, he was witnessing the start of a new national trend, dominated by teenagers and African Americans. There is no clearer evidence for the novelty of adolescent heroin use than the fact that the death of a single boy stirred a major investigation into the sources of heroin use among the South Side's teenagers.[5]

FBN agents discovered a cluster of narcotics cases among Tommy Gordon's friends and schoolmates. About twenty youths, the majority of them under eighteen, had been using heroin for between one and three years. "Some started to use narcotics while in grammar school, and some while in high school or shortly after leaving school," the agents reported. They found that the boys purchased their heroin from older peddlers, Ross "Mush" Robinson and Ralph "Whitefolks" Alexander, who had been selling to five of the boys for two and a half years. Agents claimed, "In many instances they were solicited by the peddler, who gave them their first shot of narcotics thereby inducing them to become customers."[6] Here was the classic formulation that would dominate the national discussion of adolescent heroin use in the 1950s—wily adult peddlers preyed upon innocent youths and lured them into becoming junkies by supplying free heroin. But the agents' own interviews with the Chicago teenagers suggest a very different narrative.

The vast majority of youths acquired drug knowledge from relatives or neighborhood friends, many of whom attended DuSable High School. Hugh Dabney discovered his older half-brother, Charles Berry, was using heroin, "so I asked him if he would let me try some. He said he would. We were in my parents' home alone and he cooked up some narcotic drugs and then took a shot and I watched him and then I took a shot by hypodermic injection. After I took the shot I felt good and did not get sick." Dabney apparently knew that nausea was a common side effect of heroin, drug knowledge likely obtained from his half-brother, and he knew how to enjoy his first encounter with heroin. However, despite his half-brother's use of the drug, he was not sure where to score on his own. About a month later, he ran into Tommy Gordon and Bunky Gougis, both close friends who had recently started using heroin. "I met Bunky and Tommy Gordon and I asked Bunky where he was going. Bunky replied that he was going to 47th Street, and I asked him if he was going to get some stuff. So then I told Bunky that I was using stuff also." Another youth, George Anderson, was Tommy Gordon's friend and stopped by his house in June 1947. There Tommy and two other boys were in the process of shooting up. "I asked them what they were doing and they told me that they were preparing some 'stuff' and told me how it made you feel so I asked them for some." Reynolds Wintersmith, a student at DuSable High School, began using narcotics the same way. He ran into a friend "one day when he was about to take his daily shot of narcotics, and I asked him could I have some to try. He said, 'yes.'" Wintersmith was also close friends with Bunky Gougis ("I have known him since I was a little boy because we lived in the same neighborhood, and then we went to DuSable High School together") and was with Tommy Gordon the day he made his fateful heroin purchase. When agents interviewed Claude Dangerfield, also a DuSable student, they asked him the names of the peddlers he bought from. But Dangerfield answered, "I have never 'picked up' from any peddler and do not know them. Thomas Gordon always left me on the corner."[7] While Dangerfield may have been trying to protect his sources, it is clear that no insidious peddler tempted these boys to start using heroin by dispensing free shots on the corner; they were classmates, boyhood friends who traveled in the same social circles, and were active agents of their own narcotics use, even if they were largely ignorant of the drug's effects and the potential consequences of its use. It was as if one had discovered a hot new record and could not wait to tell all his friends about it, and get them to listen to it too. The news about heroin traveled fast in the social settings of inner-city neighborhoods, and curiosity, friendship, and opportunity were the only conspirators in these cases.

For a couple of youngsters, jazz created the connection to drugs, much as it did for the adolescents who hung around Times Square. Grover Hatcher, a student at DuSable High School, used heroin for the first time in December 1946, when he was seventeen. The previous summer he organized a jazz band that played regularly at the Joy Box, a local nightclub. The bass fiddle player used heroin, and he shared it with Hatcher. Charles Durgens had studied the saxophone at DuSable High School and then moved to New York to play in a small jazz band. The bandleader, Erskine Brody, was equally young and the two of them spent off hours together. "The first shot of narcotic drugs that I used was during June or July of 1947 with Brody, inasmuch as he obtained the narcotics and gave me a shot." After the band broke up, Durgens returned to his Chicago South Side neighborhood, where he continued to inject.[8] However, few of the boys needed to learn about heroin in more centrally located settings such as jazz clubs. By 1947 the drug was already freely available in African American neighborhoods.

Another youth, James Logan, followed a different path into heroin as one of the first students at DuSable, possibly the first, to begin using narcotics. Smuggling routes to the United States had not yet been reestablished in 1945 when Logan started using morphine. While he was still in high school, Logan had run around with a group of older men, several of whom had served in the U.S. Army in World War II, and had been discharged. "Most of these boys had morphine syrettes [a small tube of morphine with a hypodermic needle attached that was part of a standard medic's kit], which they had taken from the Army. They freely talked about taking morphine shots, which naturally created my desire to try one." By this time, the original supply of stolen syrettes had run out, but the group was able to purchase morphine, most likely also stolen from military sources, on the South Side. (In 1946 the FBN discovered that "dope peddlers" had been buying surplus life rafts, each of which contained five morphine syrettes, from the War Assets Administration.)[9] Logan's friends taught him to "joy pop" (inject under the skin rather than in a vein) and he began using morphine twice a week, on Friday and Sunday evenings, before going to dances. "During this time, I bought all my narcotics in capsule form from a man known as Pops, who stood near the hot tamale cart at 55th and Indiana Avenues. . . . Pops stopped dealing about a year ago, but I would see him several times a week on the street. I paid Pops $3.50 for a half grain of morphine, but morphine finally went out, and then I bought heroin from Pops for $3.00 a sixteenth [of an ounce]."[10] Logan had learned about opiates from older, more experienced users who had acquired their habits in the service during the war. But they were not dealers, just local hustlers and friends who injected morphine together. As Logan gained experience, he developed his own contacts with dealers that enabled him to bypass his original sources for narcotics. And, like the other youths in the Chicago group, Logan initiated his drug experimentation himself.

None of the Chicago cases conformed to the prevailing narrative in which a dealer supplied heroin to an unsuspecting youth in order to addict him. Edward Davis came closest through his association with Wilbur Cannon. Davis knew Cannon because they shot pool together at a local pool hall. One day Cannon was short of money and needed a fix, and he asked Davis for $1.50 to buy some drugs. He offered to share the morphine tablets he bought with Davis, and he showed him how to prepare the drug and shoot it with an eyedropper and hypodermic needle. But even this was more like an exchange between associates, the trading of cash for drug knowledge and experience in a local setting where such exchanges could take place, rather than the model promoted by the FBN and the popular media. In one of the only examples of direct interaction between acknowledged dealers and young users, the outcome was the opposite of what authorities predicted. Grover Hatcher's habit was costing him $30 a day and he had added cocaine to his heroin use. He admitted to authorities, "the peddlers whom I bought from knew I was underage." But then he added, "they did tell me that they thought I ought to quit using it."[11]

These youths took heroin because they were swayed by the example of older peers, by the growing presence of the drug and the concentration of drug users in their neighborhoods, and by their adolescent desire to be part of the hip, new happening thing. One anonymous Chicago youth, not part of the FBN study, told investigators in vivid detail how he came to learn about heroin on the street corner. His account indicates both the eagerness of young men to try heroin and the reluctance of their older friends to introduce them to it: "I used to hear them [older boys] talk about it [heroin]. . . . So-and-so and so-and-so about stuff. This about stuff, that about stuff. All I could hear was stuff." He approached an older friend to learn more, but his friend warned him to stay away: "I mean he begged me. He wouldn't even tell me what's happening, you know." But then one day his friend was without money and in need of a fix. "He's sick [suffering from withdrawal]. He wants money. So he says, 'You got any money?' I said, 'Yeah, I got some money.' He said, 'Loan me a couple of dollars.' I said, 'How many dollars?' He said, 'Three.' I said, 'For what?' He said, 'So I can make up.' I said, 'Make up? What do you mean?' He said, 'Get high; I'm sick, man.' I said, 'What are you talking about, man?' He said, 'You know I'm hooked, I'm sick, man.' I said, 'I'll loan you three [dollars], but depending that you get me high.' The older boy finally agreed and shared two caps. "I gets high, I gets real twisted, I'm feeling nice. I never had no kick like that before."[12]

With all of its individual variations, this was a story told again and again: heroin did not need to be pushed, for the experience sold itself. Not even the "sickness" of addicted users dissuaded youths from trying it.

The FBN used the information they had gathered in the Chicago case to arrest several low-level street dealers, all of whom were African American and probably addicts. Two of those arrested, Ross Robinson and Horace Washington, went to municipal court charged with contributing to the delinquency of a minor. "Horace Washington admitted selling narcotic drugs to minors, but Ross Robinson, after a long series of questioning, admitted that he had made such sales because he was prevailed upon by the minors." The FBN and the U.S. attorney decided that they wanted to protect the boys from having to testify in court. Without corroborating witnesses and physical evidence, the dealers could only be charged with contributing to delinquency, for which the maximum sentence was one year in Cook County Jail and a one-dollar fine. Several other dealers had previous charges pending against them for narcotics sales; the statements of the youths were placed into the case file for use in sentencing on these other charges. Generally, the FBN was interested in avoiding publicity in the case, noting with relief that a printer's strike in Chicago had kept the matter out of the press.[13]

The FBN agents conducted a remarkable study that traced the origins and spread of heroin use among a group of youngsters at the very beginning of the postwar heroin boom. While this collection of reports is more extensive than others, it is by no means unusual. Agents in New York, Detroit, and St. Louis were finding similar clusters of cases, often with similar etiologies.[14] Teenagers organized in peer groups shared the news about the almost orgiastic pleasure to be derived from heroin. They acquired their drug knowledge from more experienced users, most often only slightly older than they were, in the social settings of the neighborhood. They demanded that the drug be shared.

By the late 1940s, the agents were fully aware of how one youth's heroin use influenced another's, and were beginning to understand the social and urban dimensions of heroin use. R. W. Artis, the district supervisor in Chicago, located the heart of the problem with the African American population. "A good portion of these people have come from southern states," he wrote. "This has meant quite a large market for drug peddlers, who, very greedy after their lean years during the war, are making the most of it. The housing conditions on the south side, where all of the people have been thrown together, have exposed the young to the wiles of the drug peddlers." Artis recognized the problem of segregation as well as the marginality and spatial centrality of the African American population and its consequent susceptibility to heroin. It could have led to a discussion of poverty, racism, and underemployment—in other words, to a critical analysis of the social setting of Chicago's South Side African American neighborhoods and their relation to heroin. But Artis was writing for Harry Anslinger, who was one of the principle underwriters of the dominant cultural script of the postwar period that claimed that dope peddlers lurked near schools and playgrounds in order to seduce unsuspecting youths into drug addiction. Artis therefore went on to confirm Anslinger's view, claiming "I have talked with mothers here who have told me that their children cannot walk on the streets in certain sections unless [sic] some peddler approached them with marijuana or heroin." Despite the evidence his agents had gathered about adolescent choices, the eagerness with which they pursued heroin, and the reluctance of dealers to sell to minors, Artis, like other FBN agents, used the narrative of dealers and victims to explain the increase in heroin use. If any additional explanation were needed, it lay not in discrimination or inequality but in the primitive psyches of African Americans. "As you know," Artis commented, "by nature the great majority of these individuals are inclined to anything that they believe exciting or easy living, which makes them susceptible to drug addiction."[15] Evil drug dealers and racial tropes of a simple, pleasure-seeking people were sufficient to explain the postwar heroin boom.

More systematic surveys confirmed the FBN's anecdotal reports about the concentration of heroin use in specific low-income neighborhoods inhabited by African Americans. The Mayor's Committee in Detroit, for example, found that over 90 percent of Detroit heroin users came from just two police precincts, the first and the thirteenth, that consisted of about three and a half square miles. In New York, a massive epidemiological study concluded that 15 percent of the census tracts in Manhattan, Brooklyn, and the Bronx, home to just 30 percent of the city's sixteen- to twenty-year-old males, contributed over 80 percent of the male adolescent heroin users. These census tracts were poor, dense, and largely African American and contiguous Puerto Rican areas. Reports from Cleveland and Chicago drew similar conclusions.[16] While the FBN was right in pinpointing the social location of the postwar heroin boom, they were less successful in explaining why it happened. (To be fair, FBN agents were law enforcement officers, not sociologists, and were concerned more with interdiction than analysis.)

African American adolescents began using heroin because they associated the drug with hustlers, whom they admired for defying the square (and discriminatory) world of work, and because the historic concentration of vice markets in African American neighborhoods made access to drugs and drug knowledge easy.

The first group of heroin users, who began in the 1940s, included the neighborhood "cool cats"—hustlers, gamblers, and pimps who made their living on the street. They conveyed that heroin was hip, and that its users were an elite distinguished from the ordinary working people of the neighborhood. For example, Dharuba remembered that for his father's generation "it [heroin] was somewhat slick, somewhat of a cool thing to do. All the jazz musicians did it, all the fly niggers did it." This group affected a style that combined racial consciousness, a rejection of exploitation in the labor market, a taste for fashion, and a defiance of decorum and order. They juggled hustling and drug use successfully, enjoying a lifestyle that no workingman could match.[17] They are remembered as the generation of heroin users who were respectable, who never nodded out on the streets, and who did not leave home without being presentable. As Teddy, a former heroin dealer, put it: "They were clean, their clothes looked good, and they only stole the best. They kept money in their pockets, and nobody talked." John, another addict, reported that "the addicts of yesteryear, they had more class. . . . I wouldn't have come out of the house without a suit and a tie and my shoes shined." And, "Curtis" maintained, "back in those days, dope fiends used to *dress*."[18]

Everything about this group established that heroin and its users were cool. They were in the early stages of heroin use, still able to control it. Later, some may have become full-blown addicts, similar to the popular stereotype of the junkie, willing to do anything for heroin, but in the early years these men managed their habits, supported themselves as hustlers or pimps, and succeeded in maintaining themselves on the streets in a certain style, all attributes that adolescents admired.[19]

Equally important, heroin was there, readily available to anyone who wanted to try it. "Heroin had just about taken over Harlem," according to Claude Brown. Heroin's casual use was a measure of its popularity. People invited you to get high, Brown recalled, just as nonchalantly as they might have invited you over for a drink. An adolescent could pick up drug knowledge and drugs anywhere in the neighborhood should he decide to become a cool cat.[20]

The historical association of African American neighborhoods with vice districts made heroin more readily available to adolescents like Claude

Brown, Tommy Gordon, and their peers elsewhere. Police regulation and political corruption segregated vice, gambling, prostitution, and illegal liquor sales in African American neighborhoods even as they were (at least periodically) cleaned up elsewhere. Lenox and Seventh Avenues in Harlem, Central Avenue in Los Angeles, and Pennsylvania Avenue in Baltimore were among the streets that served as the main thoroughfares of neighborhoods as well as places where after-hours clubs, gambling joints, and other illegal activities concentrated. Like the Chinatowns of the nineteenth century, African American ghettos centralized vice services, and since these vice districts were located in residential neighborhoods, as heroin became available there, it began to permeate the neighborhoods. Heroin seeped from the underworld into the homes of ordinary working people and their children.[21]

Harlem provides the perfect example of this. Drugs were relatively easy to find, and not just in nightspots frequented by musicians. May, a prostitute and heroin user, recalled in an interview: "Buying the heroin was the easiest thing in the world. I was living at 111th Street, between Fifth and Lenox. All you had to do was walk out the door on Fifth Avenue. The Spanish boys and the black boys had nothing but drugs." Her experience was not unusual; a witness before an investigating committee in 1951, which looked into New York's shocking increase in heroin use, provided a tour of Harlem's drug emporia, which were scattered throughout a twenty- to thirty-block residential area. She reported that dealers hung out at the Lotus Bar, the Rendezvous, the Solar Cafeteria, the Empire Cafeteria, the Pelican Bar, and the Reno, all on Lenox Avenue between 112th and 133rd Streets. On Eighth Avenue and 126th Street, one found the Braddock Bar, the Pasadena Bar, and Bank's Bar, all equally notorious. Across the street was the Sheffield Luncheonette, where "most of the peddlers hang around . . . from about four o'clock [when the bars closed] to seven in the morning, because that is the place where the prostitutes and pimps hang out, so naturally they make a good deal of money there." The famous Apollo Theater on 125th Street attracted drug sellers who mingled backstage with the performers. Local hotels also offered convenient meeting places for dealers and their customers. No one was immune. Even on the famous Strivers' Row (138th and 139th Streets, between Seventh and Eighth Avenues) dealers and gangsters lived in the same buildings as Harlem's cultural and economic elite.[22] The spatial logic of inner-city drug markets concentrated and perpetuated drug use and sales in these neighborhoods, and this social setting preserved and transmitted heroin use over time.

Policy makers in the 1950s ignored the evidence for a sociological expla-

Bickford's Cafeteria at Broadway and 145th Street, picketed by members of the Eleanor Roosevelt Democratic Club, June 18, 1963. Cafeterias were ideal meeting spots for heroin dealers and their customers because of the casual anonymity of their use and their large plate-glass windows, from which dealers could observe the streets. *New York World Telegram and the Sun.* Photograph Collection, Library of Congress.

nation of heroin's spread. The FBN and local police blamed drug dealers for the increase in heroin use and demanded greater enforcement powers to deal with them. Political leaders responded to the enforcement community by passing legislation that established increasingly stiff penalties for narcotics trafficking. In their view, adolescents were the victims of heroin abuse, who became the poster children to justify criminal justice approaches to heroin. Ironically, despite evidence of where drug use was increasing, most of these adolescents were white.

What was most notable about white heroin users is how few of them there actually were. For example, of the 172 users seen in the Detroit Psychopathic Clinic in 1951, only about 20 percent were white with the remainder African American or of "mixed" race. Statistics from other cities and the federal narcotics hospitals were similar. In the 1930s, the ratio of whites to African Americans was nearly reversed, with whites constituting over 80 percent of the heroin-using population. There may have been some undercounting of white users, but it is unlikely that whites suddenly went unreported after World War II: the FBN tracked down drug users ruthlessly, regardless of color. Even accounting for some hidden white heroin use, it is clear that they were a small minority among the cohort of new users.[23]

White heroin users shared similar characteristics and pathways into drug use with African Americans. In a sample of heroin users in Detroit (eleven white and fifty-three African American), both groups were about twenty-four years old on average and had used drugs for a little more than five and a half years. Most had initiated drug use with marijuana and then switched to heroin, although eight of the African Americans started with heroin or morphine as opposed to only one of the whites.[24]

The only important difference between white and African American heroin users was where they began using heroin: white users more frequently learned about heroin in central places outside of their immediate neighborhoods, in entertainment districts such as New York's Times Square, which helped limit the extent of white use, while African Americans found heroin locally. This helps explain not only why there were more African American heroin users, but also why more started drug use directly with heroin. Social setting determined who had access to heroin and drug knowledge and who did not.

In order to learn about heroin, whites had to frequent central places such as jazz clubs; FBN agents blamed jazz itself ("They are devotees of 'Bebop' music") and the racial mingling in these nightspots for the increase in white heroin use.[25] In a group of twenty white heroin users in Detroit, both male and female and all between the ages of eighteen and twenty-five, the males were "in most instances, musicians" and the women their girlfriends and acquaintances. Here the association seemed to be simply between jazz and heroin use. But then the agent investigating the case added: "I have noticed in the last six months a tremendous increase in the number of young white persons frequenting the colored district in Detroit, particularly colored night clubs of which five or six advertise themselves as 'Black and Tan' and even advertise over the radio to attract white clientele." The agent clearly linked whites' drug use to their association with African Americans in the clubs, which were also places of "race mixing" and possible miscegenation.

Young white women were thought to be particularly susceptible to charms of African American musicians; this was the case with at least one young woman in this group. Mary Lou Schaefle told agents that she started drug use with smoking marijuana while going to the Paradise Theater and the Musicians Club. "I was a great admirer of musicians and Bee Bop [sic] music," she confessed. Eventually a musician friend gave her an injection of heroin; after not using heroin again for several months, she purchased some at the Blue Bird Inn, another Detroit jazz club, and became a regular user thereafter. As her habit grew, Mary Lou and another girl in the group began to hustle in order to raise money to buy dope. "Peggy Bondy and Mary Lou Schaefle alias Mary Lou Hunt, who were reputedly about sixteen to eighteen years old, had been addicted to the use of drugs for some time past and both girls are believed to be prostituting themselves in the East side colored district."[26] The young women's attendance at the "Black and Tan" jazz clubs, according to the agent, led to addiction, prostitution, and interracial sex, thus confirming his worst fears.

While some agents may have blamed integration for the increase in drug use, others thought there was something about jazz itself that promoted heroin experimentation. When police found twenty-one-year-old John Samuels unconscious from a heroin overdose in a Minneapolis public restroom, FBN agents soon found a jazz connection. After interviewing his stepfather, agents concluded that "this is another case where association with that special breed of humans who idolize the style of music known as 'bee-bop' [sic] and 'boogie-woogie' leads to experimentation and subsequent dependence on both marijuana and heroin." Agents pieced together Samuels's history and discovered that he began playing in a jazz band in Minneapolis in 1946, at age eighteen, when he first came to the attention of authorities for using marijuana. Samuels "hurriedly" joined the U.S. Air Corps to get out of town, but enlistment apparently did little to curb his use of marijuana: he was discharged from the service in 1948, after being found in possession of some reefers. Samuels returned home, began playing jazz again, and eventually started using heroin. Despite being arrested and incarcerated for a short period in Los Angeles, Samuels simply could not stop his drug use. Shortly after he got out of jail, he overdosed. Samuels's case was serious enough that the agent concluded, "His craze for that style of music is a fundamental part of his constitutional make-up, and I doubt his ability to overcome it." It is interesting that the agent was referring to his love for bebop, not his use of heroin. The two were so interconnected in the agent's mind that it went without saying that as long as Samuels was addicted to jazz he would continue to use heroin.[27]

FBN agents again correctly pinpointed who was using heroin and where they learned about it. But neither jazz nor integration explains the increase in white heroin use. Whites had to be motivated to search out drug knowledge; they wanted to join a cultural elite, the white hipsters, who valorized jazz musicians and rejected the square world, and their heroin use was a cultural statement as well as sign of belonging. The only place where whites could acquire this experience was in the social setting of the jazz clubs in urban entertainment districts.

Rita Palmer, a seventeen-year-old Jewish girl from the Bronx, was another such youngster who had grown alienated from her parents and yearned for new experience. Rita began smoking marijuana while in high school after attending a dance at a basement social club, a common social setting for urban adolescents. Several young men were smoking reefers, and since Rita did not like to drink, smoking marijuana became a way to relax and socialize. Gradually she moved into a slightly older social circle, whose members would get high and listen to music at parties. Apparently her choice of friends led to increasingly bitter and alienating fights with her parents, who tried unsuccessfully to control her behavior. At one party in Greenwich Village, she suddenly entered a room where she observed a young man shooting up. Buddy Palmer (no relation then), a few years older than she, and a trombone-playing musician in a jazz band, became her boyfriend and eventually her husband. She begged Buddy to give her a shot, but he refused for several weeks. Finally, she threatened that she "would get it somewhere else if he didn't give it to her," and Buddy relented. Rita claimed that heroin allowed her to concentrate on the intellectual aspects of the music and not just to the "sensations" it produced. She also maintained that heroin allowed her to ignore her parents' complaints.[28]

Over the next several months, Rita increased her heroin use and decreased her school attendance, eventually dropping out and getting married to Buddy. Although Buddy warned her that she could become hooked, Rita believed that she was "different than other people" and eventually took a shot "whenever the drug was available." She and her husband worked steadily and earned about $60 a week, but on weekends they spent about $30 on heroin. This meant borrowing money from their parents as well as pawning various household and personal items. When Rita's father took a job in Florida, the couple moved in with her mother to save money. Shortly thereafter, police raided the apartment and arrested Buddy, who had been observed purchasing heroin. "The police did not determine that subject [Rita] was an addict, although she has obvious hypo needle scars on both arms."[29]

Rita, when interviewed by FBN agents, admitted that she knew of a dozen high school girls who started using drugs about the same time she did. Most of them, however, just smoked marijuana and had not tried heroin, perhaps for lack of access. Although the agents offered to have her committed to the federal narcotics hospital in Lexington, her mother refused, saying that she was taking Rita to Florida to rejoin her father. Since Rita was not charged with a crime, claimed to be drug free, had the support of her parents, and perhaps because she was white, the agents acquiesced.[30]

Rita in many ways exemplifies the experience of this early generation of white users. Like the young women in Detroit, Rita ran with a fast crowd, embracing new experiences and learning to use heroin from her jazz-loving friends. Although there were increasing numbers of white heroin users, especially in working-class neighborhoods like Rita Palmer's in the Bronx, their heroin use was dependent on being inducted into the select circles of white and black hipsterdom and participating in the social settings of jazz clubs and other night spots. Even here Rita did not have any contact with narcotics peddlers. In all likelihood, she procured heroin through her husband and his social circle. Because whites tended to rely on central places, rather than their own neighborhoods, to find heroin, they did not have the same level of access to either drugs or drug knowledge as did African Americans and Latinos. As a result, patterns of using and dealing remained somewhat secretive in white neighborhoods, which limited drug knowledge to the more adventuresome, and sheltered the majority of white youths from heroin.

Suddenly, almost as quickly as it appeared, the postwar wave of heroin use was over. Reports from New York, Detroit, Chicago, Los Angeles, and other major cities generally agreed that 1951 was the peak year for heroin initiation. In New York, new cases among adolescents stabilized at about five hundred per year; in Chicago seventeen- to twenty-year-olds had accounted for a quarter of those arrested for heroin use in 1950; by 1956 they accounted for only 10 percent as the first wave of heroin use passed. Heroin use declined most rapidly among working-class whites, who replaced "hard" drugs with soft ones, and who found more economic and social opportunities than did African Americans. On the other hand, heroin was not going away, particularly in African American and Latino neighborhoods that housed heroin markets.[31]

By the early 1950s, the first cohort of heroin users had largely burned itself out. They had been active for about five years, long enough for addiction to set in for those most heavily involved with heroin. Just as youths in neighborhoods where drug use was rampant had the opportunity to learn about and begin using heroin, they also had the chance to observe its effects, and the warning of older youths that heroin was not something to mess with finally became tangible. Not all youths were deterred, but enough were that the number of heroin users stabilized and the number of new adolescent users declined.

The "fad" aspect of heroin also waned. It was no longer the mysterious "stuff" of neighborhood conversation that no one knew anything about and everyone wanted to be the first to try. Heroin remained alluring because of the intense pleasure it delivered, because of the challenge of using it without succumbing to addiction, and because of the promise of release from the troubles of everyday life, but younger people also learned from the experience of the older generation that experience had its costs. Even though adolescent heroin use was no longer increasing, the panic was just beginning.

CHAPTER FOUR

The Panic over Adolescent Heroin Use

WHETHER THE MEDIUM was a comic book, popular nonfiction, a news report, or a public hearing, the message was the same: American teenagers were in trouble and heroin was responsible. Authorities ranging from Congress to city council members to journalists reacted to the rise in teenagers' drug use with understandable alarm. They authorized investigations in which they paraded addicts and dealers before public audiences and cross-examined them on television. They studied individual heroin users, seeking to probe the family dynamics that led to narcotics use. They created a moral panic about drug use that focused on the sinister efforts of adult dealers, and agreed on the existence of two worldwide conspiracies, the international Mafia and the Communist Chinese, that delivered heroin to the United States. Together these sources reflect the production of a cultural script, a way of framing questions about heroin use and interpreting the answers, that was shared broadly across American society and that shaped America's response to heroin in the postwar period.

Trapped, an educational comic book produced by the Welfare Council of New York City for distribution in the schools, is a typical artifact of this cultural script. *Trapped* was an attempt to compete with the sensational "crime comics" that became popular in the postwar period. It tells the sad story of Bill Jones, a white high school student in an affluent community that could be anywhere in the United States.[1] Bill, like the other students depicted in the comic, wears a suit and tie at the beginning of the story, although he becomes progressively more disheveled as he begins to smoke marijuana and then use heroin, suggesting both his middle-class status and the danger heroin posed to all of America's youth. His friend Jack gives him a puff on a reefer one day in the school bathroom; soon Bill is lighting up whenever he has the chance, and his life begins to fall apart. First his grades suffer since he can no longer concentrate on his schoolwork. He then gets fired from his afterschool job because customers complain about his lackadaisical attitude. Finally, his girlfriend drops him because she dislikes his marijuana use and is disturbed by the change in his behavior. His parents make well meant but ineffectual inquiries into the source of his frequent wild rages, but their intervention only infuriates him. Bill alienates or withdraws from everyone until Jack, a former high school track star who is given six free reefers in return for every twenty-four he sells, is his only "friend."

Jack has moved on from marijuana to heroin, and he soon persuades Bill to do the same. When Bill is feeling morose about his run of bad luck and is looking for a way to feel better, Jack tells him, "you'll find that reefers lose their kick . . . just like they did with me," and he offers to share his heroin. He warns Bill that heroin is more expensive than marijuana, and even confesses to having stolen his father's gold cufflinks to pay for his recent "deck," but asserts that there is no thrill like it. In the background lurks Charley, an adult drug dealer who looks like a seedy saloonkeeper, wearing a vest and smoking a cheap cigar. Charley runs a little store, a teen hangout with magazines and pinball machines, which serves as a front for peddling marijuana and heroin to teens looking for "kicks."

Naturally, all of this ends badly. Jack, Bill, and Jack's girlfriend, Dotty, also a heroin user, go for a ride in Jack's car and get into an accident caused by Jack's drug-induced wild driving. Bill and Dotty run away from the scene while Jack skips town, but because he is their heroin source, the two of them become increasingly desperate for a fix. They go to Charley's store and threaten to kill him if he doesn't sell them some dope. Cowering before the enraged Bill, Charley thinks "he's a hop-head all right! If I don't give him the stuff he'll blow his top . . . and the cops'll be on my neck!" ("Hop head" is a curious anachronism since it refers to an opium smoker, and opium had long disappeared from the American market.) While the immediate crisis is solved, the problem of how to pay for their future heroin needs remains. Dotty tells Bill that she has met a fellow who will give her all the dope she wants if she comes to Chicago with him; Bill protests, but Dotty threatens, "Try and stop me." Although it is never stated explicitly, the suggestion is that she will become a hooker.

Meanwhile, Bill's parents call the family physician because of Bill's erratic behavior and his flu-like (withdrawal) symptoms. The doctor rolls up Bill's sleeve, sees the track marks from his injections, and confirms that he is drug addict. The physician then arranges for Bill's admission to a hospital for detoxification, but Bill can't stand the thought of being without heroin and escapes after two days. He goes to see Charley, who refuses to give him heroin on credit when, suddenly, Jack reappears on the scene. Jack has a gun and apparently intends to shoot Charley, but before he can fire a shot, two narcotics agents walk in and arrest everyone. Jack and Bill land in jail, where Jack, in despair at a life ruined, hangs himself in his cell. Bill, through the intervention of the Juvenile Aid Bureau, is sent to the federal narcotics hospital in Lexington, Kentucky ("The judge has already promised to parole you . . . if you'll promise to go to a federal hospital for six months! They'll help you lick this thing!"). Bill tells his parents and girlfriend, "All I want now is to get this thing out of my system!"[2] Bill has rejected the alien substance ("this thing"), the heroin that has been imported to corrupt his body, and he will find his redemption by trusting in the fundamentally benevolent adult/ government authorities who have nothing but his best interests in mind.

Trapped, despite the official sponsorship of New York's Welfare Council, could easily have been mistaken for one of any number of comics or fictional pieces written for entertainment and profit rather than for drug education. The publication contains tropes that are shared across the literary spectrum from educational pamphlets to sensational exposes: white, middle-class youngsters succumbing to heroin after smoking marijuana, evil dealers plotting in teen hangouts to addict the unsuspecting, and faith in the progressive medical-judicial authorities. *Trapped*, written to compete with comic books for the attention of youth, reflected many of the same themes and contained much of the same misinformation.

A comparison to *Holiday of Horrors*, published by Orbit Comics in its *Most Wanted* series and one of the "crime comics" so many commentators worried about in the 1950s, shows how similar these genres are. In *Holiday of Horrors* a wealthy young man, Larry Newson, falls in with the wrong crowd and gets involved in a holdup to support his extravagant lifestyle. In order to calm his nerves before his first "job," Larry smokes marijuana, but it makes him go wild when the victim resists the holdup. Here criminal activity precedes drug use, although the two are inextricably linked as Larry begins to shoot heroin and enters a downward spiral. Eventually the police arrest him after a series of criminal escapades, and he is sent to a prison hospital to cure his heroin habit. After a short stay, Larry escapes, only to die in a shootout with his pusher friends after they refuse to give him any heroin.[3]

Trapped and *Holiday of Horrors*, despite their different intentions, are both unmistakable products of 1950s popular culture and reflect the cultural script about drugs. They both portray the increasing (physical) dependency on marijuana, the inevitable switch to heroin in a search for greater kicks, the turn to crime, the use of violence by males, the resort to prostitution by females, and the death of one of the main characters as a result of heroin use. The entrapment of these middle-class white youths in drug addiction makes clear to readers that heroin, like the other social problems of youth, posed a threat to everyone, regardless of race or class or locale, and were not confined to poor adolescents living in decrepit city neighborhoods. *Trapped* and *Holiday of Horrors*—with the sinister (ethnic) underworld and the sense that deviance knew no bounds—reflected the cultural fear that American prosperity and power were threatened from without and within by dangerous, hidden forces that targeted the young as the best means of undermining America. Such works did not explain who used heroin or why, but they helped shape America's response to heroin.

Trapped and other publications from the period share a remarkable amount of misinformation about drugs. Their depiction of marijuana was similar to that found in the film *Reefer Madness*, a 1938 classic that portrayed murder, rape, suicide, and mental illness as the inevitable outcomes of marijuana smoking, and featured warnings from the FBN that "narcotics" were gaining popularity among American high school students.[4] The Welfare Council's Committee on Narcotics might have been presumed to have some expertise on the subject of narcotics, yet *Trapped* largely mirrors the views of the FBN, which sought simply to scare young people away from drug use. In *Trapped*, the characters are physically dependent on marijuana and always on the verge of violence. When he is having difficulty in school, Bill thinks to himself, "Gotta get a couple of drags fast or I'll blow my top," and his hands shake when he has gone for some time without smoking, suggesting withdrawal symptoms. It seems that Bill is close to a nervous breakdown or a maniacal outbreak. When questioned too closely by his parents, Bill lashes out and knocks his father over before storming out of the house. Bill vows to his girlfriend that he can quit at any time, but of course he never does, and a reasonable reader would conclude that he was unable to do so.

The FBN made the same claims about marijuana, even though there was no evidence for them, something that was known at least as early as 1944, when the New York Academy of Medicine published the findings of its marijuana study.[5] As late as 1961, FBN director Harry Anslinger wrote "Much of the most irrational juvenile violence and killing that has written a new chapter of shame and tragedy is traceable directly to this hemp intoxication."[6] For the FBN, propaganda was more important than evidence, and the effect of this propaganda was to blur the distinctions among drugs, much to the detriment of America's youth.

The Narcotics Committee was equally misleading about heroin. *Trapped* portrays heroin as a stimulant, rather than as a depressant. Bill perks up immediately after snorting some heroin, feeling more cheerful and striding off purposefully with Jack, without going into the euphoric but dreamlike nod that usually characterized the use of heroin. Nor did he display the nausea that frequently attends opiate use in its early stages. *Trapped* also shows the protagonists sliding into heroin inevitably from their experimentation with marijuana. The switch in drugs is almost uneventful: the physical effects of the marijuana are such that heroin does not seem so different, a peculiar message for an avowedly antinarcotics agency to be sending, but one similar to that found in *Holiday of Horrors* and other 1950s cultural productions. Both marijuana and heroin cause the males to exhibit high levels of aggression and barely controlled violence, as occurred with Larry Newson. In another publication, an ostensibly sober journalistic account of heroin trafficking called *Dope, Inc.*, Joachim Joesten claims: "Under the influence of dope, a man who normally would shrink from committing a serious crime will rob, assault, rape, and perhaps even kill without qualms." A *Newsweek* article conveyed the same message when it quoted a teenager saying that he would not hesitate to kill his parents if they stood in the way of a fix.[7]

Other works of nonfiction were equally ill informed about the drugs they discussed so authoritatively, stressing the similarities between marijuana and heroin and arguing that one led inevitably to the other. Alwyn St. Charles, in *The Narcotics Menace*, a book aimed at an adult audience, maintained that marijuana was equally addicting and just as dangerous as heroin. A youth named Bill "begged, borrowed and stole all the money he could get from his mother and their friends. But still he could not obtain enough money to satisfy his reefer habit." Like the Bill in *Trapped*, this youth acted more like a desperate junkie than a marijuana smoker, but St. Charles did not seem to understand the difference. He also implied that marijuana might be even more dangerous than heroin. Marijuana was, he said, "the 'killer' drug" not because it led to a user's death, but "because of its use by killers" in a refrain that echoed the theme of the prewar marijuana panic. Another author, in a warning to parents, intoned: "Marijuana is so stimulating to some smokers that they have been known to run amuck." Equally important, it was the first essential step toward heroin. Marijuana was a "physical go-between," a required intermediary that "conditions the body for heroin." Without first smoking marijuana, a "normal kid" taking heroin would become "so sick he'd never touch the stuff again."[8] Given that adolescents were experimenting with marijuana and finding its effects to be completely different from those shown in educational, news, and recreational materials, there should be little surprise if warnings about heroin were disregarded as nonsense.

And once a youth had started on heroin his descent into addiction was inevitable. St. Charles wrote that the "Big Boys" in the dope racket targeted adolescents in order to expand their market. "The drug Czars reasoned 'kids will try anything once.' And with heroin, 'once' is enough." Other accounts suggested the same unavoidable end. Eventually, as one author concluded, the addict "is just a human pincushion with an infinite capacity for agony and a short life expectancy." These works confirmed the popular belief that heroin users were bound to become prostitutes, thieves, and desperate junkies.[9]

Trapped and the other works aimed at popular audiences fit the cultural script of the 1950s about pushers and adolescents. In *Trapped*, Charley rewards Jack for enticing Bill into using marijuana ("if you sell enough you get your own reefers for free"), which turned Jack and Bill's meeting in the men's room from a chance encounter into a planned marketing strategy. Although Jack's shift to heroin is not portrayed, once Jack begins using, he follows the same plan he employed with marijuana, and introduces Dotty and Bill to the drug, presumably with the expectation that they will help him pay for his own use. Adult dealers like Charley are not users themselves, and "kid pushers" like Jack are their tools. Jack's sharing of a deck with Bill in the booth of a candy store fits the experience of many users, in which friends shared heroin with their peers in a social setting free from adult supervision. But in this instance, giving free samples of heroin was simply a ploy to get others hooked. Dealers, parents were warned, sent youths to teen social gatherings to troll for victims. "Roll up the sleeves of every teaparty [marijuana party] regular, and at least one of them will show the needle marks of a 'mainliner.'" Why might a "hardened heroin addict" attend a teen marijuana party? The answer was simple: "He is on the prowl for more customers."[10] In the pulp

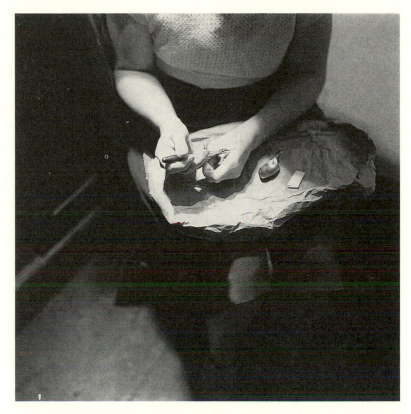

A young woman shooting heroin in her hand represents the panic over heroin use by white adolescents in the 1950s. *Look,* 1953. Photograph by Earl Theisen, *Look* Magazine Photographic Collection, Library of Congress, LC L92–53–1368 197.

novel *H Is for Heroin* ("a teen-age narcotic tells her story"), Amy Burton claims that an experienced user gladly shares heroin with others: "He lets you have a cap free and maybe two caps, and then you get loaded and like it, but then you don't get any more caps free, you buy them."[11] By cultivating new customers and then selling to them, the experienced user might make enough to support his habit or to get a discount on a "bundle" or a "load." And, in case a youth did not know how to use the heroin they supplied, a group of pushers in Philadelphia, according to *Newsweek,* ran a school to teach adolescents how to shoot up.[12]

At a time when heroin users were poor African Americans and Latinos, most popular works portrayed them as white and middle class. Frank in *Trapped* has no problem borrowing his father's late model convertible and his father has a sufficient supply of cufflinks so as not to miss the gold pair that Frank pawned. Bill's parents live in a nice, suburban home with a big front porch and comfortable furnishings. Larry Newson in *Holiday of Horrors* is portrayed as a society kid, while Amy Burton's parents are middle-class southern Californians, as were her fellow dope addicts. In *The Narcotics Menace*, Alwyn St. Charles contended that "teenage dope addicts" are not just juvenile delinquents. "Most of them," he warned parents, "are regular children, like yours and mine." The implication was clear that heroin could "infect" anyone's children and suburban life would not insulate them.[13] Since the works focused on the threat to middle-class whites, heroin use occurs in "teen space," the high schools, ice cream parlors, and playing fields of middle-class adolescence, in the hometowns of "Anywhere, USA," rather than in the urban social settings in which it was actually used. Because heroin was decontextualized, the only explanations for drug use are the adolescent search for "kicks" and the actions of adult drug dealers acting at the behest of international conspiracies. There is no attempt to understand the production of heroin use in urban social settings, to portray the real users of heroin, or to provide adolescents with information about the dangers of heroin. Instead, the intended audience was the American middle class, whose children were least likely to take heroin, but who were most likely to be enlisted in a moral panic about narcotics and the underworld.[14]

Perhaps because *Trapped* was intended for a middle-class readership, it exudes confidence about the ability to cure addicts. Despite Frank's suicide and Dotty's disappearance, authorities interrupt Bill's inevitable descent. Bill's case ends on a hopeful note as he gets ready to board the train to the federal narcotics hospital in Lexington. He has the support of his parents and girlfriend, who express no doubt that Bill will be fine in the hands of benevolent experts ("And when you come back cured, darling, I'll be waiting for you"). In this account there is no conflict between medical and criminal justice views of addiction; police officers, court officials, and physicians all cooperate to figure out what is best for Bill and to cure his illness. Middle-class parents could be expected to believe in the good intentions of authorities and the effectiveness of their interventions—even though Lexington had a failure rate of about 90 percent. For Latino, African American, and working-class white users, especially as they aged, physicians rarely intervened in a court process, the role of criminal justice agencies was less benevolent, and the outcome of intervention was not so optimistic.

If the audiences for these publications wanted to verify the message, all they had to do was read the daily press or view the new medium of television. One of the first investigations into narcotics use occurred in New York, where the *New York World Telegram and Sun* began a series of articles in April 1950 alerting readers to the increase in adolescent drug use. The paper made the usual sensational claims that teenagers progressed from marijuana smoking to mainlining heroin, that they mugged and robbed doctors and pharmacists to get narcotics, that they would become killers to secure their dope ("Roving bands of drug-hungry, berserk addicts . . . spell crime and murder"), and that parents had to fear their own children ("If I had the urge," claimed one teen addict, "and even my own mother and father stood between me and a fix, I'd kill them to get it").[15] The series caught the attention of both New York City Mayor Vincent Impellitteri and New York State Attorney General Nathaniel Goldstein, who ordered investigations into the problem. After an extensive examination of heroin use among teenagers, the Attorney General held public hearings in New York City and in Buffalo the following spring.[16] At approximately the same time, Tennessee Senator Estes Kefauver began his televised hearings into organized crime in the United States, including a half dozen sessions on narcotics. These hearings were widely covered in the local and national news media, forming a continuous loop of sensational headlines from the popular press to investigators and back again in a classic example of an escalating moral panic.

The hearings and media coverage reflected the themes found in popular works and comic books, including the presence of drugs in public schools, the role of peers in encouraging drug use, the activity of pushers, and the widespread availability of heroin in social settings frequented by adolescents. Asked at the New York Attorney General's hearings if children learned about narcotics in school, Dorris Clarke, a probation officer in New York's Magistrate's Court, replied, "Well, if it is not directly in the school, it is the neighborhood candy store or it is the alleyway alongside the school." The New York City Welfare Council's James Dumpson also testified at the hearings that heroin was available near school grounds. "The pusher stands in a hallway [of a nearby building] and passes the goods to the girls both on the way to school and coming from it." Teenagers claimed that young people acquired drugs and drug knowledge in high school lunchrooms, bathrooms, and hallways, which were natural gathering places that were relatively secure from adult observation. Investigators asked seventeen-year-old A.N.: "Where did you see heroin sold? A. Sometimes they sell it in a sweet shop across the street [from school]," while fifteen-year-old W.G. claimed he first saw heroin "in the lunchroom [in school]," and he started using it in school bathrooms. According to one student, he and his classmates passed heroin around in the back of the classroom:

> Q. How many boys would be with you when you used to pass heroin back and forth?
> A. Inside the school?
> Q. In the classroom?
> A. Yes, about five.
> Q. You would all go to the back of the class?
> A. Yes.[17]

This testimony was directly contradicted by the most extensive study of adolescent heroin use in the 1950s, *The Road to H*. The clinical team found that heroin use was initiated by adolescents in the homes of friends, on the street, or on a rooftop, and only "rarely on school property."[18] However, claims about drug selling and using at school made better headlines.

Candy stores, movie theaters, pool halls, and other recreational sites ostensibly controlled by adults were more likely to be the venues where adolescents tried drugs, sometimes without the owners' knowledge. According to news reports, when police arrested seventeen-year-old Jay Leifert, a clerk in a Brownsville (Brooklyn) candy store, they announced that in addition to egg creams and banana splits, Leifert dispensed heroin capsules for $1.50 each to those youths who knew the password, "Yankee Doodle." He ran a thriving business for several months, apparently without the owners catching on. Movie theaters were also favorite places to score, as business could be transacted under the cover of darkness and other patrons would be unlikely to notice someone nodding out. The Coney Island boardwalk, a location that attracted summer crowds enjoying the beach, the rides, and the arcades, allowed users and sellers to meet discreetly precisely because it was so public, much like Times Square. A nineteen-year-old woman told the Attorney General's investigators about the "meets" that took place there. Small groups of youngsters would gather along the boardwalk and wait for the connection to show up. When he arrived, he would indicate with a shake of the head or some other sign that he was ready to sell drugs.

> Q. Where did he give it to you; on the Boardwalk or off?
> A. Yes, on the Boardwalk. One of them would walk up and catch up

with him. The connection would walk along first, one of the junkies would follow slowly and they'd catch up with each other and
that would be it. . . . Sometimes they'd shake hands like they just
met.

Q. And the money would pass and the heroin would pass?

A. Yes.

On the boardwalk, sellers and users shared a set of codes to identify one
another: a way of walking and loitering, a furtive meeting of glances, long
sleeves to cover the track marks left by use of a hypodermic needle. As in
these other social spaces, adolescents created a parallel universe in which their
use of the area to exchange drugs and drug knowledge was largely invisible
to adults.[19]

Despite the testimony that teenagers learned about drugs from their
peers, witnesses were frequently questioned about adult pushers. They responded precisely as was scripted by the popular media and according to the
expectations of their interrogators. For example, Dorris Clarke claimed: "We
have in our files any number of instances where the user, the addict, would
make arrangements to get five or six other users or addicts, and . . . his or her
own supply is given to them." A youth in Buffalo went further and claimed
that a dealer approached him at a dance and said, "I've got something to pep
you up." The two went into the men's room where the man pulled out a
reefer and gave it to him. "I didn't know what it was, and he says, smoke it,
so I smoked it." The boy claimed: "That's the way these so-called 'big shot'
peddlers do it. They give you one free and then gradually you need it." Then
at another dance yet another stranger offered him some heroin to snort:
"We went into the bathroom and he pulled out this capsule from his inside
pocket—this white capsule—and he poured out this white powder on my
hand and told me to sniff it." These were weekly dances and three or four
times over the next few weeks he was able to get free heroin to snort until
finally he was hooked and had to purchase the drug for himself.[20]

That this account (and others like it) was entirely implausible never
seems to have crossed anyone's mind. This young man described marijuana
as an addictive substance with the same buildup of tolerance as occurred with
opiates ("then gradually you need it"). That corresponded neither to medical
evidence nor to the experience of other users, but it did fit the cultural script
promoted by the FBN as well as the popular literature on the subject. Another youth testifying at the same hearing revealed that he and his marijuana-

smoking friends resorted to crime and violence in their desperate search for money to purchase reefers, echoing another theme from popular culture.[21] In both of these cases experience seems to have been transformed to fit cultural expectations.

It also did not strike investigators as unlikely that adult strangers would loiter unnoticed at teenagers' dances and then hand out free heroin samples in the hope that a random youth might sometime become a customer. This young man's account only seems plausible if one believed that heroin was both so pleasurable and so powerful ("And with heroin, 'once' is enough") that a single dose would cause the user to become addicted, and even then it defies common sense. How could a pusher ensure that he would ever have any return on his investment given the number of people attending these dances, and the lack of assurance that a particular teen would attend a later dance and come searching for additional heroin? More important, how would he know which youth to trust with an offer of an illegal substance? Evidence even in these same hearings—had officials paid attention to it— indicated that youths eagerly sought the opportunity to try heroin, that they begged older acquaintances to share narcotics with them, and that drug use cycled through adolescent peer groups. Yet the Attorney General ignored this in favor of testimony that adult dealers waited around teen dance halls, found unsuspecting youths, then ordered them to try unknown substances, which they blindly and obligingly did. It is more plausible that a young man, eager to defer blame for his heroin use on to unnamed strangers, and undoubtedly hoping to please the authorities who questioned him, simply responded according to the cultural script he was handed.[22]

Adults were less obliging and sometimes sparred with their questioners even when it was obvious that they had been carefully coached for their appearances at public hearings. "Woodrow" appeared before Estes Kefauver's Senate Committee to Investigate Organized Crime in Interstate Commerce, and he both confirmed the script and denied the interpretation placed on his testimony. Woodrow obligingly told the committee that he had been introduced to heroin through a free sample supplied him by a pusher. Woodrow testified that pushers knew that musicians, conmen, and the sort of slick people who hung around theaters, clubs, and pool halls—in other words, in the social settings of urban hustlers—were the most likely to use heroin, and so pushers congregated near the market. In one of these locations Woodrow met a dealer who offered him a "deck" to snort. Richard Moser, the committee's chief counsel, asked, "Did somebody give it to you or did you have to buy it?" Woodrow replied, "They would give it to you the first couple of times." Just to make sure of his point, Moser followed up: "That was, in order to make you a customer, they would give it to you?" Woodrow answered, "Yes sir, until you got the habit." Yet when Moser encouraged him to blame a pusher for his heroin use, Woodrow resisted the inference that he had been misled or manipulated. Woodrow told Moser, "A lot of people figured as though the sellers were the ones that were to blame for the users, causing people to use it." Moser asked, "That is true, isn't it?" But Woodrow disagreed, "I wouldn't just say that." Despite the expectations of the committee, Woodrow maintained his own agency in the process, insisting that he wanted to use heroin ("Like I said, I was inquisitive") and that he was responsible for his own choices.[23]

Another witness, Bill, went through the same steps, and resisted the interpretation committee counsel placed on his comments. First he denied ever using marijuana, which led attorney Moser to ask how he then got started on heroin. Bill replied, "I was managing a poolroom, and there were quite a few fellows in the neighborhood who would use it [heroin]." Moser then asked, "Did somebody suggest that you try it just for the fun of it?" and Bill answered, "Well, it was more out of my own curiosity, I guess." Bill confounded the expectation that he had been led into trying heroin, and he perplexed the committee when he stated that he did not progress through the expected stages of heroin use. He began by snorting, but after about three months he began to mainline. Moser twice asked, "You never tried skin shots?" but Bill insisted his friends gave him a shot directly in the vein. This led Moser back to the question of whether someone "gave" Bill heroin, but Bill repeated, "Nobody gave them [shots of heroin] to you. I mean, once you get into it, you pay for what you get."[24]

Moser also had the opportunity to question a Baltimore heroin peddler, Charles, who tried to give the committee a more realistic perspective on dealing. Charles rejected the notion that pushers went out searching for new people to addict. Moser asked him, "How do you get customers? Do you go around to persuade people to buy drugs from you?" Charles answered "No, sir, you don't go around persuading people. Most of the people I grew up with, somehow or other along the line was addicts, most of my friends. . . . You can just sell to your friends mostly, that is how I got into it, through another friend." After discussing other topics, the chairman asked Charles again whether he would go looking for new customers. Charles said, "I was getting along all right. I never wanted to meet anybody new. That is the danger in meeting new people, because you don't know who you are meeting with. I figure that if I deal with people I know, there was plenty of them, and I did a pretty good business." Later in the questioning Charles twice more denied searching for new business, stating, "In this business, the less people you deal with, the better it is."[25] Charles told the committee what common sense might have suggested, namely that no dealer in his right mind waited around schoolyards, bathrooms, or candy stores handing out free heroin samples to unsuspecting youths. It was simply too risky and entirely unnecessary. Instead, Charles confirmed what the users had said: no pusher had tricked them into using heroin. It was a matter of "choice"—to be sure, a choice heavily mediated by opportunity, the concentration of drug sales in certain city neighborhoods, and the influence of one's peers, something to which witness after witness testified, even as the committee found it hard to believe.

Here again, the evidence existed for an urban interpretation of heroin use. Users and sellers identified the urban social settings of clubs and pool halls that supplied hustlers, gamblers, and players with an opportunity for conviviality as well as a chance to share drug knowledge and to buy and sell heroin. Cool cats rejected the discriminatory work world that defined them as unequal for the excitement and independence of the hustling life, and heroin was an integral part of the style.[26] But questions about the inequalities of American society and the concentration of markets in African American neighborhoods were unasked, precluded by the cultural script of the postwar period, as were questions about heroin that had nothing to do with individual drug dealing.

Even while blaming pushers for the spread of heroin use, authorities wanted to know why some adolescents were susceptible to heroin's lure and others were not. Instead of examining the discrimination and isolation of African American youths in ghetto neighborhoods, analysts instead emphasized heroin users' psychological difficulties, especially in their relationships with their mothers. This analysis fit the increasingly Freudian character of social work, it expressed the fear of "momism" common in the period, it individualized the problem of heroin use by focusing on the defects within the user and his family, and finally it made plausible the fear that was omnipresent in the cultural productions of the period that heroin use could spread to middle-class youth: after all, everyone had a mom.

Early studies of male heroin users emphasized their passive, almost effeminate, nature—a product of their mother fixation. The authors of *The Road to H*, one of the earliest, most authoritative, and most extensive studies, argued that addicts shunned violence and street activity. They were not the street toughs who joined gangs, but boys with interests in music, clothes, and style. They were "soft-spoken, well-mannered, and graceful," and a large number could be described as "pretty boys" who "would not appear out of place in a musical comedy chorus." Naturally they suffered from problems of sexual identity, and were overly close to their mothers, with whom they had a narcissistic relationship. As another group of researchers put it, "all of our addicts have a close empathetic relationship with the mother" and distant and even hostile relationships with their fathers, who were either physically or emotionally absent in their lives. Heroin-using boys identified "domestic occupations," such as cook, baker, or tailor, as their future goals. The implication was that they simply were not masculine enough ("they do not try to appear manly, rugged, vigorous, energetic, rough-and-ready") and desired to regress to dependent and passive relationships with their domineering mothers. A hypodermic needle penetrated their flesh and ejaculated its contents deep within them, allowing them to float in a postorgiastic bliss. While the research teams did not state that these young men were gay, they certainly implied it, and they did note that several of the young men had prostituted themselves to support their habits.[27]

This failure of masculinity among adolescent male addicts suggested the threat to middle-class youths. Like their lower-class counterparts, middle-class males suffered from momism and the absence of fathers. Women ruled the suburbs where many middle-class youths lived; suburban residences were women's domains, as were the schools in which adolescents enrolled. Fathers were absent wage earners who returned home tired and distracted at the end of a long workday and after a taxing commute, and they were a distant presence in the everyday lives of their sons. If dominant mothers produced an insecure adolescent masculinity, and if that insecurity was related to drug abuse, then here was a recipe for the production of "perverts" and addicts.[28]

The inadequacy of psychological explanations for heroin use is apparent in the text of *The Road to H*. After demonstrating that heroin users were concentrated in low-income, high-delinquency, high-unemployment areas, the authors concluded that "all addicts suffer from deep-rooted, major personality disorders." Such an analysis failed completely to account for the high incidence of drug use in particular occupational groups (such as physicians) or for their own data showing a high concentration in inner-city African American neighborhoods. Only if it were presumed that white doctors and low-income African Americans shared the same personality defects could heroin use be explained as a psychological disorder. There was a clear disconnect between the authors' urban ecological analysis and their conclusions about individual psychological states.[29]

In the end, the individual psychological explanation for heroin use prevailed over one that emphasized the concentration of economic and social disadvantage in particular urban neighborhoods. Parts of *The Road to H* corresponded to earlier scientific studies about heroin addicts that emphasized their psychopathic personalities, and those were the parts of the study that were most influential.[30] Interpretations of drug use, like interpretations of other forms of deviance, stressed the individual and familial sources of the malady. Problems lay not in American society, not in class and racial inequality, unemployment and marginality, or the urban social settings of heroin users, but in the inabilities of American mothers to prepare their sons for the world.

At the same time, threats from the outside world promised to capitalize on the failures of American families. Female-dominated homes produced sons who had personalities ill fitted for modern life and who could not resist the lures of adult pushers. These pushers in turn symbolized the larger peril to American life posed by communism and the Mafia.

Heroin had to be imported to make its way into the veins of American adolescents, and the FBN identified two suppliers, Communist China and the Mafia. FBN Commissioner Harry Anslinger played the key role in popularizing these threats to American youth through public testimony before Congress, in press releases to newspapers, in stories planted in popular magazines such as *True Detective*, and through leaks of official documents to columnists such as Jack Lait and Lee Mortimer, whose *Confidential* series purported to reveal the secrets of the urban underworld. Anslinger orchestrated the release of this "evidence" and promoted the FBN (rather than J. Edgar Hoover's rival Federal Bureau of Investigation) as the frontline of defense against the alien forces of international communism and equally international Mafiosi.[31]

Communists and Mafia members both belonged to powerful, shadowy, international conspiracies that reached unseen into American communities.[32] Popular writers at the time linked the two threats to American liberty, using the same language to describe them and arguing that the work of the Mafia in corrupting local officials and subverting the processes of criminal justice could serve the interests of international communism well.[33] To be sure, no one suggested the Communist Chinese distributed heroin through the local hand laundry or the nearby Chinese restaurant, nor could anyone show how the Italian-American underworld acquired Chinese-manufactured heroin. Rather two parallel cases were made, one against China for producing large quantities of heroin that it exported for hard currency in order to fund its drive for world domination, and the other focusing on Charles "Lucky" Luciano and his alleged masterminding of the importation of heroin into the United States. The links between the two were made through metaphor, through the juxtaposition of images, and in the flamboyant rhetoric of the narcotics bureau rather than through evidence or logic.

Concerns about Chinese heroin had some basis in fact. As early as the 1920s, heroin manufactured in Tienstin, China, and smuggled through Shanghai, made its way via the Suez Canal and the Mediterranean into New York City. World War II disrupted this trade, but after the war ended, both Nationalist and Communist Chinese traded in opium in order to raise funds for the civil war that followed. Once the Nationalists were expelled from mainland China, the People's Republic of China aggressively suppressed opium growing and use (although some illegal opium production continued in southern Yunnan province). Opium from southern China and Southeast Asia entered the world market through the Nationalist Chinese, who used the profits from the narcotics trade to fund their efforts to destabilize the communist government. Thus much of the heroin the communist Chinese were accused of producing actually came from America's Nationalist Chinese allies, but Anslinger and other public officials ignored or suppressed this information in the name of Cold War solidarity.[34]

In hearings, publications, and public statements, Anslinger repeatedly tailored his remarks to underscore the country's Cold War agenda. In 1950 he claimed that all the opium-producing nations "except Russia" had agreed to curtail its production. Then China replaced the Soviet Union as the target of Anslinger's ire until 1962, when suddenly Fidel Castro's Cuba was charged with exporting opium (with Chinese help) to the American market.[35] Despite these occasional forays against other targets, Anslinger remained focused on "Red China" throughout the Cold War period. Appearing in 1955 before the Senate Judiciary Committee, which was holding hearings on the involvement of Communist China in the narcotics trade, Anslinger declared: "Certainly all this enormous trade that is taking place out of Communist China now would have to have official direction. Otherwise it would be slowed down." Anslinger went on to claim that heroin in Japan was coming from China and North Korea "and, of course, some of it finds its way as a backwash into the

United States." Heroin in San Francisco and in Hawaii, the commissioner maintained, was 70 percent and 85 percent pure, respectively, "which will show you that the closer you are to Chinese traffic, the purer heroin becomes."[36]

On other occasions Anslinger made more expansive claims. He argued that the Chinese had a twenty-five-year plan to "finance political activities and spread addiction among free peoples through the sale of heroin and opium," and he maintained that the United States in particular was a "target" to be supplied with "a flood of foreign-exchange-earning, health and morale-devastating heroin" as part of an "insidious, calculated scheme" to "spread the debauchery of narcotic addiction." Red China had become "the dope-vending dragon of the East."[37] Again and again the commissioner accused the People's Republic of China of poisoning the free world's youth by addicting them to heroin.[38]

Following Anslinger's lead, the American press repeated assertions about Communist dope dealing. Stories published periodically throughout the 1950s used the same story lines. Headlines blared "Red China Exports Opium to Make Dope Addicts of Our Boys in Asia!" "Dope Flows from Red Sources," and "Mao—Big Time Dope Peddler." In the midst of the Cold War, few bothered to question the commissioner's statistics or doubt his rhetoric. The press, especially its politically conservative wing, acted as the mouthpiece for the FBN's propaganda.[39]

Anslinger's campaign against Communist China served the institutional interests of the FBN. In the midst of the Cold War, Anslinger positioned the agency front and center as the defender of American homes and families. J. Edgar Hoover's FBI may have infiltrated the American Communist Party and cracked Soviet spy rings in the United States, but it did not have the mandate to fight communist drug dealing. Anslinger was adept at cultivating the press and keeping his agency in the news, thus building an influential constituency and defending the FBN's status and budget through both Democratic and Republican administrations. Anslinger also marginalized those who favored a medical approach to handling addiction. After all, who could legitimately question the utility of a criminal justice approach to narcotics when both the future of American adolescents and that of the free world were at stake? The FBN promised to get dealers and users off the streets, which would dry up the market for "red" heroin and protect America's youth from both heroin and communism.

The Mafia was the only equal to Communist China in the narcotics world, and for Harry Anslinger that meant Lucky Luciano. FBN agents provided the investigative staff for Senator Kefauver's public hearings on organized crime, and they served as star witnesses in the decade's many public hearings on crime and narcotics. Their testimony about the Mafia was powerful in itself and it received confirmation in 1957, when a New York state trooper's investigation into a gathering of out-of-state visitors to a local mobster at Apalachin, New York, turned into the nation's biggest roundup of organized crime figures. Few thereafter (with the notable exception of J. Edgar Hoover) could reasonably doubt the existence of largely Italian and Jewish organized crime families, who cooperated in illegal activities and were heavily implicated in the importation of heroin.[40] Anslinger's charges against Luciano undoubtedly seemed more credible in this context.

Lucky Luciano, thanks largely to Harry Anslinger (whom Luciano called "Asslinger"), assumed nearly mythic proportions in the 1950s as America's most powerful gangster, and his career prepared him well for this starring role. Luciano had been convicted of running a prostitution ring and received a thirty- to fifty-year sentence when World War II intervened. Italian organized crime figures controlled the Brooklyn waterfront, an important shipping point for supplies intended for Europe, and U.S. Naval Intelligence proposed using the underworld to protect New York's harbor. Luciano was credited with using his contacts to maintain labor peace and enlisting dockworkers to look out for potential saboteurs. After the war, Governor Thomas Dewey, who had prosecuted Luciano for being New York's master pimp and then used the celebrity he gained in the case to win the governorship, commuted Luciano's sentence on the condition that he be deported to Italy.[41]

Controversy immediately arose over Luciano's release from prison. Naval Intelligence denied having received any substantial aid from Luciano, thus making the commutation of his term seem suspect. Several of Dewey's prosecution witnesses were rumored to have recanted their testimony, claiming that Dewey had pressured them into testifying, thus throwing suspicion on the prosecutor's case. Dewey, soon to embark on a campaign for the Presidency, probably wanted to avoid questions about his prosecution of Luciano and was no doubt glad to be rid of him. Besides, Luciano had already served nearly a decade in prison. But if Dewey hoped that the Luciano case would fade away, he was wrong. Instead, Dewey faced allegations that he had taken a bribe or had succumbed to influence peddling.[42]

Luciano's actions almost immediately cast doubt on Dewey's decision making. When Luciano waited to sail out of New York, he had several notorious visitors aboard ship, including Frank Costello, reputedly the "prime minister" of New York's underworld, and the equally infamous Meyer Lansky, who was in charge of minding Luciano's interests. Clearly the gangster retained the loyalties of powerful figures, and his wartime "service" had not rehabilitated him. Once Luciano settled in Italy, FBN agents discovered that "friends" in New York were sending him gifts of cash, an automobile, and different luxury items, which the press portrayed as subjects' tribute to their exiled kingpin. Then the FBN discovered that Italian pharmaceutical companies, which were allowed to produce heroin legally, had "lost" large quantities of their heroin, which resurfaced in New York City. Who, the FBN asked, was better able to organize such a scheme than Lucky Luciano? Finally, two Italian Americans, who were arrested in Rome with three kilos of heroin in their possession, purchased their supply from a dealer who was alleged to be Luciano's right-hand man. All of the evidence was circumstantial, but constructing Luciano as a powerful criminal mastermind who had control over organized crime even from his prison cell, who had successfully fooled the Governor of New York into releasing him from prison, and who now commanded a worldwide heroin smuggling network, was not simply an act of the imagination.[43]

However, no one ever indicted Luciano for drug smuggling. The voluminous FBN and FBI files on Luciano reveal extensive surveillance of his activities by American and Italian agents from the moment he returned to Italy in 1946 until his death in 1962. In addition, several undercover operatives worked their way into Luciano's confidence and sent reports to the FBN. Despite these investigations, no evidence was ever produced against him. As agent Charles Siragusa put it, "We have numerous moral proofs . . . however, unfortunately we do not have the legal proof to arrest and prosecute Luciano."[44] In the classic logic of conspiracy thinkers, the absence of evidence itself "proved" Luciano's involvement: only a criminal as clever as Luciano could hide all evidence of his activity.

Legally admissible evidence was not necessary, however, to convict Luciano in the press and before the public. In addition to the testimony at hearings, during which FBN agents asserted that Luciano controlled the narcotics trade, newspaper accounts of heroin seizures routinely identified the narcotics as belonging to Luciano's organization—based only on agents' claims.[45] Harry Anslinger referred to Luciano as "Il Capo" and declared that "hoodlums carried narcotics to America and returned to Italy for the next consignment, on orders from Il Capo." Luciano ran an "assembly line"

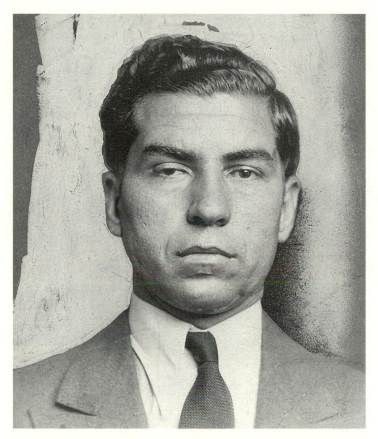

Charles "Lucky" Luciano, who became the alleged mastermind of the world heroin trade, 1936. *New York World Telegraph and the Sun.* Photograph Collection, Library of Congress, LC-USZ62–123539.

bringing Turkish opium to Italy, where it was manufactured into heroin and smuggled into the United States. Anslinger linked Luciano to the local dealer in the playground in a vast and evil international conspiracy. Luciano's heroin shipments "poured into the United States, sucking into addiction thousands of postwar adolescents."[46]

When describing the Mafia, Anslinger emphasized the "organized" in organized crime and linked it to international communism. Using the most popular metaphor of the era for corporate executives, Anslinger argued that the "killers in gray-flannel suits" used the profits from their drug empire to gain control over legitimate business and to extend their corrupt corporate

Harry J. Anslinger testifying before a U.S. Senate Foreign Relations Subcommittee, 1954. *New York World Telegraph and the Sun.* Photograph Collection, Library of Congress, LC-USZ62–120804.

tentacles into all facets of American life. Like the communists, who were supposed to have infiltrated unions, Hollywood, and youth and teachers' groups, organized crime moved into seemingly innocent front organizations. Because of the vast sums earned from the addiction of American youth, the Mafia was "beginning to obtain a creeping control over some major industries of America and Europe." While the communists sought world domination, the aim of the Mafia was not political transformation, but simply economic dominance. Since the Mafiosi had no political ideology, they also had no compunctions about cooperating with the communists if it was advantageous to them. While no evidence existed for the claim, Anslinger linked Chinese heroin to Italian crime organizations, declaring that "the syndicate crowd does not object to dealing with the Reds, as long as the profits are big in terms of dollars." As long as the Red Chinese had the Italians distributing heroin for them, they had no need for their own organization.[47]

Convinced of the presence of Mafia dealers in the nation's playgrounds and with visions of red heroin sapping the nation's strength, Congress engaged in a bout of bill writing in the 1950s. In 1951, on the heels of the Kefauver hearings and news of increasing numbers of adolescent heroin users, twenty-six bills were introduced in Congress to provide for stricter controls and harsher penalties for drug dealing. With the approval of Commissioner Anslinger, who provided public testimony on the necessity for longer drug-trafficking sentences, Representative Hale Boggs of Louisiana introduced the Boggs Act, which Senator Kefauver shepherded through the Senate. Penalties for first-time offenders were established at two to five years, with a mandatory five- to ten-year sentence with no possibility of parole for someone caught twice. A third-time offender faced a mandatory twenty-year sentence, again without any provision for a reduced sentence or parole. The Boggs Act did not discriminate between addicts who peddled narcotics to support their habits and big-time traffickers who moved kilo-sized lots of heroin into the United States. While it may have been aimed at the latter, the former were far more likely to be caught and imprisoned.

Another flurry of bills followed in the mid-1950s as Anslinger continued to emphasize the twin sources of America's heroin problem. In 1955 Congress considered fourteen bills, with sixteen following in 1956, when Senator Price Daniel of Texas used public hearings to bolster support for what became known as the Narcotics Control Act of 1956. Daniel's bill raised the ante higher still by increasing sentences for heroin dealing and, more important, establishing severe penalties for heroin possession that effectively made criminals of any users. Those convicted of possession for first, second, and third offenses received sentences of two, five, and ten years, respectively, with probation or parole available only for first offenders.[48]

Congress and the FBN had engaged in acts that were largely symbolic and self-serving. As a result of this legislation, the playground dealers who populated the imaginations of comic book and pulp fiction writers, the international traffickers who the FBN argued sipped cappuccino in Italian piazzas while counting the profits from their drug deals, and dope-dealing Chinese Communists who allegedly plotted to subvert American freedom were now all subject to lengthy prison terms. Threats both foreign and domestic had been contained.

The chief beneficiaries of this early war on drugs were Hale Boggs, Price Daniel, and the Federal Bureau of Narcotics. Hale Boggs was locked in a political battle with the remnants of the Huey Long machine in Louisiana and figured he could use the narcotics issue to promote his gubernatorial ambitions. The patently political purpose of Daniel's hearings is obvious when one considers that his committee spent five days in New York City, the national center of narcotics use and trafficking in the United States, and ten days in Texas, where even officials testifying before the committee admitted the problem was a small one. But Daniel, like Boggs, needed an issue to promote his candidacy for the governorship. Anslinger and the FBN were the other big victors in the legislative process. Daniel's bill significantly increased the power of the FBN, bringing the agency more on par with the FBI and allowing agents to carry arms, serve search warrants, and request wiretaps on phone conversations among drug traffickers.[49]

The legislation of the 1950s established that American drug policy would be focused for the foreseeable future on incarcerating heroin users. This hard-line approach reflected the cultural script of the postwar period, but it failed to stymie heroin use. The spread of heroin occurred in specific populations and traveled from peer to peer among groups with good reason to be alienated from American society. Marginal populations, undeterred by antinarcotics legislation, continued to ingest heroin, and not just in traditional centers of narcotics use such as New York and Chicago.

CHAPTER FIVE

Ethnicity and the Market

THE CITIES OF the East Coast and the Midwest dominated the postwar wave of heroin use, and drug users in those cities consumed Turkish heroin imported through New York. In this hierarchical market, coalitions of Italian, Jewish, and African American gangsters delivered heroin to local market-places. However, in the West there were other sources of heroin. Entrepre-neurs in Los Angeles, in the borderland cities of the Southwest, and in San Francisco had access to heroin supplies from Mexico and Hong Kong. Al-though heroin from New York remained highly desirable, users in the West and Southwest made decisions about what heroin to ingest based on cost, availability, and most important, ethnicity. Demand organized the market-place and sometimes made entrepreneurs cross ethnic lines to form alliances, but more frequently New York, Asian, and Mexican heroin shipments were controlled by and sold to distinct groups in an ethnically stratified market-place.

Los Angeles led the nation in narcotics arrests in 1954, surpassing New York City by about 50 percent, even though it had only about one-tenth as many users. Experts estimated that about three thousand "addicts" lived in Los Angeles, or about 5 percent of the nation's total heroin-using population, according to the Federal Bureau of Narcotics.[1] A very active police force produced many arrests, and their efforts contributed to the concern among the public over adolescent narcotic use.

A closer look at police statistics, however, reveals that the moral panic of the 1950s was misplaced. The public had no idea who was using heroin or where that use was occurring. Arrests were concentrated among twenty-five-to twenty-nine-year-olds and were actually falling among younger age groups. While the cohort of young men who had begun shooting heroin in the years after World War II continued to use drugs and get arrested, the overlooked good news was that fewer adolescents were joining them. This indicated that, contrary to the beliefs of alarmists, the postwar heroin wave had crested in Los Angeles, as it had elsewhere in the country.[2] In addition, citywide arrest figures were misleading because they did not reveal either the location or the ethnicity of heroin users. Although heroin consumption occurred among all ethnic groups, as will be seen below, it predominated within the concentrated market provided by socially and economically marginal populations. In post-war Los Angeles, the social setting of the Mexican American barrios produced heroin use and sales.

The barrios were spatial islands within Los Angeles, kept insular by the hostility of the dominant Anglo community, by attitudes that associated Mexicans with violence and crime, by aggressive policing, and by the land-scape itself, as the barrios frequently developed in older, interstitial, and un-desirable areas that had been bypassed in the city's growth.[3] New arrivals from Mexico, who used familial and village contacts to settle and find em-ployment, as well as migrants and their children, who returned to Mexico periodically, kept ethnic identity and ties between Mexico and the barrio alive. This cross-border movement also supplied potential smugglers with cover and contacts.

By 1940 three-quarters of Los Angeles's Mexican population was native-born. This second generation particularly resented the distance between the promise of American life and its delivery in Los Angeles's barrios. Chicanos were largely confined to low-wage and low-skilled sectors of the economy, such as day laboring, construction, and transportation. Memories of forced repatriation to Mexico during the Depression added to the sense of insecurity and alienation within these communities. In this context, illegal enterprise offered an attractive alternative for young men willing to risk participating in it. The workforce for the drug trade came from the nearly ubiquitous barrio street gangs, who were the most alienated from Anglo-dominated society and most used to defying Anglo authorities.[4]

Members of Chicano gangs began their involvement in drug smuggling in the early 1940s with barbiturates and marijuana. Migrant farm workers had most likely introduced marijuana smoking into the barrio when it was still legal, and it became part of a "pachuco," street-tough style adopted by some Chicano adolescents. Barbiturates also became popular as "party drugs" among the young because they were less expensive and more readily available than alcohol. Some barbiturates were manufactured by American pharmaceutical companies and disappeared into the underground marketplace on their way to being exported, while Mexican manufacturers also supplied the "yellow jackets" Chicano gangs peddled in the barrio market. Other barbiturates, called M&M's because of their small size and resemblance to the candy, were manufactured in Mexico expressly because they were compact enough for smuggling into the United States.[5] Trading in marijuana and barbiturates provided the organizational structure and experience for heroin smuggling, which began in earnest during World War II.

Although opium had been available in Mexico for decades, Mexican heroin entered the United States in noticeable quantities for the first time during the heroin-starved 1940s. Chinese merchants had smuggled opium into Mexico and then across the border to supply Chinese opium dens on the West Coast in the early twentieth century. Mexican farmers began cultivating opium poppies, but little of their crop was converted into heroin.[6] Then during the war Mexican opium poppies became a highly desirable commodity as the only source for heroin accessible to the U.S. market, and Mexican growers took advantage of the opportunity. Poppy cultivation exploded in the states of Sonora, Sinaloa, Durango, and Guerrero. Border towns, such as Mexicali and Tijuana, which had been homes to a cross-border vice trade since before the turn of the century, now became centers for heroin smuggling into the United States. By the mid-1940s, Mexican heroin was widely available in the Southwest and California and even as far east as New York City. (New York's heroin shortage eased when "lines of communication reformed and heroin began coming in from Mexico," according to William Burroughs.) While the restoration of "normal" smuggling routes after the war drove Mexican heroin from the marketplace elsewhere in the country, it retained its market niche in the Southwest and southern California, where heroin had not been a significant problem prior to World War II.[7]

Heroin use began in the barrios of Los Angeles in the same way it started in inner city neighborhoods elsewhere. The drug gradually became associated with adult hustlers and pimps. Eventually Chicano gangs (unlike gangs in the East and Midwest) began both using and selling heroin, finding it to be a source of income and a "clean" and cool alternative to barbiturates and the messy drunkenness of the older generations. By the late 1940s, heroin use was as well established in the barrios as it was in African American ghettos in other parts of the country. Over time, experience with heroin became so

widespread among Chicano youth that one scholar, who collaborated with
ex-gang members and ex-addicts in conducting her research in the 1970s,
concluded "most of the young men in most barrio gangs become narcotics
users."[8]

Chicano gangs created a market that was quite distinctive when compared to heroin markets in New York and elsewhere in the country. Proximity to Mexico meant that the market was "horizontal" and decentralized in
form. Individuals could cross back and forth over a nearby and relatively
porous border, and they did not require particular expertise or much capital
to enter the drug trade. Unlike in the East, where "entry costs" were high
because smugglers had to cultivate contacts in Marseilles and elsewhere in
Europe, and distance added to the expense and difficulty of smuggling, in
the Southwest there were few barriers to entering the heroin marketplace.
Chicano gang members had the advantage of sharing language and ethnic
backgrounds with Mexican dealers, there was a history of cross-border trafficking, and the gang provided an organizational structure that abetted entry
into the drug trade. Low-level smuggling across the border remained a char-
acteristic of the heroin marketplace in the Southwest from the 1940s on.

Gangs used stolen merchandise as a form of "currency" for exchange in
the cross-border trade. Some barrio gangs became specialists in car theft, and
drove stolen automobiles into Mexico to be bartered for drugs or sold for the
purchase of heroin. One gang member described the mode of operation used
by his friends. "These guys were running cars over to Tijuana at that time,
or maybe Mexicali, because jeepsters had come out that year and the guys
had taken a jeepster over and in the jeepster they put a motorcycle. When
they dumped the car over there, they just came back on the motorcycle. One
guy got about 2½ ounces of heroin," which was worth several thousand dollars in the retail market.[9] Raymond Chandler in *The Long Goodbye* included
a car-theft scheme that shipped cars from Los Angeles to Mexico: "The procedure is routine. Mostly the money comes back in the form of heroin."[10] It
was difficult for anyone to establish a monopoly over the supply of heroin in
such a highly decentralized marketplace. As one police official commented,
"The wholesale dealer from the West Coast does not have to handle large
amounts. This availability also makes it possible for many small peddlers to
engage in the traffic without having to produce a huge bank roll." The result
was "hundreds of independent narcotic peddlers."[11]

The relative impurity of brown Mexican heroin also contributed to the
decentralization of the market. The profit margin in heroin trading lay in the

dilution of the product at each step on its way to the consumer, but Mexican opium poppies had a lower opiate content than those grown in the Golden Crescent, and Mexican heroin was about one-third less pure than New York heroin. This placed a de facto limit on the number of "steps" it could take on its way to the market if it was to retain any value to users.[12] Trading in Mexican heroin thus remained localized, except in times of national heroin shortages such as those of the 1940s and the 1970s, and it produced smaller, though steady, profits. Usually Chicano gangs had the market to themselves and supplied their own communities.

Despite market decentralization and competition among barrio gangs, the drug-trading networks organized by the gangs formed a closed trading system. Barrio gangs, because of ethnicity, family, neighborhood, and friend-ship, were bound together more tightly than most criminal organizations, and gang affiliation retained meaning well beyond adolescence and into adulthood. Many gangs, such as White Fence and El Hoyo Maravilla, were quite large and sustained themselves over several generations with nephews and sons following uncles and fathers into the gang. Incarceration did not disrupt gang membership, but rather formed the basis for organizing inmates in California youth reformatories and adult prisons. These closely knit gangs avoided dealing with outsiders and used Mexican ethnicity and barrio resi-dence as markers of trustworthiness in selling heroin. At a time when there were few Mexican American police officers, selling only to other Mexican Americans effectively limited the risk of police infiltration and arrest.[13]

State and federal enforcement agencies found the closed organizational structure of barrio gangs frustrating. Narcotics agents claimed that they had a difficult time recruiting informants from Chicano heroin users. For an informant, cooperating with police meant turning one's back not only on peers but also on relatives and neighbors, and suffering a social death in the community that was worse than doing time in prison. When investigators looked into the smuggling activities of El Hoyo Maravilla, they commented that "constant efforts over the years to gain entre [sic] to this group through subordinates and customers of the Leyvas brothers were unsuccessful. Persons in a position to assist in the investigation of this group preferred to go to the penitentiary." While police eventually got cooperating witnesses, it took twelve years before California authorities were able to make a case against the leaders of El Hoyo Maravilla, who were able to smuggle a very substantial average of forty ounces of heroin per week during that time period, according to law enforcement officials.[14]

The modest penalties for drug dealing, especially in the 1940s, meant that there was little incentive to cooperate with police. Federal penalties increased in 1951 in the moral panic that followed the discovery of adolescent heroin use, but during the early postwar period, sellers had little to worry about. One dealer recalled, "At that time you only had a six-year top [sentence]. . . . That's what it was across the board for selling, possession or whatever. That's whether it was weed or hard stuff. You knew you had a ceiling of six years and if a guy did 2½, he had a right to 'bitch.' It was more often the case that a guy would do 18 months or two years. Nobody was too excited [about the penalties for drug dealing]."[15] With "doing time" almost a rite of passage among gang members, even the increased penalties for narcotics dealing in the 1950s did not deter gang members from the trade or induce them to "snitch" to the police.

With gang membership and involvement in heroin distribution and consumption overlapping phenomena, the Mexican American barrios became the geographic centers for heroin in southern California. The California Civil Commitment Authority, which maintained statistics on known "addicts," reported in the late 1960s that half of the state's addict population was Chicano and that two-thirds of the addicted Chicanos resided in Los Angeles. East Los Angeles, the heart of the barrio, was the center of both heroin selling and heroin consumption in the city. The social setting of East Los Angeles—the insularity of the barrios, the social marginality of the population, the ubiquitous gangs, the alienation promoted by the discriminatory practices of Anglo society—supported the perpetuation of the heroin trade from one generation to the next.[16]

Of course, Mexican Americans were not the only heroin users in Los Angeles. African American and Anglo heroin users were largely shut out of the barrio heroin networks. They had to find Mexican American intermediaries to purchase drugs for them, or they had to obtain heroin elsewhere. One possibility was to purchase New York heroin even though it was more expensive; the other was to cross the border themselves and buy heroin in Mexico. It is not clear how much cross-border traffic existed among Anglos and African Americans, but there was a long history of "vice tourism" in southern California. Public hearings in 1955 into the heroin problem in southern California revealed that some Americans traveled regularly to Mexico to purchase drugs. In addition, American officials all but admitted that it was impossible to control the flow of pedestrian and automobile traffic from Mexican border towns, so clearly individuals took advantage of the proximity of the border town marketplaces.

American heroin users claimed that they could purchase heroin in Mexico without worry about arrest, and FBN and police sources agreed. Bebe Phoenix, a prostitute in Los Angeles, maintained that the heroin dealer "Big Mike" was well known in Tijuana. "He must be well known if you can just ask a cab driver to take you to Big Mike's, and they arrange it." American narcotics officers added that they had frequently tried to make purchases from Mike Barragon Bautista, but "we have always been steered to one of his runners." Big Mike used cab drivers and others to make pickups and deliveries. When Americans arrived in town and wanted to purchase narcotics, "They get in a cab, and the cab will take them to wherever he deals and the deal is made. They either fix there and come back to the line in the cab or they will bring some [heroin] back with them." While Big Mike was well known to Mexican authorities, he seemed to be immune to arrest and was a relatively public figure. In addition to owning a fleet of taxicabs, he operated one of the largest brothels in Tijuana, where his wife served as the madam, and he had a collection of racehorses as well as a vast estate.[17]

Dealers such as Big Mike and wealthy opium growers were not only socially accepted in Mexico, but even admired for their ability to make easy money from the American drug trade. Local cabdrivers took tourists to Sierra Blanca, across from the town of Culiacan, to admire the expensive homes of local narcotics traffickers, who were lionized as "Los Valientes." These individuals prospered because they enjoyed the protection of local officials, who treated opium growers, heroin dealers, and vice lords as businessmen who simply catered to Anglo weaknesses while helping the local economy. City treasuries and local merchants depended on the cross-border vice and drug trade, and federal police earned extra money by abetting or at least ignoring it. Mexicali and Tijuana were "very profitable to the Mexican Federal Agents," American officials maintained. They supplemented their pay by working as bodyguards and informants for drug-smuggling operations.[18]

The presence of "injection specialists" in Tijuana provided further evidence of a flourishing cross-border drug trade. Investigators for the Senate Judiciary Committee found fifteen spots, which were run by practical nurses and "unlicensed doctors" who administered shots of heroin hypodermically for between one and five dollars per shot. "Most of these places are located in a section of Tijuana immediately adjoining the border fence between Mexico and the United States where they are easily accessible" and which eliminated the danger of attempting to smuggle drugs across the border.[19] While there is little information about who patronized these places, the two most likely groups were drug tourists and inexperienced users. Individuals with money and time headed for Tijuana and went on a three- or four-day heroin binge without worrying about carrying "works" or smuggling drugs. Drug tourists most likely held steady jobs and enjoyed reasonable incomes; they were most likely working-class users who found Mexican heroin more affordable than heroin imported from the East, and managed to control their heroin use except for their occasional binges.

Individuals who did not have the expertise to inject themselves were the other logical customers. This group, since they were novices, aroused the most concern among those worried about the spread of drug use in the young. Customs officials found that when they made random stops of adolescents returning to the United States, they discovered that several showed "fresh needle marks on their arms indicating that they had received heroin shots." An experiment with heroin, authorities feared, was becoming another illicit thrill that southern Californian teenagers could find south of the border, even though they had no evidence that heroin use was increasing among adolescents.[20]

Drug tourists and novices alike faced inspection upon their return to the United States. Customs officers estimated that approximately twenty-five addicts a day crossed over the border from San Diego to Tijuana to score heroin. Border control officers checked suspicious-looking returnees for telltale "track marks" on their arms, which could be used to detain them. California law permitted authorities to arrest individuals with track marks (until the United States Supreme Court overturned the statute in *Robinson v. California* in 1962), and customs and border control officials did not need any probable cause in order to inspect for them. Addicts resorted to different subterfuges in order to hide track marks. Most wore long-sleeved shirts, but on a hot day that was an immediate source of suspicion; other users had elaborate tattoos drawn on their arms that incorporated the lines of needle marks. Some injected in spots less likely to draw attention, such as in the groin, the penis, or between their toes, or had other parts of their bodies tattooed and injected there. It was possible to find these track marks, but only through a careful physical examination: "Our means of detecting that is that if you run your thumb over the tattoo, you will find the raised scar tissue, which is very difficult to detect by sight."[21] Of course, authorities had to have reason to believe that someone was a user before investigating body

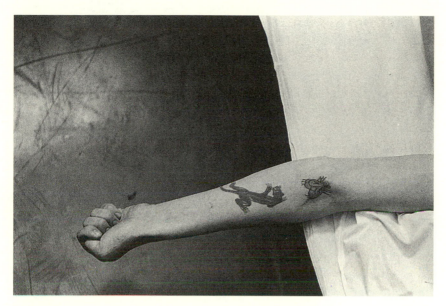

Heroin users in California used tattoos to hide evidence of drug use at a time when narcotics users could be arrested solely on the basis of the track marks. Photograph by Cal Bernstein, *Look* Magazine Photographic Collection, Library of Congress, LC L9-57-7382-F9.

parts, thus unless one crossed the border frequently and became recognizable to border control officials, or acted suspiciously, there was little likelihood of detection.

As both the FBN and the Customs Bureau pointed out, it was nearly impossible to find individual smugglers coming across the Mexican border. Approximately one million people per month, about a third of them pedestrians, crossed the border from Mexico to California during the mid-1950s; it was not feasible to search even a small minority of them. Weekends were particularly difficult, as the number of cars and pedestrians swelled. "On Sundays and holidays, they have races and bull fights, and also jai alai down at Tijuana. The result is that it is not unusual for six to eight thousand automobiles to come back from Mexico from 3 o'clock to about 6 o'clock in the afternoon." Traffic backed up for two to three miles and even with three times the manpower, officials claimed that they would not be able to examine the cars much more than they did, "except that we don't examine them at all."[22] In addition, an estimated six thousand servicemen from San Diego's military bases headed over the border on payday to drink and carouse in

Tijuana's bars, dance halls, and brothels.[23] Border control officers had little hope of finding smugglers in this throng.

Given the availability of heroin in Mexico and the ease with which individuals could move across the border, it seems surprising that there would be a demand for New York heroin at all. There are three reasons why New York heroin could penetrate this market. First, the higher opiate content of Turkish heroin made it a consistent favorite among consumers, and those who could afford it no doubt sought it out in the marketplace. Second, this was not an open marketplace and discrimination was a vital factor in determining who had access to which heroin. Sellers occupied ethnic niches and preferred selling to other members of the same group; African Americans in particular were suspect in transactions with Chicanos, and therefore needed an alternative supply of heroin. As a marginalized population concentrated in specific neighborhoods, they were a natural market for heroin, and their demand was large enough that white and African American gangsters formed partnerships to bring heroin from New York to Los Angeles. Third, individual smuggling ventures, even though they were the focus of investigative hearings, could not supply the demand for heroin in southern California. This created an opening for New York heroin.

Marketplaces existed in African American communities, particularly in South Central Los Angeles, which was the largest area of African American settlement. Wartime had transformed African American Los Angeles, bringing thousands of migrants, mostly from Texas, Louisiana, Mississippi, and Arkansas, into the city in search of work in the shipbuilding, steel, and defense industries as well as the docks of Terminal Island. The migrants settled in two principal areas: the industrial corridor of South Central Los Angeles, where the Southern Pacific line even opened a temporary station for migrants with nearby relatives, and in Little Tokyo, emptied of its Japanese residents during the war and conveniently located blocks from Union Station. White areas near South Central and Watts resisted any expansion, and what had once been multiracial neighborhoods turned into largely black communities by the 1950s.[24]

Shoeshine parlors and newsstands, sometimes tied into the underworld as fronts for prostitution, sold marijuana and "bennies," and then picked up on the trade for "dope" after the war. As happened in African American communities in the East, jazzmen, gamblers, and pimps viewed heroin as part of a cool style and heroin use seeped into African American nightlife, with adolescents eventually copying what the hustlers were doing. At first sleeping-car porters, acting as individual entrepreneurs, purchased heroin in the Harlem retail market and brought back small quantities to the Central Avenue jazz clubs and after-hours joints as well as to the brothels of Little Tokyo to sell for extra cash. Anyone looking for dope started in the hangouts for "high rolling pimps, gamblers, and dope-dealers" around Central Avenue. However, the initial low-level trade could not support many users, and as demand for heroin grew, so did efforts to increase supply. By the 1950s, white entrepreneurs with connections to New York formed partnerships with African American distributors that ensured more reliable and larger supplies of the prized New York heroin.[25]

Jewish and Italian gangsters dominated the wholesaling of New York heroin in Los Angeles. Since only a few dealers had reliable connections, the market for their heroin was hierarchical and centralized, with limited opportunity for newcomers to enter the trade, and the market looked more similar to those found in Eastern and Midwestern cities. The hierarchical organization ensured a high profit margin and narrowed the risk of arrest, since these entrepreneurs sold in wholesale lots to only a few partners. Heroin passed through many hands before being retailed, but since this heroin had a high opiate content, it could be adulterated more heavily while still ensuring a good product. The distribution system for New York heroin, with its inter-ethnic character and vertical organization, could not have been more different from the market organized by Chicano street gangs.

FBN investigations into heroin trafficking illustrate the organization of the New York–Los Angeles distribution system. Since these were failed part-nerships, in the sense that they ended in arrest and prosecution, it is possible that they are not representative of drug-trading enterprises generally. How-ever, all enterprises faced the same challenges in connecting wholesalers in one part of the country to regional distributors and retailers in another, and in establishing trust in illegal enterprise across ethnic lines. Some were only luckier or more skilled than others.

Drug traders tried to use ethnic background as a basis for trust, although they frequently had to make alliances with gangsters of different ethnicities. For example, Abe Allen (alias Abe Elenevitch or Abe Dolan) was a Los Angeles drug dealer who was allied with Italian suppliers in New York. Ac-cording to the FBN, Allen was considered "an important violator in this district for a number of years" with "well established connections with dealers throughout the country." In this case, Allen told an informant that "the stuff now in town was not much good" and proposed that they organize a joint purchasing venture. The informant introduced Allen to two colleagues, FBN Agent Michael Piccini and Joseph Pitta, a heroin dealer turned informant, with the suggestion that they participate in the deal instead. Although Allen was initially suspicious of Agent Piccini, within a week he had made arrangements for Piccini and Pitta to purchase heroin from his connection in New York. It is not clear why Allen took such a risk, but his brother, who had died recently, was also a dealer and owed their New York connection $16,000, a debt for which Allen may have been responsible.

If Allen thought he could control the transaction, he was mistaken. Allen, Pitta, and Piccini were to travel from California separately, then rendezvous in Manhattan at the Hotel New Yorker on Eighth Avenue and 34th Street. While Allen was driving from Los Angeles, Piccini and Pitta flew to New York and checked into the New Yorker, where they contacted Allen's New York connection, Frank Tornello, before Allen arrived. After several negotiating sessions, in which Tornello's associates checked the pair out and Piccini and Pitta received a heroin sample to test, the group finally met at the Casa Corsi restaurant. Tornello allegedly told the men, "If you boys work out all right we will put you in charge of the west coast and you can take care of all the supply in that part of the country. You don't have to touch it, just wholesale it." This would produce a smaller profit (a mere 100 percent!), but Piccini and Pitta would have to deal with only fifteen or twenty wholesalers, thus reducing their risk. "We will give you as much stuff as you want and turn over all our customers on the west coast but you will have to work it our way." Piccini agreed to an initial deal; a couple of days later, he met one of Tornello's associates at his hotel and advanced him $6,400 for a half kilo of heroin, with pickup to be made the next evening.

Most of the arrangements were made over dinners at the Casa Corsi, and the group agreed to use the restaurant for future transactions. They decided that Piccini and Pitta would call the restaurant from Los Angeles every Monday night at 9 P.M., and one of Tornello's men would await the call and get the shipping order. It is not clear if any other deals were made; several months later Tornello was in custody and awaiting trial.[26]

The Tornello case illustrates organizational structure of the New York–dominated heroin trade. This marketplace was vertical in organization, with New York transmitting heroin to Los Angeles, where it was redistributed and eventually reached the retail level. In an effort to ensure trustworthiness, these entrepreneurs relied on ethnicity: they met in an Italian restaurant, and more significantly, the Italian-American Tornello decided to trust his fellow Italian-

Americans, Picci and Pitta, even though they were strangers, rather than the Jewish Allen with whom he had prior dealings. Ethnicity, at least in this case, proved to be a slim reed on which to rest a large enterprise in an inherently unstable business.

While the Tornello case provides rich detail about the wholesaling of heroin, investigators did not follow the drug into the retail market. It is not clear if Tornello's heroin remained in the white community or entered Los Angeles's South Central neighborhood. Fortunately, an example of another one of these partnerships, also seen from the perspective of the Italian-American gangster who organized it, illustrates how heroin from New York entered into Los Angeles's African American community.

Louis Fiano began trafficking in narcotics as an afterthought. While serving time in the federal penitentiary at Leavenworth, Fiano became friendly with a New York gangster with the alias of Jimmy Valentine (also known as Jimmy Colonna). After being released from prison, both men returned to their homes, but Valentine soon found himself in trouble again and called on his prison acquaintance for help. Valentine wanted his friend to find work in Los Angeles for the only witness to a murder in which Valentine was implicated. Fiano obliged, and Fiano's attorney, G. Vernon Brumbaugh, a well-known criminal defense lawyer who had many Los Angeles bookmakers and professional criminals on his client list, managed to block the extradition proceedings against the witness. As a result, charges against Valentine were dropped.

In return for this favor, Valentine supplied Fiano with a kilo of heroin to be sold in Los Angeles. According to the FBN, "Fiano did not know what to do with the kilo of heroin. He went to attorney Brumbaugh, who told him to sit tight and he would make some inquiries and let Fiano know what to do." Brumbaugh consulted with another attorney and told Fiano, "He would have the entire concession for the colored narcotic traffic, further that no one would be permitted to bring any heroin from New York to be distributed among the colored trade except himself." Thus Fiano was promised a virtual monopoly over the African American market in Los Angeles. This arrangement was approved by Johnny Roselli, a well-known gangster in Las Vegas, who apparently looked out for the West Coast interests of some New York mobsters.

In order to link Fiano to a distribution network in the African American community, Brumbaugh arranged a meeting with Billy Briggs at the Hi Lo Grill on Western Avenue in South Central Los Angeles. Briggs was a well-known bookmaker in the African American community, and as such had many local connections, such as bars, corner stores, and newsstands that served as "drops" for his betting slips, and which could also serve as distribution points for Fiano's heroin. Briggs gave Fiano $4,500 for the kilo upon delivery, and paid him an additional $2,500 after the initial lot was sold. Fiano sent $5,000 back to Valentine to pay for the heroin, gave $1,000 to Brumbaugh as a "finder's fee" for making the connection to Briggs, and kept a thousand for himself. With this lucrative deal, Fiano entered the narcotics business permanently.

The heroin business turned out to be more difficult to organize than the promise of a monopoly implied. Fiano had to make his own arrangements for New York suppliers, rather than rely on Valentine, and problems arose almost immediately with his distribution system in Los Angeles. Because Briggs was a gambler, not a narcotics dealer, he did not know much about cutting heroin, and he "ruined some of the heroin by over-adulterating it." For that reason, Fiano decided to find someone with more experience to distribute heroin for him in the future. Brumbaugh introduced him to another possible partner, who had received heroin from an Italian gangster in New York and distributed it through an African American network. Fiano now arranged to become the new source of supply for this African American trading group through which heroin entered distribution points in South Central Los Angeles.[27]

Once Fiano had his distribution network set up, he started buying heroin from a variety of New York sources. Some of these were Italian, others were Jewish (at least as suggested by surnames), and still others were of indeterminate ethnicity. Fiano constantly changed suppliers, buying a few kilos from one source, and then turning to another in a series of shifting short-term partnerships. Sometimes the arrangements were interrupted by arrest, sometimes by disputes over the quality of the heroin, and sometimes by temporary shortages. Therefore, although Fiano sold New York heroin in Los Angeles steadily for about six years without getting caught, there was none of the longevity and continuity that having the "concession" for heroin sales to African Americans suggested. Rather, Fiano created transitory partnerships with individuals from a variety of ethnic backgrounds that lasted for only a few deals.

There was more continuity among his distributors in Los Angeles, which may have been more important for Fiano. As a white man, Fiano could not sell heroin in African American neighborhoods, nor would he have wanted to encounter small-scale wholesalers or, even worse, retail customers. Fiano wanted to limit his contacts to as small a number of intermediaries as possible who in turn handled the cutting, repackaging, and reselling of the heroin in retail outlets; therefore, partnerships with African Americans were essential. Fiano distributed many kilos of heroin between 1955 and 1961, when he was finally arrested.[28]

Gangsters such as Fiano and Tornello found a market in Los Angeles for their heroin despite the city's proximity to Mexico. The social setting of the barrio produced the vast majority of Los Angeles heroin users, and Mexican heroin was more important—at least in terms of volume—than New York's in this marketplace. Although Mexican Americans dominated both heroin using and selling, and individual cross-border transactions provided additional supplies, the stratification of the marketplace along ethnic lines left a large unmet demand for heroin, especially among African Americans. African American and white gangsters therefore organized interethnic alliances in order to meet the demand.

Heroin trading in Texas was organized in three distinct ethnic patterns. As in California, cross-border ties with Mexico determined the structure of the market. Officials estimated that 90 percent of the heroin in the state originated in Mexico and the majority of heroin users were Mexican American. However, trading patterns were dependent on ethnicity, shifting as one moved farther away from the Mexican border. African American entrepreneurs in Houston and Dallas established a second type of ethnic network that exchanged marijuana from the borderlands for heroin purchased in Harlem, which they then sold to fellow African Americans. The third grouping in Texas consisted of white narcotics users, who took opiates prescribed by physicians or stolen from pharmacies, hospitals, or doctors in a pattern that was left over from the prewar period and indicates the importance of race and class. While Texan cities had large numbers of Chicano and African American users whose demand for heroin structured the market, whites predominated in small-town or rural settings, they consumed legally produced narcotics, and they were somewhat protected in their interactions with the market.[29] They constituted an exception to the urbanized and marginalized populations associated with heroin in the postwar period, although ethnicity still structured how the heroin market worked.

Chicanos made up the vast majority of users in borderland cities such as San Antonio and El Paso in a pattern very similar to that found in Los Angeles. Mexican Americans in south Texas lived in segregated communities that serviced Anglo commercial farming interests and supplied the need for low-cost labor. Migrant workers moved back and forth across the border as growers sought to increase labor supply and keep wages and costs as low as possible, and law enforcement and border patrol agencies regulated this labor flow. The social setting of the barrio, produced by police repression, a highly segregated society, and economic exploitation, reinforced a sense of social marginality, while cross-border mobility provided an opportunity to engage in smuggling as an alternative way to make a living.[30]

San Antonio, the largest city near the Mexican border, organized the heroin trade with Mexico and served as a trans-shipment point where smugglers and dealers met. Mexican smugglers brought heroin from different border towns in Mexico up to San Antonio, while Chicano dealers from Austin, Houston, and Dallas came down to San Antonio to purchase heroin for resale in their home cities.[31] There is no evidence of street gang involvement in smuggling, but the trade was so specialized that specific families in San Antonio engaged in heroin distribution as an exclusive and collective enterprise that was at least as tightly knit as any organized by barrio gangs. Chicano wholesalers only dealt with Chicano retailers, which minimized the risk of penetration by law enforcement officials. Mexican Americans dominated the trade so thoroughly that informants knew of only three African American dealers in all of San Antonio who were said to be fairly small scale.

Chicanos often discriminated against Anglos and African Americans, who were seen as being particularly untrustworthy. One user, a white woman, said that in Houston, "It is pretty hard to buy heroin . . . unless you know the people. Sometimes [even] then . . . you can't buy it." Non-Hispanic users therefore had to find Mexican American intermediaries—junkies needing money or heroin for a fix—to purchase drugs for them. When they were able to buy heroin, African Americans accused Chicanos of short-changing or "burning" them: selling heroin of poor quality or simply taking their money and not selling any heroin at all. As in southern California, marketplace discrimination (along with the relative weakness of Mexican heroin) opened a market opportunity—this time for African Americans.[32]

African Americans used ethnicity and their Texas "hometown" connections to set up drug trading networks that ran between the major Texas cities and Harlem. African American entrepreneurs found a market niche exchanging Mexican marijuana, highly prized in New York, for New York heroin, equally prized in Texas. Texan expatriates arranged to have friends or relatives purchase marijuana in fifty-pound bags, and then repackage it for

shipment north. Dealers packed suitcases with one-pound bricks of marijuana, wrapped in burlap and covered with wax paper to hide the odor, and
then took the train to New York, where they sold the drug by prearrangement
to local wholesalers. George Hall, for example, grew up in Dallas and moved
north with his family when he was a teenager. Hall completed high school in
New York and worked as a baker and restaurateur, and as sideline, he created
a seventeen-member big band and a smaller "George Hall combo" that
played in various jazz clubs in the city. A fellow musician who had also
moved to New York from Texas wanted to dispose of twenty-five pounds of
marijuana, and Hall agreed to use his music connections to sell the drug. It
was a fateful decision, because Hall began to focus more of his attention on
the drug trade. He sold ever-larger monthly shipments of Mexican marijuana,
becoming the largest marijuana dealer in the city. Either Hall or one of his
Texas associates flew to Houston every couple of weeks to transport $5,000
or $6,000 in cash that represented the profits from the previous weeks' ship-
ments, while couriers showed up in Penn Station with suitcases full of weed.
Hall himself steadfastly maintained that he was satisfied in his position as a
marijuana distributor and that he never dealt in heroin, but two of his Texas
suppliers made arrangements to trade marijuana for heroin instead of cash.
Leonora Henderson, the wife of one of Hall's original partners (who was by
that time incarcerated in Texas), traded a portion of the monthly marijuana
shipment for heroin and laundered the profits from the marijuana-heroin
exchange through a restaurant she opened in Houston.[33]

This extremely sophisticated drug enterprise operated through a series of
shifting partnerships beginning in 1945 with the initial marijuana transactions
and functioning until 1954, when most of the major partners were arrested.[34]
Structurally this Texas–New York ring resembled the drug networks that
moved heroin from New York into Los Angeles, with businessmen creating
short-term alliances at both ends of the network, except that marijuana
moved up the urban hierarchy as the medium of exchange and all the partners
were African American. Ethnicity, supplemented by a shared regional or
hometown identity, created trust among these African American dealers operating in a stratified market.

Small-town white opiate users existed in their own world. They constituted a unique group that was too isolated to form a community of users and
traders, and they frequently had access to legal narcotics. In other words,
social privilege—class and race—limited their exposure to the illegal market.
Some whites were medically addicted and were maintained informally on

morphine by physicians, which reflected the continuance of an older and particularly Southern pattern of drug use. Like Mrs. Dubose in *To Kill a Mockingbird*, they were protected by the social mores of small towns, where their identities were frequently known. They tended to be older and most of them became habituated to heroin in the years before World War II rather than in the immediate postwar years.[35] The case of Perry Milton Turner illustrates the general pattern.

Perry Milton Turner became addicted to morphine in 1932, at age nineteen, while he was hospitalized in Austin, Texas, and he continued to use morphine with the help of his physician for some period of time after his release. Turner presented himself as a respectable workingman despite his troubles with narcotics. "I've worked and I have got that drug and used it in moderate amounts and it didn't interfere with my work because I could buy it in a manner, get it from a doctor, getting the prescription filled in a drugstore." While some white users patronized the illegal marketplace in a pinch, they more commonly used morphine or synthetic opiates prescribed by physicians. In a study of narcotics addicts in Kentucky, one-third of the male users and two-thirds of the females reported that physicians supplied their narcotics in a typically Southern pattern. These users either relied on a sympathetic doctor who was willing to maintain them, or they visited several physicians, feigning illnesses or claiming that they were using opiates as a treatment for alcoholism. Few of these physicians were fooled into prescribing narcotics. While some of them treated addicts as patients and levied regular charges, others took advantage of the market (and perhaps justified their actions because of the risk of losing their narcotics license) and charged a premium for writing prescriptions for addicts. As one woman commented, physicians charged three or five dollars for a regular visit, but "as much as $25" if they knew she was an addict.[36]

If these addicts had problems getting physicians to prescribe narcotics for them, they pocketed a prescription pad and submitted forged prescriptions to pharmacies. Usually criminal involvements increased with the length of time spent using narcotics, which was the case with Perry Turner. Turner found that it became too expensive to pay physicians for narcotics prescriptions during the Depression, thus he started forging prescriptions, which led to his first arrest. Eventually he switched from morphine to heroin, which he could purchase in the illegal marketplace without encountering the scrutiny of Austin pharmacists, who probably recognized him after several years of narcotics use. Turner purchased heroin cheaply in Mexico and tried to insulate himself from arrest by having his supply delivered to him in Austin. Despite his precautions, Turner's involvement in the illegal marketplace led to an increasing number of arrests, totaling fifty-two by the mid-1950s (his wife had accumulated an additional 122, mostly on narcotics possession charges). While the FBN generally treated Southern, frequently elderly, whites maintained by physicians differently than young, urban working-class males—whether white, African American, or Latino—Turner lost this advantage when his economic fortunes dipped and he began patronizing the illegal market. Middle-class addicts maintained by physicians were immune from the worst abuses of the heroin marketplace, including police harassment. They received morphine or dilaudid, and as long as it happened quietly, they did not arouse the ire of the FBN, which considered them "medical addicts." For Turner downward mobility was as much a problem as his narcotics addiction, as he lost the essential protections provided by class.[37]

Heroin users in Texas, despite their small number (approximately 1,800 in 1955), created distinctive patterns of participation in the marketplace. Although the marketplace was predominantly urban and Chicano, and organized around heroin imported from Mexico, discrimination forced other users to create their own heroin trading patterns. The underground economy was organized into ethnic niches, and ethnicity determined whether one purchased Mexican heroin from a Chicano dealer, New York heroin from an African American dealer, or legally manufactured drugs from a white pharmacist.

The San Francisco heroin market was also ethnically stratified, but the city's heroin users had a demographic profile that was distinctly different from that of any other city in the country. The San Francisco police estimated that about seven hundred heroin users lived in a few sections of the city; slightly more than 40 percent were white, about 15 percent were Chinese, and almost 40 percent were African American, with only a few Mexican Americans.[38] The combination of white and Chinese constituted a majority of users in a pattern that was more similar to the prewar period than to anything that came later. About 95 percent of the city's heroin was imported from Hong Kong, according to police, which reflected the importance of San Francisco's Asian trading partners as well as the traditional role of the Chinese in organizing vice. This otherwise small city had the nation's largest Chinatown and was dominated by its waterfront and port—the second largest in the country. Individual entrepreneurs, usually Anglo or Chinese merchant seamen, smuggled narcotics and then resold their merchandise in Chinatown or in the seedy districts that catered to the waterfront trade.

Asian heroin first appeared in San Francisco in the 1930s, when entrepreneurs began shipping it from Hong Kong. Although the volume of imports was unknown, Martin Scott, the supervisor for the U.S. Customs Bureau in San Francisco, declared that "practically all the seizures we make are on vessels from the Orient." Merchant ships presented "almost unlimited opportunities" for concealing narcotics, and in most cases only a single customs agent guarded a vessel after the initial landing. Frequently smugglers left the narcotics on board for several days and waited for the most opportune time to bring the contraband off the ship. "If it appears too risky, the attempt to unload can be abandoned at the first port, awaiting a more favorable opportunity at another port of call. At the worst, the narcotics can be retained on board for another voyage when the situation will be more propitious."[39]

Some 200,000 seamen entered the port each year, each having the opportunity to supplement his meager wages through smuggling contraband. Usually seamen smuggled drugs by prearrangement with someone who then served as a distributor, but if they acted as individual entrepreneurs, they sold heroin in the flophouses and bars that serviced an army of single male laborers in the city's large Tenderloin district. California narcotics authorities cracked one ring of twenty-five Anglo sailors who smuggled more than 70 kilograms of heroin into San Francisco between 1948 and 1954. The sailors worked on the American President Line ships, which arrived in San Francisco from Asia every three weeks, and they seldom smuggled more than a single pound on a trip. Usually only one or two seamen knew the details of each venture and participated in the smuggling, although each member of the group contributed money toward the purchase of heroin in Hong Kong, receiving a corresponding share once the drugs were sold. Because of the limited nature of the partnerships, each individual knew only a few details about a single venture, and risked only a relatively small sum on each voyage. The sailors avoided suspicion by rotating the responsibilities for smuggling the heroin, with delivery occurring in one of the Tenderloin's seedy bars. By 1954, when one of the ring members was arrested, many of the others had already retired and were engaged in legitimate enterprises on shore.[40]

Arrests and convictions were rare, however, especially in the case of small-scale transactions. Resources and personnel were too limited to search most sailors and ships, and even if customs inspectors found illegal narcotics on board a vessel, it was difficult to prove ownership over the contraband.

For example, a squad searching the *San Louis Obispo* found 118 ounces of opium hidden in a fire extinguisher. They arrested a Chinese steward, Dong Lin Dee, but the courts acquitted him because it was not possible to determine if he actually possessed the opium or if it had been hidden by other crew members. Without catching Dong in the act of removing the opium from the ship, the inspectors had no case.[41]

As these examples show, smuggling was frequently a small-scale business in which many individuals participated. They smuggled high-quality, relatively pure Asian heroin, which would be cut and redistributed for the first time in San Francisco. Individuals then sold heroin in small lots using occupational status or ethnicity to establish connections in a pattern that seemed well suited for the small population of heroin users in the city.

Once the heroin entered the distribution system, street dealers of different ethnicities handled it, but it is notable how many were Chinese. This ethnic niche in the heroin trade reflected the history of San Francisco's Chinatown in particular and Chinatowns generally. In the era of the "bachelor society" and legally enforced discrimination, which did not end until after World War II, working-class Chinese were a marginal and isolated population, exploited by white and Chinese society alike. The residue of elderly male opiate users formed the base for the expansion of the heroin trade after World War II, when new vice entrepreneurs built on the experience of their predecessors.[42]

Chinese heroin wholesalers relied on ties of ethnicity, region, and dialect in their business relations and created closed trading networks that were extremely difficult to penetrate. Neither the San Francisco police nor the FBN had many Chinese agents, thus ethnicity and language were effective means of limiting risk. One young man, arrested with an ounce of heroin in his possession, worked as a courier and received twenty dollars for each package he delivered. He said of his ring, "We were all Chinese, only Chinese to Chinese." When asked if there were many Chinese addicts and if the number was increasing, he replied, "Older Chinese addicts were hooked before they left China—the younger Chinese don't know anything about it." Most of these elderly Chinese had been opium smokers who switched to heroin because it was more available, easier to smuggle, and less expensive than opium, again indicating that the Chinese in San Francisco created a unique niche in the heroin market.[43]

There were not enough Chinese, however, to absorb the heroin imported into San Francisco, and Chinatown became a place where heroin crossed ethnic lines. San Francisco's population of Chinese heroin users was largely stagnant, as there was an insufficient number of younger Chinese (until immigration reform in 1965) to replace elderly users. Therefore even if importers wanted to create a closed system in which they sold heroin only to other Chinese, such distinctions were difficult to maintain. Chinatown became a retail marketplace where Chinese heroin users supported their habits through street sales to Anglos who were part of the larger North Beach bohemian and working-class white market. One female addict, a white woman named June Lindsay, was asked how many Chinese dealers she encountered over the past four years. "About 10," she replied. "And how many Negroes have you known who sold heroin in San Francisco?" she was asked. "About 3 or 4." When pressed, she acknowledged that there was at least one white dealer but no Mexican Americans. Her experience was representative of a broader pattern in which Chinese retailers sold to white users in Chinatown.[44]

With supply in the hands of other groups, African Americans faced the most discrimination in San Francisco's heroin marketplace. This discrimination provided African American entrepreneurs with an opportunity to organize their own trading system selling New York heroin. It is not clear from FBN records how much heroin was shipped to San Francisco from New York, but enough of a potential market existed that entrepreneurs were willing to set up distribution rings. In one case, Charles Johnson, who traveled from the West Coast to New York periodically to attend boxing matches, formed a partnership with Sebastian Bonnano to distribute New York heroin in San Francisco and Seattle. His San Francisco partner was Willie "Chocolate" Dandridge who sold the heroin, most likely in the African American community in the Filmore.[45] After distributing at least twenty-five ounces of heroin through Dandridge, as well as seventeen ounces of heroin and eight ounces of cocaine through a dealer in Seattle, Johnson retired from the business.[46] (Apparently unable to resist illegal earnings, Johnson later returned to heroin dealing and was caught.) Marketplace discrimination in San Francisco provided an opportunity for enterprising African Americans to establish ties with New York and distribute its heroin in a market otherwise dominated by others.

San Francisco's historic ties to China determined the organization of the city's heroin market, just as proximity to Mexico structured the market in Los Angeles and San Antonio. Although heroin supplies were relatively plentiful, they were not equally available, and this marketplace discrimination opened up opportunities for African American entrepreneurs. Ethnicity served as an exclusionary factor in determining access to the market, and it shaped both consumption and distribution patterns for heroin.

In the postwar period, Mexican and Asian heroin became a permanent part of the market in the Southwest and in California, even if they were rooted in particular ethnic niches and their use was localized. Patterns of ethnic discrimination were not permanent, however. Mexican and Asian heroin formed heroin "reservoirs" that could be tapped in times of shortages, when entrepreneurs crossed ethnic and geographic boundaries to create new trading partnerships. The interactions between the heroin trade from New York and its local "ethnic" rivals demonstrate a truism of markets: where there was a demand, a supply always followed. And in the early 1960s, the demand was once again starting to grow.

CHAPTER SIX

The Rising Tide

IN 1962, PRESIDENT John Kennedy convened a White House conference on drug abuse, and cautious optimism characterized the discussion. Reports from police in Chicago and Washington, D.C., for example, provided evidence for a decline in heroin use and most jurisdictions reported fewer young narcotics arrestees.[1] There were other reasons for optimism that year: the Supreme Court ruled in *Robinson v. California* that addiction was not a crime and heroin users could not be incarcerated simply because of their status. Rumors of Harry Anslinger's retirement from the Federal Bureau of Narcotics proved to be true, and it seemed that a retreat from the incarceration and punishment of drug offenders might be possible. But the moment of optimism was short-lived: young African Americans and Latinos—and toward the end of the decade, young whites—began to use heroin in larger numbers, creating a new wave of heroin use that dwarfed the one that had followed World War II.

The baby boomers, that demographic bulge that has affected so much of postwar American society, reached adolescence beginning in the early 1960s. Fifteen- to nineteen-year-old males comprised 7.1 percent of the nation's population in 1950; in 1960, they comprised 7.5 percent, and by 1970 their share increased to 9.7 percent. Since adolescent males between the ages of fifteen and nineteen were the most prone to experiment with heroin, their swelling number in American society signaled danger. But the geographic distribution of these young men was more important than their mere number.[2]

The African American, Latino, and white teenaged populations were all

TABLE 1. CHANGE IN MALE POPULATION, AGED FIFTEEN TO NINETEEN, SELECT CITIES, 1950–1970

	New York	Chicago	Detroit	Philadelphia	Washington, D.C.
Whites, 1950–1960	−1.20%	−2.20%	−16.00%	−6.10%	−23.40%
Whites, 1960–1970	+7.00%	+0.67%	−12.70%	+2.44%	−40.75%
Nonwhites, 1950–1960	+47.80%	+65.60%	+67.00%	+43.30%	+46.40%
Negro, 1960–1970	+128.33%	+117.83%	+125.55%	+77.60%	+97.54%

Source: U.S. Census, 1950–1970, Census of Population, Tables 20, 24, 33.

growing, but in different places: whites in suburbs and African Americans and Latinos in cities. The white populations in major cities began declining after 1950, the trend being most notable among middle-class families.[3] Parents who moved to the nation's burgeoning suburbs did not have protecting their children from heroin in mind when they did so, but that was the effect. Suburbanization, at least initially, effectively separated white middle-class adolescents from the urban ills of crime and drug abuse.[4] African American and Latino populations, located in neighborhoods where drug trading occurred, enjoyed no such immunity. These youthful populations provided a spatially concentrated potential market for narcotics.

The five American cities at the center of the postwar heroin wave illustrate the trends in population growth. They all showed sharp increases in their African American adolescent populations and little change or even declines among white adolescents, a group that should have been growing. The "nonwhite" adolescent male population increased well above the national average in these cities: anywhere from 40 to 70 percent during the 1950s (Table 1). In the 1960s, the pace of change accelerated, with only Philadelphia experiencing less than a 100 percent increase in the population of "Negro" adolescents.[5] At the same time, the percentage of white adolescents was stagnant. In New York City and Chicago, for example, the white male adolescent population remained level between 1950 and 1960, while in Detroit, Philadelphia, and Washington, D.C., it declined, sometimes precipitously. In the 1960s, only New York and Philadelphia showed real increases in the percentage of white adolescents, as middle-class white families continued to leave the city.[6] As a result, young African Americans became an increasingly large percentage of urban populations: African Americans, sixteen to twenty-four years old, comprised approximately 40 percent of populations in central cities with more than one million residents in 1960, and about 55 percent of the populations of those cities by 1970.[7]

Adolescents living near centers of drug use and sales were at a higher risk than any other group for using heroin; the shift in population meant that those adolescents were largely African American and Latino. While a national sample of young men revealed that 14 percent of African Americans reported experimenting with heroin (as compared to 5 percent of whites), the differences for those living near copping zones was startling: in a sample of young men residing in Manhattan neighborhoods characterized by high drug use, nearly 40 percent of African Americans (versus 11 percent of whites) used heroin.[8] Race, class, and place intersected to shape adolescents' experience, as young men residing near drug markets were two or three times more likely to begin using heroin than were adolescent males more generally. In analyzing the swelling wave of heroin users in the 1960s, the social setting of the inner city was the most important determinant of who used heroin.

While demographic change and location explain the vulnerability of specific populations, they are insufficient by themselves to account for the increase in heroin use. Other social factors, including the decline in peer influences against heroin, played a role in adolescents' decision making. The postwar generation of heroin users actively discouraged their younger siblings and acquaintances from taking the drug. While the impact of this social learning was modest, by the 1960s the effects had worn off completely. The cohort of young men that had begun taking heroin between 1945 and 1950 was thirty or older in the 1960s, many were in jail or in rehab, and they were distant enough in age and experience to have lost their connection to young teens in the neighborhood. More important, street gangs had actively dissuaded members from using heroin in the 1950s, but in the following decade, the influence of gangs was waning.

In the heyday of teenage street gangs, suspicion of heroin users kept heroin at bay. (Los Angeles's Chicano gangs were an exception.) Gang members believed that hardcore heroin users were unreliable because, if arrested, heroin users might trade information for release once they began to suffer from withdrawal symptoms. In addition, since heroin users had to move freely across territorial divisions in order to raise money and to purchase drugs, they could not afford to be identified with a group organized around the defense of turf. As author Claude Brown put it, "Everybody knew that junkies didn't go around bebopping [gang fighting]." Gang members assumed that loyalty to the gang diminished as dependence on heroin increased. Therefore gangs warned their narcotics-using members that if they wished to continue to be part of the gang, they had to quit using heroin.[9]

However, the relationship between gangs and drugs was not as clear-cut as the opposition to heroin implied. Gang members ingested a variety of drugs from alcohol to tobacco to marijuana to "uppers" (amphetamines) and "downers" (barbiturates), while older gang members sometimes experimented with heroin on their way out of the gang. According to a study of heroin use in New York gangs, about a third of the members surveyed had experimented with heroin, and about a quarter were currently using it, but some gangs experienced no heroin experimentation at all. What differentiated the two groups was age: non-heroin-using gangs were younger and more cohesive, they participated in delinquent activity as a group, and engaged in more fighting with other groups—in other words, they acted like a gang. Gangs with heroin users not only were older, they also did more in small cliques of two or three members rather than as a group, and they rejected gang-fighting as "kid stuff," a phase that they had already passed through.[10] These were gangs that were slowly disintegrating, and heroin use was part of the process. While gangs were clearly not impermeable barriers to heroin, their presence in a neighborhood provided some peer-organized resistance to its spread among those youths most active in the gang.

Public policy, which had defined gang fighting as the paramount problem facing young men in the 1950s, upset the precarious balance between gangs and heroin. The rising toll of adolescent gang violence led the New York City Youth Board (and similar organizations in other cities) to flood conflict-ridden neighborhoods with gang workers to mediate disputes, while the police broke up groups of teenagers on the streets. At the same time, settlement houses, churches, and teen centers hired street workers to make contact with gangs, to provide recreational and employment opportunities, and to isolate core members while encouraging peripheral ones to return to school or to enter the workforce. These initiatives combined to suppress a peer group that was hostile to heroin in the very neighborhoods where drug use was most concentrated.

Disrupting gangs undermined adolescents' mode of collective resistance. Gangs may not have been politically astute in their understanding of the effects of inequality and poverty on the lives of individual members, but they offered a group response to the problems of poor adolescents. They were a buffer against unemployment and labor market discrimination, they resisted police harassment, they encouraged members to skip school and to defy social service agencies' demands for obedience and decorum, and they offered relief from life in an impoverished household. In the absence of gangs, adolescents substituted individual responses, such as heroin use and hustling.

Hustling was an important source of income in the face of limited opportunity in the legitimate labor market. The combined impact of demography and migration expanded the pool of African American teenagers in American cities beyond the capacity of the labor market to absorb them. The group would have strained the resources of a healthy urban economy, but in fact, urban economies were not healthy. Older eastern and midwestern cities were shedding jobs—particularly the manufacturing and warehousing jobs most suitable to an unskilled workforce—to the suburbs and to the Sunbelt, making the plight of young workers more dire. New York City teenagers had an unemployment rate of 9.6 percent in 1960, or approximately double the adult rate. However, unemployment rates varied, with males experiencing higher unemployment than females, and with African Americans having higher rates than whites. White fourteen- to nineteen-year-old males had an 11 percent unemployment rate, while "nonwhite" males in the same age group had a 19 percent unemployment rate.[11] In a study of sixty "ghetto" labor markets in 1970, researchers found that the unemployment rate for African American teenaged males was 35 percent, or nearly twice what it had been in New York at the start of the decade.[12] In light of a bad market growing worse, the underground economy had obvious appeal.

One response to a deteriorating labor market was to remain in school, and whites chose that option more than African Americans did. Between 1940 and 1960 the number of African American dropouts increased slowly, while white adolescents remained in school in larger numbers. As a result, in 1960 only slightly more than half of black male teens were in school as opposed to over 70 percent of whites. Young men who were not enrolled in school and excluded from the labor market were prime candidates for inclusion in an underground economy.[13]

Working off the books has a long history in socially and economically isolated communities. The underground economy includes a range of activities from the obviously criminal to those that are illegal simply because they are unregulated: neither employer nor employee reports income; no attention is paid to minimum wage or maximum hour legislation; and zoning, permit, and health and safety regulations are ignored. Working as a prostitute, num-

bers runner, gambler, fence, drug seller, or a pimp is more widely recognized
as illegal, although the "victims" are usually consenting partners in the transactions. Burglars, shoplifters, and muggers earn a living in ways that most
would regard as criminal because wealth and property are being expropriated
and redistributed, although such distinctions blur considerably in communities that have limited access to legally provided goods and services. Finally,
there are specialists in violence whose role it is to regulate the marketplace in
the absence of other regulatory institutions, as well as predators whose presence makes the underground economy insecure.[14]

The underground economy changed in the 1960s—new workforce opportunities in illegal drug selling developed just as the number of unemployed young men increased. Ironically, policing was a factor in the creation
of new jobs in the heroin trade. The growth of both city and federal narcotics
squads during the 1950s forced a reorganization of the retail end of the drug
business, which ultimately opened up more job opportunities for youth.
With more pressure on retail sales, dealers organized the trade into several
different constituent parts in order to limit exposure to arrest and prevent
the seizure of product and assets. They employed lookouts who would signal
when police were nearby, steerers (or "touts") who informed customers of
where to purchase, someone who took a customer's money, another who
handed over the drugs, and a runner who periodically replenished supplies
and picked up cash. Others might run a shooting gallery, where users not
carrying "works" rented syringes, got water, and found a space to shoot up.
While older hustles—such as pimping, gambling, and running the numbers—continued to flourish, drug dealing not only began to offer more employment opportunities, it also became the apparent path to riches.[15]

The life of Ellsworth "Bumpy" Johnson illustrates the transformation of
the underground economy and the lure of heroin selling. Johnson began
dealing heroin late in his underworld career after he had already achieved
success and fame. Born in Charleston, South Carolina, in 1906, Johnson
moved to New York City in his teens, where he became a burglar and stick-up
man. After serving time in a reform school, Johnson turned to the numbers,
pimping, and hustling for a living. He secured his reputation as a feared
member of the underworld through his defense of black numbers operators
from a takeover by the white gangster Dutch Schultz in the 1930s. Johnson's
doings were reported in the African American press throughout the country,
as he was a suspect in a number of stabbings and shootings, but he also
earned notice for his dress, generosity, manners, and extravagant lifestyle.[16]

Johnson was a noted "race man," who supported civil rights initiatives, and as a policy banker, he employed many Harlem residents in what was a semi-respectable profession. Johnson's rise to prominence was interrupted when he went to prison in 1937 for stabbing a man. Johnson served his entire ten-year sentence, apparently preferring that to being paroled and remaining subject to state supervision.

Upon leaving prison, Johnson took advantage of the expanding market for heroin in Harlem in the postwar years. Johnson partnered with Italian crime families in New York to distribute heroin to African American retailers, but was in business only for about a year before being rearrested; after a conviction on a narcotics charge, he returned to prison for a fifteen-year stint. The *Amsterdam News* recounted that when he finally was released from prison the second time in the early 1960s, he was greeted like a conquering hero with champagne corks popping. Johnson returned to the narcotics business and became a big enough entrepreneur that he was able to explore setting up his own international connections. New York police accused Johnson of importing "narcotics" (probably cocaine) from Peru for sale in Harlem, and he was awaiting trial on the charge at the time of his death from a heart attack in 1968.[17]

In a measure of Johnson's larger-than-life persona, crowds lined Harlem's streets to watch his funeral procession, and three priests and a bishop led his high-church funeral services. They eulogized Johnson as a man of honor with a code of ethics to which he held fast, who decided "early in life not to be a clown, a flunky or a beggar." Johnson himself was unapologetic about his choices, asking, "What would you have me do? Go down to Grand Central Station and carry bags for dimes? . . . White people ain't left us nothin' but the underworld."[18] Accounts of his life have been fictionalized in the films *Shaft* (1971), in which the title character, John Shaft, helps "Bumpy Jonas" get his daughter back from Mafia kidnappers, and *Hoodlum* (1997), which recounts Johnson's struggle against Dutch Schultz.

Several generations of young African American men became enamored of Bumpy Johnson because of his wealth, uncompromising code, and style. Claude Brown remembered Johnson, the defiant numbers runner, as a hero and compared him favorably to contemporary drug kingpins, who were ruthless "negative idols" for young people. Ignoring Johnson's role in the heroin trade, Brown wrote, "a teen-ager now grows up in a community where the digits [numbers] have been supplanted by scag, blow, smoke." Ironically, one of the men Brown disparaged, heroin dealer Frank Lucas, idolized Bumpy

Johnson for taking him under his wing when he was a teenager newly arrived from the South. Lucas recalled that street toughs and cops alike left him alone, and he acquired a certain swagger. Walking into a jewelry store he had robbed earlier, Lucas believed that the owner recognized him, but merely asked if he wanted some help. "Because now I'm with Bumpy Johnson—a Bumpy Johnson man. I'm 17 years old and I'm *Mr.* Lucas." Writer Frank Chapman included in a review of *Hoodlum* his recollection that "in the ghettos where I grew up—in Chicago and St. Louis—Bumpy Johnson was definitely a hero and, for want-to-be criminals, a role model."[19]

Bumpy Johnson was a prototypical "bad man," someone who commanded fear and respect from most members of the African American community.[20] While upstanding families might distance themselves from his violence and drug dealing, even they could admire his defiance of the white legal and illegal power structures. Bumpy Johnson and the many lesser-known local dealers who dominated the street corners of inner-city neighborhoods showed that one path to esteem and power was through the heroin trade. Valorizing men such as Bumpy Johnson inevitably enhanced the allure of the underground drug economy for marginalized young men.

Smuggling also changed in the 1960s, which increased the amount of heroin that was available for sale. Older addicts complained bitterly about heroin's declining quality, which suggests that heroin supply lagged behind the growth in the user population. While an increase in supply was probably not a major factor in the growth of the heroin market in the 1960s, customs and enforcement personnel argued that they were playing catch-up with smugglers and that more heroin was slipping through border controls. Air travel grew exponentially in the decade and changed the means, the volume, and the speed with which heroin could be smuggled. Airline staff sometimes supplemented their income by secreting packages aboard a plane and leaving them to be removed by ground personnel. Other enterprising smugglers hid a supply on a plane, waited until a flight cleared customs at New York or Philadelphia, and then reboarded the flight and removed the drugs at a subsequent inland destination where there were no customs inspections. Several couriers might be dispatched on the same flight, and even if one were captured, it simply drew attention away from the others. Customs officials believed that smugglers began using cargo containers to move larger amounts of heroin into the United States in the mid-1960s. Shippers hid the drug in a container of legitimate goods, in which parts were removed and replaced with an equally weighted parcel of heroin, making detection nearly impossible. Such shipments were not chaperoned, but they allowed a much larger volume to be smuggled at a time.[21]

And smugglers knew to change their routes. In the 1960s, Latin America became a prime transshipment point for heroin ultimately destined for New York. Heroin arrived in Montevideo or Buenos Aires and was then transferred to commercial flights bound for Miami or Houston, where no one would be looking for heroin from Marseilles. On other occasions, shipments were loaded on small private planes that hopped across Latin America before landing at small airstrips in the southern United States. The multiplication of routes, couriers, and traffic made the task of interdicting heroin more difficult and resulted in increased availability.[22]

The last factor in the increase in heroin use in the early 1960s was the nearly complete corruption of narcotics police—the New York City Police Department (NYPD) and the New York office of the Federal Bureau of Narcotics. All markets require regulation, and in the absence of the state, illegal markets develop their own informal regulatory systems.[23] Accounts of the underground economy have frequently overlooked the fact that the police have played a vital role in regulating the marketplace—in the early twentieth century as part of the political machine and in the late twentieth century as individual entrepreneurs. The growing heroin trade altered fundamentally the ways in which police interacted with the illegal marketplace. Narcotics changed policing because it generated so much cash that it obliterated the traditional distinction made by police between clean and dirty money, and because the very act of policing the narcotics market encouraged even honest officers to act in ways that were corrupting.

The police have played a crucial, but changing, role in the organization of illegal markets. In the heyday of the political machine in the early twentieth century, the machine, rather than the police, regulated the vice market. The police served as another source of patronage appointments for politicians and collected graft as agents of the machine. Precinct captains owed their appointments to the local ward leader, thus they turned over a substantial portion of the graft collected from madams, pimps, gamblers, and professional criminals to the party coffers.

Police reform in the twentieth century focused on insulating the police from politics and severing the connection to political machines. Reformers stressed professionalism, created bureaucracy, and militarized police training to make the police more independent of political control and more immune to corruption. Over time, reformers succeeded in creating a police department in which career advancement relied more on standardized exams than political litmus tests.[24]

Machine politics changed as well. By the mid-twentieth century, the political machine lost its traditional role as a result of electoral reform, the growth of a welfare state in which assistance was a right rather than a gift from the ward leader, and a greater federal role in municipal politics more generally. At the same time that the machine declined, the police became an increasingly independent force, more distant from politics than at any point in the past. These simultaneous developments changed the locus of corruption.

In the postwar years, police increasingly acted as independent regulators of the city's vice markets, filling the void left by the end of machine politics, ensuring the orderly operation of the illegal market, and in the process, enriching themselves. Dishonest officers eagerly sought out appointments to units or beats that offered money-making opportunities. Officer William Phillips recalled paying bribes in order to get choice assignments, and Detective David Durk, although not interested in collecting graft, wondered why he always patrolled in front of a midtown store, until an older officer told him that he needed to slip the desk officer a few dollars in order to get a better post. Uniformed officers sought promotion to plainclothes, not only because it was a step toward becoming a detective, but also because of the income-producing opportunities it promised, which officers discussed openly.[25]

In addition to specific assignments or squads that promised to be lucrative, officers identified some precincts for their high-income possibilities. Harlem's precincts generated so much cash that police referred to them as the "Gold Coast."[26] William Phillips collected enough graft that after he was transferred out of Harlem he was able to make the down payment on a house. Other officers eagerly sought the opportunity to be posted there. Congressman Charles Rangel reported that he had been approached by an African American policeman who complained bitterly that he could not get an assignment to Harlem. He expressed his hope that Rangel would intervene on his behalf: "I'm starving to death," he complained in a lament echoed by other African American officers, asking why white officers got all the opportunities to collect graft.[27] The Harlem market was such a treasure trove that corrupt officers went to great lengths in order to be assigned there.

Most police departments accepted a certain amount of graft as inevitable, and some officers came to expect it. Businesses offered free meals ("eating on

the arm"), discounted merchandise, gifts during the holidays, and cash gratuities with the expectation that officers might pay extra attention after closing
or ignore a delivery van's parking violation. Managers of construction sites
paid officers to overlook violations of city ordinances, while towing companies paid premiums to be called in case of a traffic accident. These informal
licensing fees, which were paid into a kitty that was then divided among the
officers with the size of shares depending on rank and length of service, were
considered "clean money" and did not imply any corruption on the part of
the officer. They were a form of market regulation that allowed the ordinary
business of the city to proceed smoothly.

Illegal enterprise had an equal interest in running smoothly and also
provided gratuities to police. A madam might have her "girls" gratify officers'
sexual desires at no charge, knowing that they could be called upon to remove
unruly patrons, or the owner of an after-hours club might supply free drinks
for off-duty police, realizing that he was less likely to be robbed with them
on the premises. Bookmakers and other gamblers provided a monthly payoff
for police to ignore their activities. Police generally considered such gratuities
as unproblematic as payoffs from legitimate businesses.

The extent of corruption within the NYPD became apparent after
Mayor John Lindsay reluctantly ordered an investigation into allegations
published in the *New York Times* that police received millions of dollars
annually in payoffs. This systematized form of corruption had developed over
at least a decade, and the Mayor's Commission to Investigate Corruption,
better known as the Knapp Commission, eventually concluded that half of
the city's police officers were corrupt.[28] While police reform had succeeded
in severing ties between the machine and the police, it still left the police
with the job of regulating the illegal market. Clearly, a large number of officers took advantage of the opportunity.

By the late 1960s, the collection of money was organized so systematically
that it formed the chief occupation of several officers within each precinct.
Precinct captains had "bag men," particularly trusted veterans, who made a
monthly round of illegal enterprises to collect the "nut," a payment that
could run to several thousand dollars. Vice entrepreneurs who were "on the
pad" were not harassed in the ordinary conduct of their business and would
be given warnings prior to any raids in return for their monthly payment.
New officers had to wait sixty days before receiving their shares of payoffs,
but those transferring to other assignments received an extra two months'
allotment. The payment was a return on loyalty and silence, and it allowed

an officer to get established in his new precinct while forming bonds with new colleagues. At first a new officer was "like a wallflower. Nobody even says hello to you." But if someone passed the background checks with a former precinct and responded appropriately to colleagues' hints, he was accepted as "one of the guys" and given earning opportunities.[29]

The process of corruption occurred gradually, but after a while the whole routine looked normal. In the words of detective William Phillips, slowly "your conscience changes, your sense of values changes. So keep your mouth shut, and it begins to look real easy." Payoffs were the norm, simply what turn-of-the-century Tammany Hall leader George Washington Plunkitt had called "honest graft," opportunity seen and taken, the added perks of public service.[30]

While many police officers accepted the spoils of office, they did not engage actively in crime themselves. If accepting money from vice purveyors could be justified as regulating services that the public clearly desired, and ignoring traffic or blue law violations justified as something arguably within the public interest, police officers recognized that other activities were more unambiguously corrupt. Some officers, called "meateaters" in the evocative language of the Knapp Commission, went beyond the arrangements of honest graft. "Meateaters" were distinguished from "grasseaters" for the aggressive manner in which they sought out economic opportunity. They shook down violators, pocketing cash to be split with a partner, in return for releasing someone caught in a criminal act. Arriving first at a burglary scene, they might steal several items, or raid the cash register if it had not been completely looted by a burglar. While shunned by some, others eagerly sought these men as partners because they had reputations for finding "scores" with verve and imagination.[31] By the 1960s, police had honed graft into a well-organized business.

Most police officers, even the more venal, drew the line at money earned from narcotics. The very term "clean money" made it clear that some money was dirty, that some behavior was wrong. In the mid-1960s, patrolman Robert Leuci asked advice from future police commissioner Michael Codd about accepting a transfer out of the tactical police force and into plainclothes. Leuci, like most officers, had heard about corruption among plainclothesmen, and he asked Codd how he would advise his son about a transfer. Codd told him to stay put. Later Leuci asked him about a transfer into the narcotics division, and Codd allegedly told Leuci not to worry. "There's not a cop in the world who would take drug money," Codd assured him. But even as Codd was making the classical distinction between clean and dirty money, this line was disappearing, as Leuci and later the public discovered.[32]

Narcotics graft was exceedingly lucrative and provided far greater payoffs than the pads paid by gamblers and madams. The temptation for officers who had already accepted payoffs in other vice markets was simply overwhelming. In a department characterized by routine corruption, there was a slippery slope in which each decision had a cumulative effect until what had once been a major line of demarcation could be crossed with a fairly small step.[33] As Detective Leuci recalled, "All that was once my honor fell from me piece by piece." In the case of the narcotics market, police overcame the traditional distinction between clean and dirty money because of the increasingly large sums generated by the market, and because of the very nature of narcotics policing.[34]

Policing the narcotics market was so difficult that officers found it virtually impossible to avoid violating their professional and ethical codes. Police discovered that perjury was practically a job requirement when testifying at a street dealer's court hearing. In order to prove possession, an officer had to connect specific packets of heroin seized in a raid to an individual dealer. Since dealers rid themselves of whatever heroin they had as soon as the police appeared, officers had to testify that they observed a suspect dropping heroin packets and that they kept both the suspect and the heroin in sight when making an arrest. However, in the turbulent and potentially dangerous atmosphere of a raid, it was nearly impossible to keep an eye on both the heroin and a suspect anxious not to be connected to it. Prosecutors and judges must have realized the formulaic nature of officers' testimony, but they avoided drawing conclusions about perjury. Since cases rested on their testimony, officers felt pressured to take the steps necessary to secure a conviction in the name of a larger sense of justice.[35]

Once officers became inured to perjury, augmenting the evidence against an "obviously guilty" suspect followed logically. Police used confiscated heroin to "flake" or "pad" arrestees. "Padding" involved adding some additional heroin to that seized from a dealer in order to change an arrest from a misdemeanor to a felony (in New York possession of more than one-eighth of an ounce of heroin was defined by law as possession with intent to sell), while "flaking" meant planting evidence on a suspect and then arresting him. Officers rationalized their behavior by arguing that suspects were clearly guilty and that the police merely provided some extra help in convicting them. Street dealers rarely carried large amounts of heroin; as officer Edward Droge testified, "It was a common practice for dealers . . . to carry bundles on them which added up to less than the amount necessary for the felony—just a couple of bags shy." Police viewed padding a dealer as part of the cat-and-mouse game played between criminals and police, justifiable in preventing drug defendants from taking advantage of legal loopholes.[36]

While they turned in sufficient quantities of heroin to gain a conviction, police held some back for their own purposes. In addition to having heroin around for padding and flaking, the most important use of stolen heroin was to pay informants. Narcotics detectives had a "four collars a month" rule, which meant they had to return to uniform if they did not make four arrests per month, and informants made buys or provided the information needed to make arrests. Police jealously guarded their prize informants and were willing to supply them with high-quality heroin in order to keep information flowing, especially since any money given to them would be spent on drugs anyway. In addition, heroin users traveled in limited circles, often confining their purchases and activities to a small group of dealers or a single neighborhood. As Detective Leuci argued, over time informants became suspect and dealers refused to sell to them. "They have habits that they have to take care of every day," Leuci noted, "and now the only people who will give them drugs are cops." In the eyes of the law, gifts of heroin were considered sales and treated as a felony, but police believed that supplying heroin to informants was a necessary, even justifiable, part of doing business. The conclusion was inescapable that "corruption" was integral to policing narcotics markets.[37]

Gradually, the demands of narcotics policing shifted officers' perceptions and involved them almost inevitably in graft. Stealing cash from dealers before arresting them became a widespread practice within the narcotics squad. Police rationalized stealing from dealers as retributive justice, especially when they suspected a dealer might forfeit a bond and skip bail before a hearing. Waverly Logan, a member of an elite squad of African American officers operating in Harlem, contended, "The general feeling was that the man was going to jail, was going to get what was coming to him, so why should you give him back his money and let him bail himself out." Logan maintained, "We kind of felt he didn't deserve no rights since he was selling narcotics." Another detective also commented that the money was "ill-gotten" and it was a rough form of justice to steal it. "The drug dealer doesn't deserve it—I have a family and I deserve it. Those were the practices. It wasn't viewed as such a terrible thing."[38] While these may have been rationalizations made up after the fact, they have a ring of truth. A dealer felt the loss of his wad immediately, while criminal justice proceedings, if they resulted in a conviction, dragged out for months before delivering any jail time. Where drug dealers' money had once been too dirty for a police officer to touch, an "etiquette of corruption" gradually developed around narcotics. David Durk recalled that if detectives scored money from dealers, they divided it equally, while the sergeant and lieutenant would get a share and a half or a double share. In order to set up such scores, police used informants, illegal searches, and illegal wiretaps to gather information about who might be carrying large amounts of cash and drugs. Detectives then raided dealers knowing they could not make legal cases against them.[39]

Once police began letting dealers go after stealing their drugs and cash, the next step was to put a dealer on the pad. Police officers allowed certain dealers to operate with regular payoffs, provided protection to dealers, and opened their own narcotics franchises, becoming dealers themselves. Investigators from the Knapp Commission concluded that regular payoffs could reach $3,000 per man per month in an elite squad, while an individual "score" in which an officer happened to catch a dealer might range from a minor shakedown to as much as $80,000.[40] Detective Phillips noted the gradual evolution of police practice, from taking money while arresting a suspect to "not only taking his money, taking his junk or half of it, [but] . . . putting the guy on the pad. That's giving a guy a license to deal."[41]

Dealers on the pad enjoyed the full protection of the police department. The Knapp Commission concluded that police tipped off dealers about raids, sold the contents of police files to suspects, sold information about the location of wiretaps, sold the identity of informants, listed favored dealers as informants in official department files in order to protect them from arrest, provided armed escort for the delivery of narcotics, and rented automobiles for the transportation of narcotics, so that if the tags were checked they would show that the car had been rented by a member of the NYPD. Besides protecting dealers' operations, some police went into narcotics retailing themselves. One officer, appearing before a state investigating commission, confirmed testimony given by addicts that he supplied them with drugs for sale:

Q. Did you ever give narcotics to Diane [an informant]?
A. I did.

Q. For what purpose?

A. She's supposed to sell it on the street for me.[42]

Here the police did not even offer the pretense of regulating a market; they were full market participants.

The demands of policing narcotics and the tremendous amount of money produced by the narcotics market combined to generate enormous pressure on officers to act corruptly. The small steps that started with committing perjury and planting evidence ended with police retailing heroin. These steps began and perhaps were even justified as part of a war on drugs, but they ended with police officers acting in ways indistinguishable from the dealers they policed. Lieutenant Durk argued that by the end of the 1960s, there were two major heroin-marketing operations in New York City. One was the Lucchese crime family's traditional wholesaling center in East Harlem, while the other was in the New York City Police Department and "operated out of the fourth floor of the First Precinct station house in lower Manhattan—the headquarters of the Special Investigations Unit [SIU] of the police department's Narcotics Division." When the SIU was finally disbanded, it was in the wake of revelations that 180 kilos—approximately $32 million worth of heroin—had disappeared from the police evidence room to be resold on the streets of New York, with the profits divided among police officers.[43]

The market for illegal narcotics shaped the police department more than the police department shaped the market. The narcotics market generated the conditions for its own regulation, and the police responded to the market's overwhelming power in ways that were profoundly different from what they had done before. In the past, the police may have had gamblers on the pad, but they did not take policy slips; they may have accepted sexual favors from prostitutes, but they were not pimps; they may have protected burglars, but they themselves did not burglarize; they may have kept criminals out of jail, but they did not direct their illegal activities. The narcotics market erased the line between clean and dirty money, between honest and dishonest graft, and ultimately, between police officer and dealer.

The FBN was the other major law enforcement agency that had responsibility for policing narcotics in New York City, and it was as corrupt as the NYPD. The two organizations worked closely together, sharing intelligence and going on joint raids, and they employed many of the same methods. Not surprisingly, with the most important office of the FBN utterly corrupt, New York easily retained its position as the heroin import capital of the nation.

Corruption was apparent in the New York office of the Treasury Department's Narcotics Division—the FBN's predecessor—as early as the 1920s. Federal agents padded their arrest records and associated with drug dealers, while the son and son-in-law of the chief of the Narcotics Division, Levi Nutt, were accused of aiding heroin importer Arnold Rothstein in evading federal income taxes. The scandal led to the reassignment of seventeen agents as well as the closing of the Narcotics Division and creation of the FBN under the leadership of Harry J. Anslinger. The reorganization apparently had little effect, as three agents were soon arrested for attempting to bribe one of their colleagues into perjuring himself at a drug dealer's trial. Minor scandals erupted periodically, and by the 1950s, the bureau's most important office had a reputation for corruption.[44]

The FBN employed corrupt practices similar to those in the NYPD. Agents working in small teams raided apartments, looted cash (which they kept for themselves), and held back narcotics seized on raids. Bureau policy unintentionally reinforced these practices. Agents who were burned in their drug purchases had to repay the money out of their own funds, and so they began keeping stashes of heroin to supplement the heroin content in their buys. New agents worked in small teams with experienced men during their first-year probationary status, which provided on-the-job training but also ensured that new agents became acculturated to the practices of their peers. In order to retain their jobs, new agents generally went along with established practices even if these were legally questionable or blatantly illegal. Agents held meetings in bars owned by members of organized crime, and they rarely paid their bills in these places. Finally, agents experienced great pressure to make cases, even if they had to sacrifice long-term investigations for immediate arrests. As a result, agents were tempted to cut corners and engage in the same flaking and padding done by the city police.[45]

As in the NYPD, agents routinely sold cases—that is, information about investigations and informants' identities were revealed for a price. Security was very lax: any agent could read an informant's file since those filing cabinets were unlocked. And while the role of the informant was necessarily dangerous, the loss of life among FBN informants was striking. Between forty and fifty informants were murdered during the 1960s as drug dealers learned their identities.

Nor were federal agents immune from death threats and intimidation.

At least three agents received narcotics overdoses when having drinks with fellow agents, not because they were going to inform on corruption, but because they tried to shake down heroin importers without the prior approval of corrupt colleagues. Honest agents were threatened or transferred out of the New York office, and allegations of inappropriate practices against the investigator sidetracked at least one probe into corruption. Agents suspected of corruption were transferred rather than fired and sometimes gained positions of authority over those who had previously investigated them. Moreover, Commissioner Anslinger, with his intimidating style, would brook no criticism of his agency or its operations, making whistle-blowing unlikely. "Corruption within Treasury," concluded former agent Tom Tripodi, "was almost a tradition." An internal investigation in 1968, the results of which were never released, indicated the extent of corruption in the FBN. The probe incriminated one-fifth of the FBN's agents nationwide and led to the resignation of forty-five agents and criminal indictments of an additional twelve.[46] Just like their police counterparts, federal narcotics agents acted as individual regulators of the market in cooperation with the international traffickers they were supposed to arrest. The conclusion is inescapable that the flow of heroin into users' veins would have been impossible without the assistance of the city's police force and the New York office of the FBN.

In the absence of any other governing structures, the police and federal narcotics agents stepped forward to regulate the narcotics market. Officers acted more individually and entrepreneurially at precisely the moment when narcotics markets expanded and generated enormous amounts of cash, which changed the ethos of policing in ways that traditional vice regulation had not. In the war against drugs, some of the biggest dealers were the warriors themselves.

By the end of the 1960s, New York City's population of known heroin users had doubled, with a minimum of 60,000 living in the city, a rate of increase that far exceeded the growth of the adolescent male population. The social setting of the inner city with high rates of unemployment and an expanding underground economy based around heroin lured young men into both heroin sales and use. The corruption of police agencies ensured that supplies of heroin would be ample and that New York's role as the center of international heroin trafficking would be unchallenged. The result was a crime rate that spiraled out of control and threatened the very existence of the city.

CHAPTER SEVEN

Dealing with Dope

THE RISING TIDE of heroin use in the 1960s produced an urban crime wave of vast proportions. New York was particularly hard hit, and its seeming collapse into crime and chaos came to represent the fate of cities all across America. Both Democratic Mayor Robert Wagner and Republican Mayor John Lindsay proved to be completely ineffectual in combating this explosion in serious crime, and the helplessness of liberal politicians in the face of rising crime rates fueled local and national politics that were increasingly nasty and racially polarized.

Heroin's role in the crime wave is undeniable, but heroin was not its only cause. Heroin was linked to the proliferation of what might be called economic crime. In 1962 Mayor Wagner estimated that heroin addicts were responsible for the theft of $600 million in goods annually, mostly through larceny (including shoplifting) and burglary.[1] In addition, heroin users committed street crimes—robberies or muggings, which made citizens afraid to walk the streets at night and were particularly threatening to ordinary civic life. But homicide, rape, and aggravated assault, which had no demonstrable relationship to narcotics, also rose in this period, although not to the same extent. While heroin made the crime problem significantly worse, it was only part of the problem.

A geography of inequality produced both heroin use and crime. Certain urban neighborhoods concentrated the effects of poverty and racial discrimination and hosted large numbers of the demographic group most prone to both heroin use and street crime: marginalized and isolated young men. These neighborhoods were the by-products of economic development, areas

TABLE 2. INCREASE IN INDEX CRIMES, NEW YORK CITY, 1960–1975

	1960	1965	1970	1975	Increase
Murder	390	631	1,117	1,645	421.8%
Rape	841	1,154	2,124	3,866	459.7%
Robbery	6,579	8,904	74,102	83,190	1264.5%
Assault	11,021	16,325	31,255	43,481	394.5%
Burglary	36,049	51,072	181,694	177,032	491.1%
Larceny $50 or more[a]	54,213	74,983	132,572	188,832	348.3%
Car Theft	21,069	34,726	94,835	83,201	395.9%

Source: FBI Uniform Crime Reports. These are total reported crimes.
[a] The larceny categories of less and more than $50 were collapsed into one category in 1973.

left over as productive activity moved elsewhere, and they were the spatial expressions of a market economy that simultaneously concentrated poverty and wealth, marginality and centrality, disadvantage and advantage, and underdevelopment and development. These neighborhoods were not simply the containers of events, they were also their producers. Any attempt to deal with both crime and heroin use would have to address this in order to be successful.

Crime overwhelmed New Yorkers in the 1960s. Between 1960 and 1968 robbery increased over 825 percent and burglary 480 percent. More accurate accounting explained some of this increase, but even if police undercounted robberies and burglaries in the early 1960s and new reporting standards exaggerated the rate of increase, the growth of crime was undeniable (Table 2). Homicide—generally the most reliably counted crime—doubled in this same eight-year period. The crime wave of the 1960s was neither a reporting artifact nor the result of a media-driven moral panic.

Robbery played a particularly important role in New Yorkers' perceptions of safety. While most violent crime was intraracial in nature, robbery was an exception. According to an analysis of robbery victims done in New York in 1967, approximately half of robbery victims reported that perpetrators were of a different race. Robbery thus fueled racial and ethnic tensions with white New Yorkers blaming African Americans and Puerto Ricans for the increasing volume of street crime.[2]

The crime wave that started under Mayor Wagner's administration became a major issue in the 1965 mayoral campaign. A series in the *New York Herald Tribune* hammered relentlessly at the Democratic administration for the overall decline in the city's quality of life. Mayor Wagner himself had proclaimed the necessity of doing "something" about the "the drug addicts, the addict pushers, the numbers runners, the petty thieves, the muggers and others who form a special underworld of the poor."[3] Another series in the *Tribune*, begun just before election day, gave human faces to the statistics on crime: an old lady in a wheelchair attacked by a burglar, a restaurant worker mugged in the subway, a Manhattan deli owner held up by an addict, an elderly man in Brownsville attacked by a group of boys yelling "kill him, he's white."[4] Crime threatened to rub the city raw, and it demanded immediate attention.

Fighting crime became a centerpiece of John Lindsay's mayoral run. He charged that crime had gone up 15 percent in the last year of the Wagner administration, but he was careful to reject comments about crime that focused on the role of African Americans and Puerto Ricans. Lindsay argued that members of all groups committed crimes, and he pointed out that African American and Puerto Rican New Yorkers were disproportionately the victims of crime. Nonetheless, Lindsay maintained that crime was New York's most serious problem, and he was swept into office promising to solve it.[5]

Of course, as Lindsay recognized, crime was not evenly distributed throughout the city. Police precincts in poorer neighborhoods reported far higher crime rates than those in wealthier ones despite the tendency for crime in poor areas to be underreported. The likelihood of being a victim of a violent crime was two or three times higher for African Americans than for whites, while the chances of being robbed were higher for those with annual incomes of less than $6,000, regardless of race, than for those with higher incomes. A report by the New York branch of the NAACP recognized the dangers for African American residents of the city, declaring that while it was concerned about police brutality, "it is not police brutality that makes people afraid to walk the streets at night."[6]

The geography of crime is apparent in a comparison of two precincts, the 28th, covering Central Harlem, and the 19th, the so-called "silk stocking" district on the Upper East Side. These precincts were not far apart geographically, but socially and economically each was in a different universe (Table 3 and page 120). Manhattan had an overall rate of 357 robberies per 10,000 residents, the highest in the city. The 28th Precinct had a rate of 599, more than 50 percent higher than the Manhattan average, while the 19th Precinct had a rate of 86.5, or about a quarter of the borough average. Homicides were

TABLE 3. HOMICIDE, ROBBERY, AND BURGLARY RATES BY MANHATTAN POLICE PRECINCT

Precinct	Homicide rate per 10,000	Robbery rate per 10,000	Burglary rate per 10,000
1	7.87	568.67	1,749.29
4	10.39	249.44	1,278.36
5	3.28	95.34	199.44
6	2.15	214.74	459.03
7	2.11	175.45	262.44
9	3.08	303.02	473.95
10	3.86	164.05	505.99
13	0.38	121.86	378.33
14	12.87	2,378.49	4,210.61
17	0.91	178.02	795.08
18	6.49	508.25	1,383.12
19	0.74	86.3	250.18
20	1.84	178.75	335.32
23	1.78	195.31	259.64
24	1.63	267.06	347.12
25	5.98	291.99	298.08
26	2.67	259.11	236.21
28	19.68	599.31	440.82
30	2.83	264.21	329.05
32	7.75	319.9	336.48
34	0.85	78.67	186.35
Borough average	4.72	357.00	700.00

Source: New York Times, February 14, 1972, p. 1.

distributed in a similar fashion. Central Harlem's rate of 19.68 homicides per 10,000 residents was by far the highest in the city, while the 19th Precinct had 0.74. (The 14th Precinct, which appears to be an anomaly, was home to Times Square and the garment district, which had many crimes and few residents among whom to divide them, thus producing the highest crime rate in the city.) Generally, poorer residential neighborhoods reported far higher rates of crime than did wealthier ones.[7] With residents in poorer areas the most likely victims of all crime except for car theft, crime itself was highly spatialized. But fear of crime was not.

One difficulty with assessing how much heroin use added to the city's crime rate is that no one really knew how many heroin users there were. Narcotics arrests by the New York City Police Department increased steadily after 1955 (see page 121), before skyrocketing in the mid-1960s, which corre-

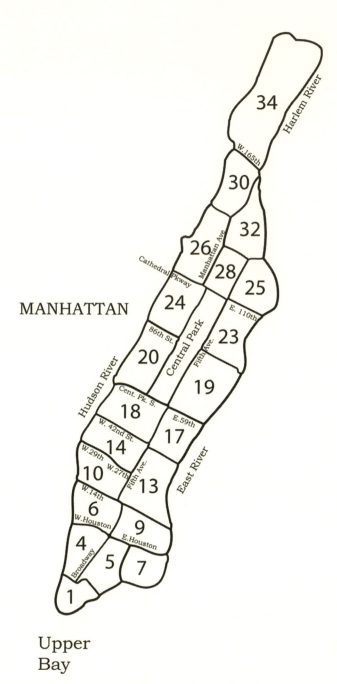

MANHATTAN

Harlem River

34

W. 165th

30

32

26

Manhattan Ave.

Cathedral Pkway

28

25

24

E. 110th

86th St.

Central Park

Fifth Ave.

23

Hudson River

20

19

Cent. Pk. S.

18

E.59th

W. 42nd St.

17

W.29th

14

W.27th

Fifth Ave.

10

W.14th

13

6

W.Houston

9

E.Houston

East River

4

Broadway

5

7

1

Upper
Bay

Manhattan Police Precincts, c. 1972. New York City Police Department.

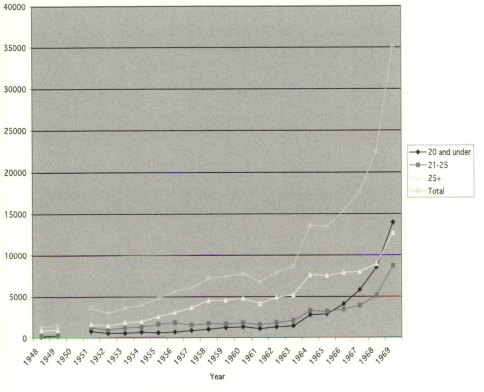

Narcotics arrests, New York City, 1948–1969.

sponds to the surge in crime. The arrest statistics suggest an increasing population of users, especially among individuals under twenty years old, even if they do not provide a clue as to their real number. According to conservative estimates by the New York State Narcotic Addiction Control Commission, there were 60,000 heroin users living in New York City in 1967, half of them African American, a quarter Puerto Rican, and a quarter white, most of them living in a few areas.[8]

Heroin use was concentrated in the city's poorest neighborhoods. The Central Harlem health district had the city's highest concentration of users, with 145 per 1,000 persons aged fifteen to forty-four (the peak years of opiate use); two health areas within the Central Harlem district reported rates of over 200 per 1,000, or nearly ten times the city average.[9] East Harlem ranked second in the city, and "Riverside," comprised of West Harlem and the Upper West Side, ranked third. No health district was entirely free of opiate users, but white middle-class neighborhoods in Staten Island, Queens, the northeast Bronx, and the far reaches of Brooklyn had rates that were so far below the city average as to be insignificant.

The geography of heroin was linked to the geography of crime. Social scientists have found that most crime is highly localized, as criminals hesitate to venture into unknown areas and tend instead to seize opportunities that arise in the course of their daily routines. Heroin users engaged in a variety of "hustles" to support their habits, combining legal jobs with roles in the drug trade, but they did not commit just narcotics-related crimes.[10] Serious heroin use demanded income-generating strategies that for unskilled, uneducated persons almost invariably involved crime, and the self-reports of heroin users include large numbers of illegal acts, even when narcotics-related offenses are not counted. Male addicts most frequently burgled, shoplifted, and stole various kinds of property, although they also committed crimes of violence, while female users shoplifted and engaged in prostitution. Studies by social scientists have found significant addict involvement in robberies and assaults; comparisons between heroin-using and nonusing felons, for example, show that heroin users were responsible for a larger number and larger variety of crimes and were more likely to carry a weapon than were nonusers.[11] Residents living near copping zones became the unfortunate targets of opportunity, which helps explain the city's distribution of robbery and burglary rates. African Americans and Puerto Ricans were heroin's principal users and its principal victims as poor communities cannibalized themselves.[12]

While John Lindsay fought crime as mayor (he increased the size of the police force by 3,700 patrolmen and made New York the first major city to install a 911 emergency call system), he proved no more able to stem the increase in crime than any other big-city mayor in the 1960s. The *New York Times*, generally sympathetic to Lindsay, repeatedly ran stories about crime leading up to the 1969 election for mayor. One letter writer, sounding more rueful than angry, captured the feelings of elderly white New Yorkers fearful of being victimized: "We were accustomed to hibernating at night and walking gingerly during the day. But recently, right in our own apartment building halls, we were averaging one mugging a week." He went on to say that after seeing several neighbors with stitched up heads, "I reluctantly decided that although retired I would have to double my rent and move into a still-segregated neighborhood." The letter writer, because of his class and race, could afford to leave his Crown Heights apartment behind, but of course not all residents were able to follow suit.[13]

Lindsay's inability to manage crime made it a major issue in the next mayoral campaign. White voters rallied around candidates vowing to make the city safer by getting tough on criminals, and only the division of the anti-Lindsay vote allowed the mayor to win a plurality (as a Liberal/Independent) for a second term. But no mayor could have managed the crime problem better than Lindsay.[14]

The crime that John Lindsay and other big-city mayors faced was produced by trends entirely beyond their control: forces that had created an unusual period of low crime rates in the mid-twentieth century unraveled in the 1960s. Mayoral responses, such as increasing the size of the police force, hiring civilian employees to put more of those officers on the streets, instituting new patrol patterns, and adopting a computerized dispatch system, among other reforms, were reasonable attempts to deal with crime, but they made only minor differences.[15]

While people did not realize it at the time, the peaceful decades of the mid-twentieth century were an aberration. Historians have identified what is known as the great U-turn, in which rates of violent crime dropped until they bottomed out in the mid-twentieth century, and then began to rise again. The most convincing explanation of the data argues that the process of industrialization subjected increasing numbers of preindustrial men to industrial discipline while limiting access to alcohol for long periods of the workweek. The public brawling and drunken spats that sent hundreds of victims each year to the morgue declined as a result, even if some of that crime moved indoors and emerged as domestic violence.[16] In addition, schooling, itself a form of social discipline that prepared youths for entry into the labor market, captured increasing numbers of male adolescents, subjected them to order for long periods of time, and thus limited their exposure to "street culture." Higher wages and stable jobs, especially in the years after World War II, encouraged marriage and family formation and corrected the gender imbalances that had traditionally supported a masculinist culture of violence.[17]

Then all of the conditions that were conducive to public order changed, and crime rates rose. African Americans were migrating northward just as the industrial economy was declining. The decision of both employers and government policy makers to export blue-collar jobs from the city to the suburbs, to other regions (particularly the Sunbelt), and then overseas had the long-term effect of removing unionized, highly paid jobs for unskilled labor when these positions finally became available to African Americans.

Minimum-wage, dead-end jobs offered few incentives for family formation, which was usually a stabilizing factor in male socialization. High truancy and dropout rates returned adolescents to the street corner, where they became involved in the underground economy, and rendered their absorption into the legal economy more difficult. Discrimination in the housing market and the location of public housing grouped and isolated the poor in geographic enclaves. This meant that large numbers of young males, unfettered from work and the responsibilities of family, and aware of their marginalization by the larger society, were concentrated in particular neighborhoods and produced high rates of violent crime, as concentrations of young men have done throughout American history—regardless of race. In other words, the large-scale economic and social trends that had converged in the middle of the twentieth century to produce a historically low crime rate began to diverge in the 1960s, with increasingly devastating results.[18] Addressing the structural fault lines of American society was a task for government, but one that was beyond the capacity of individual mayoral administrations.

Many of the communities that had once sustained poor and working-class families went into rapid decline in the late 1960s and early 1970s. The causes of this decline were complex, but the most obvious ones were heroin and crime: addicts who looted buildings, mugged the elderly, burgled businesses, and committed arson for hire drove people out of their neighborhoods. The structural roots of urban decay ran deep, but they were largely invisible to the public and the media. The actions of the city's criminals were not.

Not surprisingly, political debate focused on crime and drugs rather than on the structures of disadvantage that produced them. Demands for law and order became a way of rallying those fearful of the changing racial composition of their neighborhoods as well as those with concerns about safety and the obvious deterioration of their communities. Conservative politicians on both the local and national levels successfully isolated and marginalized their liberal opponents by taking command of the crime issue. Liberal politicians were reduced to denouncing "law and order" campaigns as code words for racism and claiming that the crime increase was a statistical artifact, which left them seeming to defend criminals while dismissing concerns about crime that were based in very real experiences.[19] The inability to articulate a progressive response to crime and heroin use that also recognized citizens' rights to security had a consequence beyond harming liberal politicians' electoral chances: the debate, by focusing on the actions of the individual criminal, contained its own solution—incarceration—that seemingly addressed the problem while leaving its causes untouched.

John Lindsay was one casualty of the political debate over crime. In 1973, battered by an abortive run for the presidency and by the bitter legacy of his eight years as mayor, Lindsay announced that he would not seek reelection. Most New Yorkers breathed a sigh of relief.[20]

At the same time, neighborhoods were not simply made by large social forces, nor were their inhabitants passive victims. Residents determined social outcomes for themselves and if government offered few solutions to the problems of crime and heroin use, residents themselves attempted to address the issues. Heroin users and sellers certainly shaped the face of the neighborhood, with their heroin dealing and criminal activities touching the lives of most residents, especially by luring young people into the heroin marketplace. However, some areas, even those with significant structural disadvantages, possessed assets, such as community organizations, churches, and settlement houses, which enabled them to mobilize political and economic resources to confront drug abuse and addiction.

Case studies of three neighborhoods with high rates of addiction provide "bottom up" examples of how communities coped with heroin and crime and the underlying problem of neighborhood deterioration that bedeviled local government. Manhattan's Lower East Side was one of the most highly organized communities in New York, and it succeeded in gaining public and private resources to combat social problems, including heroin addiction. East Harlem had fewer institutional assets, but its community activists created political alliances with other groups in the city to demand medical treatment for heroin addicts. In the collection of neighborhoods that made up the South Bronx, local politicians gained federal funding for job-training and health centers in the area, but were less successful in confronting addiction and neighborhood decline. Each of these cases presents a variation on a similar theme: heroin feasted on an inheritance of disadvantage and crime disrupted the processes of community life and civic order. Residents in these neighborhoods resisted the onslaughts of crime and heroin, but they could not prevent them.[21]

On the Lower East Side of Manhattan, a long tradition of active community organization mediated a postwar history of poverty, ethnic conflict, gang fighting, and drug use. In 1954, local settlement houses formed the Lower Eastside Neighborhood Association (LENA) in order to coordinate efforts to solve community problems, especially gang fighting as white adolescents resisted the influx of Puerto Rican and African American families. In a perfect illustration of how an organized community can garner outside resources, LENA received private and federal funds to form Mobilization for Youth (MFY) in 1962. MFY funded outreach workers, a delinquency prevention project, counseling and employment training, and recreational centers for youth, all aimed at disrupting the gangs of the neighborhood. But very quickly the community discovered that it had organized to solve the wrong problem.

By the time MFY hit the streets, gang fighting on the Lower East Side had largely ceased. The combination of outreach work, mediation sessions, and the involvement of parents and police succeeded in suppressing gangs, and in retrospect, 1959 was the peak year of gang activity. The decline of the gangs then opened the door to heroin.[22]

LENA adapted the methods of working with street gangs to suppressing heroin, but with little success. Street workers identified drug users in the neighborhood and tried to get them to return to school or complete a general education degree (GED), find jobs, utilize recreational facilities, become reconciled with their families, and find programs in which to detoxify.[23] Some of these activities were counterproductive. Bringing heroin users into recreational facilities with nonusers seemed to offer a marketing opportunity. Parents, who already feared their adolescents might experiment with heroin, discouraged them from attending. For example, MFY established several coffeehouses for young people, but the most successful of these became an addicts' hangout, and soon no one else showed up. Closing and reopening several times as well as other efforts to purge users and attract other youths failed, leading MFY to close the coffeehouse.[24]

Outreach proved equally problematic. Unlike gangs, which had known hangouts where they congregated regularly, heroin users worked with one or two partners and spent much of their time looking for "scores" and searching for good dope.[25] They did not advertise their presence with graffiti or gather to defend their turf. And if they were addicted, providing employment or supplying referrals to different social welfare agencies did not necessarily address their problems. Methods developed to suppress street gangs were not very effective with heroin users.[26]

Individual work with heroin addicts proved equally frustrating, if abstinence was the goal. Users and workers engaged in a delicate minuet, with workers never sure of a user's intentions, but nonetheless buying meals, intervening in court cases, and providing services to users' relatives. Weeks or even months of such contacts sometimes resulted in an addict's consent to enrolling in a detoxification program. But beds were scarce, waiting lists long, and addicts had to endure multiple attempts to enroll. For example, Jeffrey Chase, an MFY outreach worker, accompanied Luis to Manhattan General Hospital, where they left after waiting for several hours. Chase wrote in his field notes, "He'll be admitted tomorrow morning for certain. Waiting room filled with junkies on the nod, sleeping, don't hear their names over the P.A. system, lose their turn. . . . Man. Gen.'s waiting room: 75 addicts attempting voluntary commitment, 15 of whom were accepted today." Luis returned the next day as promised and checked into Manhattan General for the three-week treatment program. But less than a week later Chase discovered that Luis had checked himself out, claiming to be lonely and depressed. Within a couple of days, Luis returned to using three or four bags of heroin per day.

This pattern repeated itself, as happened frequently with addicts, over the next several months. When Chase arranged for Luis to detox at Metropolitan Hospital, Luis disappeared from the waiting room before his grandmother could even sign him in. Then, while Luis's habit climbed to six bags a day, Chase arranged to have his sentence in a pending larceny case suspended upon admission to the Federal Narcotics Hospital at Lexington, Kentucky. Since Luis had not been committed to Lexington by the court, he retained the right as a voluntary patient to sign himself out, and less than a month after arriving, he did so. "I'm perplexed as to what ought be done with him," Chase wrote. "Must play it by ear or not play it at all. Perhaps institutionalization [in a mental hospital] is the only positive thing toward which to work with this client." Luis was institutionalized, but not in a hospital. The last entry had Luis in the Brooklyn House of Detention awaiting trial on a robbery charge.[27]

Luis's case was fairly typical: he tried one form of treatment after another, perhaps desiring sincerely to abstain, perhaps only wanting to manage his habit and to lower his tolerance for heroin, or perhaps possessing both desires simultaneously. Social workers spent endless hours waiting in court, arranging hospital admissions, and negotiating with police and other criminal justice agencies, only to have to start all over again, without ever being really sure of their clients' intentions or ability to follow through on them. Such social work kept open the possibility of treatment and eventual reintegration into the community and depressed a user's involvement in crime (at least while in treatment), but work with addicts remained extraordinarily frustrating.

In addition to providing services to individual addicts, MFY also proposed to address the more deeply rooted causes of heroin use. MFY pursued larger goals of community empowerment that held promise as a long-term solution to the drug problem. Rent strikes, civil rights organizing, protests against police brutality, petitions for improved education, sit-ins, and organizing for welfare rights made the Lower East Side a hotbed of political activity as MFY tried to help residents take command of their neighborhood.

MFY's confrontational strategy pitted it against local political and economic powers, alienating itself from both the Democratic Party and some of its original institutional sponsors. The *New York Daily News* accused MFY of harboring communist agitators, and public hearings soon followed. Federal and state investigators looked into the organization's finances after charges that money had been misallocated. Secret wiretaps, the use of informants, and a series of public hearings disrupted the organization, undermined morale, and led to the resignation of the executive director (although no evidence of embezzlement or communist agitation was found). The political firestorm surrounding these investigations sidetracked MFY and forced it to substitute social service provision for radical organizing, with funds firmly in the hands of City Hall.[28]

The Lower East Side did not become politically quiescent despite MFY's problems with red baiting. Squatters took over buildings, and political groups used the Lower East Side as a base from which to organize. Older groups, such as LENA and the settlement houses, continued to mobilize and promoted anti-drug campaigns. On July 4, 1970, the Concerned Action Committee, sponsored by St. Augustine's Church and the Grand Street Settlement, two of LENA's original members, organized a "March Against Fear" designed to rouse the local community against drugs. "We expect to have a hearse with a coffin, cars with posters and signs, men carrying a cross, parents who are mourning the loss of children from over-doses of drugs and drummers playing a funeral march." Only parents who had lost children to drugs could participate in the parade, which traversed the blocks in the heart of the Puerto Rican Lower East Side.[29]

The impact of such protests, of organizing by radical groups, of public educational activities, and of social work generally is difficult to measure. They captured public attention, they probably prevented some youths' experimentation with heroin, they mediated relationships between residents and municipal agencies, and they secured scarce resources, such as detoxification spots in hospitals, for community members. But what community organizations could not do was stamp out heroin use.

Nor could they confront the underlying structural problems that made organizing more difficult and created a landscape that supported the drug trade. A declining population, largely poor and living in some of New York's oldest housing, did not encourage landlords to invest in their buildings. A survey done in 1960 found that 95 percent of the buildings on the Lower East Side were in need of rehabilitation or replacement. To minimize losses on increasingly decrepit properties, landlords reduced maintenance and services—including heat and hot water—and deferred paying real estate taxes. As buildings neared the end of their productive lives, some landlords sold them to strippers and "finishers" who, as the names imply, removed anything of value from the building even while they were still inhabited; others resorted to arson to collect insurance or simply abandoned their properties once nothing more could be milked from them. Other economic actors, such as banks, insurance companies, and the federal government, also withdrew from investing in the area.

The combination of private capital flight and the absence of a government response made portions of the Lower East Side virtually uninhabitable. Blocks dotted with decrepit or abandoned buildings provided havens for drug users and sellers, with shooting galleries and stash houses. This landscape rooted heroin in the neighborhood even as community groups fought to get it out. Block after block succumbed to abandonment and arson until there were not even enough buildings to sustain the drug trade. As a study done in the 1970s put it, "Eventually, the block is denuded of dwellings and residents, and the drug traffic lacking 'cover,' begins to move to another block. Such was the fate of East 11th, 10th, and 6th Streets between Avenues B and C. These streets now contain less than half of the houses that were there even two years ago."[30] Disinvestment and government indifference created a landscape ripe for drug users and sellers to exploit. Community organizing, even the radical efforts of MFY, had no viable response to these deeper structural problems. Community activists, despite all of their energy and imagination, were treading water on the Lower East Side.[31]

East Harlem did not have the institutional assets of the Lower East Side, nor did it attract the same level of external resources. East Harlem's institutional actors were successful, however, in entering into citywide coalitions to confront social problems, especially heroin use. They created services for detoxifying addicts, they lobbied public officials to change city policy and

state laws, they rehabilitated abandoned buildings, and they engaged in public education campaigns about narcotics. But here, too, they encountered an
urban landscape shaped by disinvestment and government indifference and
captured by the drug trade.

Organizing in East Harlem confronted a long history of illicit activity
rooted in the area. It had been home to Jewish and Italian bootleggers, who
later applied their entrepreneurial talent to heroin importing. East Harlem
became the center of the East Coast heroin trade in the 1940s, and remained
an important wholesale heroin marketplace at least until the 1980s.[32]

As on the Lower East Side, the spread of heroin use in East Harlem first
became apparent to community members in the 1950s. "Pee Wee" Leon, who
eventually saw nearly his entire high school class succumb to heroin, appealed
to the East Harlem Protestant Parish (EHPP) to help with the problem. The
parish organized education programs aimed at informing the young about
the dangers of narcotics, and formed a Narcotics Committee in 1956 to host
discussions for families of addicts. Subsequently, the parish opened a storefront drop-in center and a clinic where addicts received a physician's services,
referrals to hospitals, assistance in job searches, psychological counseling, and
legal assistance for those facing criminal charges.[33]

Despite these efforts, the number of East Harlem's heroin users grew
steadily, as did the demands on the Narcotics Committee. EHPP Reverend
Norman Eddy commented that he "had been talking with addicted men and
women for seven years . . . and had met only three whom he knew to be off
narcotics." While few of the visitors to the EHPP's storefront center ab-
stained from heroin for any length of time, their sheer number suggested the
need for additional services. With a staff of three and a program designed to
help only those from East Harlem, the EHPP storefront recorded visits from
2,175 individual users (or 5 percent of the nation's addicts, according to FBN
statistics). The Narcotics Committee declared a "state of emergency" in 1962:
"Normally, we used to see sixteen to twenty people a day, or between 80 and
100 a week. Now, with the same staff, we try to be of some help to as many
as seventy a day, and, on an average, 225 a week."[34]

Growing increasingly frustrated with counseling so many heroin users
with so few resources, East Harlem's community activists organized politically to demand hospital beds for detoxifying addicts. The only publicly
funded detoxification beds in New York in the 1950s were in Riverside Hospital, which had opened in 1952 for adolescent patients. Adult users who wished
to detoxify had to go to private hospitals, if they could afford it, or they

withdrew "cold turkey" in a thirty-day commitment to Rikers Island prison or the Women's House of Detention. The EHPP joined with five neighborhood drug programs to form the New York Neighborhoods' Council on Narcotics Addiction in 1959, and they asked Mayor Wagner to create hospital beds for adult addicts. When they got no response, the coalition threatened to organize a prayer march bringing religious groups from all over the city to demonstrate at City Hall. A few days before the scheduled march, the mayor agreed to set aside twenty-five beds in Metropolitan Hospital. Simultaneously, the State of New York agreed to open beds in Manhattan State Hospital.[35]

From this modest beginning, the coalition went on to lobby for an alternative to the prosecution of addicts in the criminal justice system as well as for aftercare programs for detoxified heroin users. The council organized churches throughout the state to write to their legislators ("I didn't know there were so many Presbyterian churches," commented State Senator George Metcalf) in support of the Metcalf-Volker bill that provided for addicts' voluntary commitment to a state hospital and allowed users arrested for possession to substitute hospitalization and aftercare for jail time. (The bill allowed those charged with felonies or narcotics sales to take advantage of the civil commitment procedure as long as the district attorney agreed.) Upon release from hospitalization, patients were supposed to receive community-based aftercare treatment under the auspices of the Department of Mental Hygiene.

The politically adept activists of East Harlem succeeded in creating a statewide coalition that agreed that heroin users required treatment, not punishment. Even though treatment did not address the structural problems that produced heroin use, it was a signally progressive achievement. The Metcalf-Volker bill marked a high point of liberalism, a notable retreat from the criminal justice model established by the federal government in the Harrison Act (1914) and reaffirmed in the Boggs (1951) and Narcotics Control (1956) Acts.[36]

Disillusionment set in quickly, however. Metcalf-Volker passed before the staggering crime wave rolled over New York. Equally important, there were two major problems with implementing the bill. First, few aftercare programs were created. The Department of Mental Hygiene ignored the aftercare requirements of the bill and focused instead on adding hospital beds for detoxifying users, which fit better with its institutional mission even though there was no evidence that detoxification by itself actually weaned users from heroin. What had been the heart of the bill for liberal clergy and community groups virtually disappeared. Second, few heroin users agreed to participate in the civil commitment process and fewer still completed it. A jail sentence seemed preferable to civil commitment because it almost always required less time than hospitalization and parole to an aftercare program. Liberal activists forgot that addicts too had agency, and that the life of a street addict was—though heavily mediated by social setting—also a choice, for many a better choice than living under state supervision. A state study showed that even for the minority who agreed to civil commitments, few completed its terms and 80 percent were rearrested subsequent to their hospitalization. Bureaucratic self-interest on the one hand, and the actions of heroin users on the other, doomed the progressive achievements of the Metcalf-Volker bill.

Prosecutors who had supported Metcalf-Volker somewhat reluctantly now pressed for longer jail sentences for narcotics offenders and other felons as crime rates rose. Governor Nelson Rockefeller, whose aides had worked closely with the Neighborhoods' Council to fashion a bill significantly more liberal than the district attorneys desired, now shifted to the right in the face of public concerns about crime. In 1965, New York State passed an early version of "three strikes" legislation—a persistent felon law in which a third felony conviction could lead to a term of twenty-five years to life. The following year, the governor signed the Narcotics Addiction Control Act, which increased penalties for those involved in narcotics sales and established compulsory treatment for addicts brought before the court. These measures set the stage for the passage of the draconian "Rockefeller law" in 1973 that treated heroin sales as Class A felonies (the same category as homicide) and that presaged the tougher war on drugs legislation that followed nationally.[37] The consensus that had supported the medicalization of drug addiction evaporated in a few short years as frustration with crime mounted, demands for law and order grew, and Governor Rockefeller positioned himself for a run for the White House.

In the absence of state support for aftercare facilities, EHPP established its own program at Exodus House. Exodus House was a residential community that provided high school equivalency education, vocational workshops, and group therapy sessions in a program that lasted approximately eighteen to twenty-four months. In addition to the professional staff, Exodus House hired former addicts who worked as rehabilitation aides. The program seemed effective for those who stayed, but as with similar "therapeutic communities," 90 percent of the clients dropped out in the first few months.[38] Community activists kept the faith in the face of an increasingly hostile political climate and a dim prognosis for addicts' recovery.

Nothing was more disheartening, however, than the recruitment of new users from the youth in the neighborhood, along with their involvement in crime. A study of a single block (100th Street between First and Second Avenues) that followed residents over four years found that one-third of the sixty teenagers interviewed in 1965 had become heroin users by 1968. These youths found access to drug knowledge inescapable in East Harlem, and the allure of heroin outweighed the educational programs of the EHPP as well as the example of local junkies.[39] Living in a drug-selling center shaped the lives of these youths.

The youngsters on 100th Street first encountered drug users at an early age. Nearly all of them had run into heroin users shooting up, frequently in the halls, on the landings, or on the roofs of their buildings. One boy complained that addicts came and knocked on the door of his apartment asking for water to use for shooting up; he feared that they were casing the place for a possible break-in. Another youngster recalled that as an eight-year-old, "I was playing with my friends on the roof, going up in the skylights [to] play tag, [and] there was these dope addicts taking it." Another boy was afraid to go up on the roof because he thought that addicts might throw him off, as had happened to another child on the block.[40]

In addition to an early introduction to drug knowledge, these youngsters grew up participating in acts of theft and violence. The interviews support social science findings that criminal activity existed independently of and prior to heroin use.[41] Several boys discussed snatching pocketbooks from women, usually in nearby Yorkville, a largely white, middle- and working-class neighborhood. They also participated in assaults, usually on other adolescent males, and a number mentioned that they had been assaulted as well. Property theft and larceny were routine. Teenagers went on weekend shoplifting expeditions to department stores such as Macy's or Bloomingdale's. Nearly every adolescent interviewed, regardless of eventual drug use, reported at least one shoplifting excursion, and most went quite regularly. Mike, for example, said that he and his friends went every Saturday, and "whoever don't come . . . is a chump."[42] These youths participated in crime as an adolescent rite of passage, which had nothing to do with the use of heroin. The same social setting that produced heroin use also led to crime and delinquency.

While shoplifting was a source of excitement, it also served a utilitarian purpose: adolescents stole goods for themselves, but desperately poor, they peddled what they did not want door to door in the neighborhood. Neighbors, friends, and relatives all participated in the underground economy. New clothes, television sets, and radios, the much-advertised products of a consumer economy, were otherwise difficult for poor people to acquire. When cheap goods exchanged hands, few questions were asked ("everybody buys them, [and] don't worry about it").[43]

Youths might rationalize their theft from downtown stores as a redistribution of wealth, but they also victimized local shopkeepers. Kids stole fruit or candy from the stalls in East Harlem's open-air market; one storekeeper complained that she could not leave anything on the counter in her shop or put any merchandise outside without it being stolen. But without noting the irony, this woman readily admitted to participating in the underground economy herself: when a couple of youths came through her building selling quarts of milk and cartons of cottage cheese ("They must have robbed a dairy shop"), she did not hesitate to buy them. Like other residents, she found the lure of inexpensive goods too much to resist, rationalizing that the goods had already been stolen so she may as well take advantage of the opportunity.[44]

Youths distinguished between their own petty theft and the crimes committed by local junkies, who were universally vilified for preying on the neighborhood ("with narcotics you'd rob your own mother"). Reports of the number of heroin users who lived on the block ranged from fifty to a hundred, and they supported their habits by the usual assortment of larceny, burglary, narcotics sales, and shoplifting, although a number of them were employed. The block of 100th Street was a center for the retail drug trade, and residents expressed their resentment at seeing cars and users from outside of the neighborhood come in search of drugs while sellers commandeered public space. Burglaries were a common source of complaint; one boy recalled seeing a junkie going from door to door trying to sell a neighbor's coffee table, and another recounted how a junkie scurried out of the window and down the fire escape just as he and his family returned home to their apartment. Youngsters' attitudes toward junkies reflected a distinction between crime that produced benefits for the community and crime that did not. Residents maintained a moral order as best they could, but they did so without the formal assistance of the offices of civil society.[45]

While federal authorities declined to tackle the structural problems of East Harlem and were notable by their absence, municipal authorities were notably present, but made East Harlem's problems worse. The police were the most visible face of government, and encounters with police fueled cynicism about the law and no doubt helped explain the pervasive criminality in the area. Nearly everyone mentioned that the police were corrupt, inefficient, and brutal. Respondents noted exceptions—particular officers who would not take bribes and would try to help residents, but they were notable precisely because they were so unusual. East Harlem had a flourishing numbers racket, and grown-ups and adolescents alike knew when and where the police were paid off. Police raided gambling spots or alley dice-playing groups and made off with the cash or accepted a payoff to ignore the game. Youths commented on particular officers who would accept a bribe to let them go if they were caught with "hot" goods, while residents found the police to be unresponsive to their complaints about crime. With narcotics trafficking relatively open on the block, residents speculated that the police were paid to ignore what was so obvious to everyone else. One woman said that police confiscated drugs from junkies, but then kept the heroin to plant on suspects they thought were dealers. A youth witnessed a police officer participating in the sale of narcotics, claiming "this cop saw three junkies, and he gave them the dope, and the junkies gave him about 15 dollars each."[46]

If corruption were not enough, residents' faith in the police was further undermined by the callous and frequently violent ways in which the police treated them. Residents protested police shootings of unarmed individuals, such as a youth shot in the back by an officer who had been seen drinking in a local bar while on duty. Adolescents also commented on the beatings they received both in patrol cars and the precinct house. "You get a cop [who] wants to know something," said one youth explaining the use of the "third degree," "maybe some information from a guy, so they try to grab you, smack you around so they can find out." Other times, police picked a youth up and drove him around the neighborhood, beating him in the back of the car without ever taking him to the precinct. Order and safety depended on self-reliance, on one's reputation for toughness, or on connections to others who might exact revenge on one's behalf, and not on the system of police and courts.[47]

The number of heroin users, the seeming unavoidability of crime in the area, and the unresponsiveness and even malfeasance of public bureaucracies all took their toll on the neighborhood. Community groups worked to refurbish storefronts that were vacant, and Metro North, a local housing group, raised funds to paint and renovate a group of buildings. But other residents complained that services were being withdrawn from their buildings as land-lords retrenched on their investments ("we don't get hot water on weekends [and] once in a while we don't have hot water and steam"). There were two gutted tenements on the block, burned and looted by thieves, as well as vacant apartments within several buildings. These vacant apartments became havens for drug users, whose presence then forced other residents out of their apartments. Apartment fires were a particular hazard since junkies who nodded off while smoking cigarettes set themselves and their furnishings ablaze. Over time vacancies accumulated, and in the course of four years, the block lost approximately one-third of its residents. This provided a clear signal that disinvestment combined with the actions of drug users were creating a social setting that supported the narcotics market and intimidated others.[48]

Families resisted these developments by helping their local churches organize services for addicts, demanding improvements in housing, or simply minding their own business and going to work every day. Their children rejected heroin and resisted the temptations of downtown shoplifting trips, but sometimes felt isolated from their peers. Esther explained that she was left alone because "we have been, I guess, the most cleanest persons there and nobody has gotten in trouble in our family and we have respect. Everybody respects us. And they know how my mother is." Benjamin steadfastly ignored the junkies around him ("[I] see somebody, I just keep on walking, I didn't pay no attention to them"), and Marcellino dumped his friends who were trying to get him to use heroin ("I cut them loose"). But while Esther and others like her (the two-thirds of those interviewed in 1965 who had not taken heroin three years later) were able to remain personally aloof from the chaos on the streets, they did not escape unscathed. Esther was intimately familiar with heroin since "three of [my cousins] died, and I got one who is still on it," while another young woman, who belonged to a church-affiliated group known as the "Conservatives," reported that of the twenty-seven girls in the group, six had become heroin users, as had forty of the eighty boys. Either directly or indirectly, heroin touched everyone.[49]

East Harlem was a classic "interstitial" area, a spatial leftover ignored as capital flows constantly remade the city. It had been built as a slum for poor and working-class residents, and it became a place where underground entrepreneurs were able to conduct illegal businesses unimpeded by law enforcement. This social geography had intertwined vice and poverty since the turn of the century, and it defied time, ethnic transition, and community organizing. Conditions worsened in the 1960s with the dramatic rise in heroin use, the mounting crime rate, increasing disinvestment in the neighborhood, and the inability of government to step into the breach. Residents tried political lobbying, education campaigns, and neighborhood rehabilitation efforts, but they were overwhelmed. Disinvestment, the disinterest of public authorities, and the actions of neighborhood junkies created a social setting that frustrated residents and replenished the number of heroin users and sellers even in the face of community resistance.[50]

Among New York's neighborhoods, few could rival those of the South Bronx (Morrisania, Melrose, Hunts Point, and Mott Haven) in devastation. While the South Bronx garnered federal funds and its community members organized politically, the area suffered a debilitating loss of capital and people, and by the 1970s, it had become a de rigueur stop on any visiting politician's tour of urban decline.

The South Bronx after World War II held few hints to its fate. It was a step up from the tenements of the Lower East Side or East Harlem, but it continued those areas' history of ethnic strife. Tensions among Irish, Italians, and Jews were compounded after World War II as some 50,000 African Americans and 75,000 Puerto Ricans moved to the South Bronx by 1950. Juvenile arrests tripled between 1940 and 1948, and the political scientist Samuel Lubell commented that in a day of randomly selecting individuals for interviews, "I could not find a single family which was not desperate to get out of the area." The politics of space—New York City had a 1 percent apartment vacancy rate in 1950—fed the bitter ethnic conflict.[51]

Ethnic succession in the South Bronx was no easier than anywhere else in the city, but it did not leave the area devastated. Rather, a combination of factors accelerated social change. The concentration of high-rise housing projects, with a total of ninety-six buildings, sharpened distinctions in the neighborhood and ultimately confirmed patterns of segregation as efforts to maintain racial balance failed. Clara Rodriguez recalled that in her Mott Haven neighborhood, "these ominous towers of brick rose. They were huge, they were ugly; and they were, most importantly, unsafe." New expressways (the Major Deegan, the Cross Bronx, and the Bruckner) circumnavigated the Bronx and disrupted commercial and residential areas, sending streams of refugees in search of nearby low-rent neighborhoods. The industrial zone in Hunts Point, which had provided unskilled employment to Bronx residents, suffered New York's fate in microcosm, shedding jobs with increasing rapidity in the 1960s even after it became the city's food distribution center. These forces reshaped the South Bronx, as did the decisions of hundreds of land-lords and speculators in the area.[52]

Landlords at first intensified use of available space, then withdrew services in order to maximize profitability. As landlords switched from coal to oil-fueled burners after World War II, they converted the basement coal storage areas into inexpensive but less-than-desirable apartments for the very poor—generally Puerto Rican and African American families. Other land-lords subdivided apartments in their buildings into smaller units. For example, Helen Johnson recalled that a speculator began buying up and dividing the old but still serviceable buildings on her block in the mid-1950s. "His buying of the block took three years. You had to have someone in your apartment at all times to call the police if they started up through the floor. They came through the closets with pipes so they could install bathrooms in the divided apartments. Once the pipe went through—that was it, you were done. Because then two families moved in upstairs and you had enormous numbers of people in much too small a place." The new residents generally had larger families, reflected in a one-third increase in enrollments in local schools in the 1950s, which meant more wear on the old buildings. Once the process of intensifying the use of space was complete, owners invested little in keeping up their properties, thus preparing the ground for the disinvestment that followed.[53]

Crime also played a role in neighborhood change. Although many residents associated crime with the heroin surge of the 1960s, in fact the data tell a different tale, with a clear increase beginning in the previous decade. Sam Strassfield, a patrolman in the 41st Precinct, noted: "Already, by 1954 the cops had launched Operation All-Out, doubling their manpower because street crime and violent crime was steadily rising." Data collected by the New York City Youth Board support Strassfield's recollections. Health districts 35 (Morrisania) and 40 (Melrose) had the highest numbers of offenses committed by juveniles in the Bronx in 1955. Melrose showed a 267 percent increase in offenses between 1951 and 1955, while Morrisania, already a high delinquency area, had an increase of 164 percent, comparable to the borough average. Juvenile delinquency, like crime generally, was highly concentrated in a small number of geographic areas with many young men and high rates of poverty.[54]

Adolescent heroin use added to the crime problem. In the mid-1950s heroin concentrated in ten health districts in the South Bronx, where its use was "epidemic." Approximately a quarter of citywide heroin cases involving adolescents between 1949 and 1955 came from the Bronx (as opposed to 62 percent from Manhattan).[55] The heroin problem in the South Bronx was first publicized in 1951, when investigators for State Attorney General Nathaniel Goldstein found that students at Morris High School purchased heroin in the neighborhood (Morrisania). A youthful-looking undercover investigator went with a boy to a candy store about two blocks from the school, where the boy purchased a package for him containing three grains of heroin. The agent also arranged a second purchase, this time a sixteenth of an ounce of heroin, for a few days later. Then at Sheinman's Pharmacy, at the corner of Fox Street and Longwood Avenue, they obtained four hypodermic needles for a dollar.[56]

While heroin use appeared first in Morrisania, by the late 1950s it had spread to other sections of the South Bronx. Neil Connolly, a parish priest at St. Athanasius, came to Hunts Point in 1958, where he found the white teenagers using heroin. "In 58 I do remember people pointing out some of the drug addicts—mainly then Irish and Italians left over. Even then there was a preoccupation with security and I remember we had to be very careful when those boys came to visit our pastor. He was old and couldn't see well and we had to make sure they didn't steal anything." Mercedes Melendez said, "They started robbing people [and] . . . by 1959 people were starting to complain about it." Father Louis Gigante, also at St. Athanasius parish, said that within a few years heroin was completely out of control. "I'd say '62-'63-'64 we were considered maybe the drug capital of the world."[57]

Life in the South Bronx, never easy, became worse under the onslaught of adolescent addiction. Father Connolly at St. Athanasius Church recalled, "Anything of value was taken. The rectory pipes were stolen, as were pipes and fixtures in other buildings. There were floods all over the place." According to Father Gigante, "Every kid had to grow up with addicts in their building. They were like roaches. There was a drug addict in every corner. There was a pusher every place." The accumulation of heroin users in a building became a death knell. Just as happened in East Harlem, the appearance of addicts in a building meant that other residents fled. "Once you found junkies in the building," Ralph Porter claimed, "you could almost bet your bottom dollar that within three months that building would be abandoned because no one wanted to stay there. They didn't want their kids to come through that scene." Long-time storekeepers gave up their shops in the face of repeated burglaries and robberies. Charles Lefkowitz, who owned a menswear store, was one. "Believe me, I cried when I got out. I broke down and cried. That was the only thing I did in my life and here I am leaving at 64 years old. But I wanted to get out because I figured my luck was going to end. The other merchants pleaded with me not to go, but I had to. We had two hold-ups in one week. That's when I knew I had to go." Because of the number of assaults on its employees, the Postal Service in the South Bronx sent mail carriers in pairs on days when they delivered welfare or social security checks. By 1968, Morrisania and Mott Haven together accounted for about 15 percent of the city's known addicts (and two-thirds of the Bronx's addicts). As in Manhattan's neighborhoods, crime, poverty, and heroin were spatially concentrated phenomena.[58]

Residents persisted in the face of this accumulation of social problems, but they could not withstand the plague of arson that overwhelmed the South Bronx. Beginning in the mid-1960s, owners started burning their buildings once they had been milked of their profitability and stripped of their assets. Only insurance remained as a source of extractable capital. Father Robert Banome argued, "It was the greed of the landowners, those who owned these buildings and wanted to make a quick profit, who saw that a new element was coming in. . . . And so people on drugs would be hired, they were professional arsonists who would be hired to do in a building for a hundred dollars." Engine Company 82, on Intervale Avenue in Morrisania, had the reputation of being the busiest fire company in the city. It responded to about 1,500 calls in 1957, about 3,000 in 1967, and 8,000 in 1972 as the South Bronx burned.[59]

There was resiliency in the South Bronx, but it was not always apparent. Father Gigante at St. Athanasius wanted to organize "defense groups" to confront pushers and addicts, but the effort failed: "These people do not think of the streets as theirs, but as somebody else's," he said. In other areas of the South Bronx, however, residents were more willing to organize. Proving that law and order was not just a conservative issue, Morrisania's residents wanted to confront drug dealers and defend their homes. Forty African American and Puerto Rican housewives marched on the precinct house to obtain pistol permits: "As they marched along the streets of neat one-family homes and apartment houses, they yelled: 'Gun Power, Gun Power,' 'We Want Guns,' and 'Have Gun, Will Kill!' Several people sitting on stoops called back, 'Sock it to them!' " At St. Athanasius, the parish encouraged more progressive responses to addiction by renting a building to Odyssey House for a treatment facility, which filled its thirty-five beds and had a waiting list within a week of opening. Church members also took the lead in pressuring the Bronx district attorney to take the plague of arsons seriously and form a taskforce to investigate and prosecute offenders.

In general, however, the lack of political leadership in the South Bronx was stunning. While local politicians won Model Cities money to organize community centers and develop housing, much of it was squandered in the creation of corrupt petty fiefdoms, in internecine conflict among rival constituencies, and through plain thievery. With Model Cities money frozen in 1973 and New York's near bankruptcy four years later, the trough ran dry. Together the combination of political failure and the withdrawal of public services left the South Bronx with fewer resources to face addiction than either the Lower East Side or East Harlem even as capital disinvestment and arson made the problems of the South Bronx worse.[60]

All New Yorkers suffered from the effects of the heroin trade: increasing crime rates, a debilitating fear of crime, and a racially polarized politics. But residents of neighborhoods housing the largest numbers of heroin users were especially victimized. Heroin use first appeared there in the 1950s, and in the following decade, these neighborhoods were left awash in crime and drugs. Not only did most crime occur there, but the perpetrators were their own sons and daughters. At the same time, conservative politicians used the crime issue to isolate their liberal opponents and develop a consensus around lengthier prison sentences for offenders; their success precluded a conversation about the structural causes of urban decline. By the mid-1970s, those convicted of drug offenses began serving terms similar to those meted out to murderers and rapists in a remarkably expensive, but ineffective, "solution" to the problems of crime and heroin use.

Community activists continued to lobby for more effective treatment options for heroin users, but few additional resources for the treatment of addiction appeared as long as heroin was seen as a ghetto problem. As Father William Smith of St. John Chrysostom put it, "It was a terrible, terrible problem with no support from anyone in political life or the institutional church, until . . . it spread out of the ghettos. . . . That's when . . . all the money became available because the kids that count[ed were] on it."[61] By the 1970s, there were more "kids that counted" on heroin than ever before.

CHAPTER EIGHT

Heroin Suburbanizes

In the 1970s, the directors of San Francisco's Haight-Ashbury Free Clinic discovered that heroin was no longer just a problem of inner-city African Americans and Latinos: "Heroin," they proclaimed, "is in the suburbs."[1] "Suburbs" here was a code word for white and middle class as well as a reference to the wider spatial distribution of heroin that was becoming apparent. Middle-class white youths began experimenting with the drug during the 1960s, and their use had proliferated to such an extent that physicians working in the Free Clinic dubbed 1970 as the "year of the middle-class junkie."[2]

Where did these "middle-class junkies" come from? Beginning in the mid-1960s, a "hippie" drug culture emerged in San Francisco's Haight-Ashbury and New York's Greenwich Village and East Village, organized around smoking marijuana, taking hallucinogens, especially LSD, and using amphetamines. These neighborhoods also housed small numbers of heroin and "speed" users left over from the beat generation; inevitably the groups mixed, with the hippies able to acquire new drug knowledge and experience. The story of the white "middle-class junkie" is one about social setting and the change in drug culture that occurred there.

The middle-class youth who moved into Haight-Ashbury and Greenwich Village/East Village arrived in communities where heroin users consisted of working-class white males supplemented by a few beats—generally middle-class dropouts who exemplified a hipster lifestyle.[3] The working-class whites had begun taking heroin after World War II as part of the first surge in heroin use. For example, in New York's Greenwich Village, a cohort of

Italian teens became addicted to heroin in the early 1950s, and they remained active users well into the 1960s. This population generally did not mix with the newcomers moving into Greenwich Village and did not have much influence over them.[4]

The beats were more important, even if they were fewer in number, and they opened a new market for drug use among hip young whites moving into Greenwich Village. Ethnographer Ned Polsky, who studied the Village beats in the summer of 1960, called them a "transmission belt" for the use of marijuana by increasing numbers of middle-class whites. However, he also found that a significant minority of beats—perhaps one in ten or twelve—were heroin users.[5]

The best-known beats experimented with a variety of drugs in addition to being serious drinkers, and morphine and heroin were part of the mix. Benzedrine, a form of amphetamine, was the most commonly used drug after marijuana. Experimenters broke open Benzedrine inhalers, which could be purchased in pharmacies without a prescription, and inserted the strips into drinks to get a buzz. Benzedrine fueled the writing of many beats, including Allen Ginsberg and Jack Kerouac, and Joan Vollmer, William Burroughs's companion, became seriously addicted to amphetamines. Ginsberg and Kerouac both tried morphine in 1946, although they did not become users. Herbert Huncke and William Burroughs, along with the various burglars, thieves, and prostitutes that Huncke introduced into their circle, became addicted first to morphine and then to heroin. According to poet Diane di Prima, heroin was "ubiquitous" in her circle of beat acquaintants. Allen Ginsberg memorialized the experience of some of his fellow beats when he wrote in "Howl" that he saw the "best minds" of his generation "dragging themselves through the negro streets at dawn looking for an angry fix."[6]

The well-known experimentation with heroin by some of the beats and the famous jazz musicians they admired inevitably influenced others. While some were repelled by heroin use, other beat wannabes around the country decided to try heroin as soon as they arrived at a location where it was available. As one young man put it, "When I started hearing about the beatniks and jazz guys, it was like I couldn't wait to get my hands on it [heroin]." William Burroughs, in particular, became an icon for heroin-using rock musicians, with groups taking both names and song titles from his work, and he recognized the participants in the 1960s drug culture as his progeny. (Burroughs's fame as a heroin user eventually worked against his desire for sobriety as fans showered him with gifts of heroin in the hope of claiming that they had shot up with the "Godfather of Dope.") The beats' example did not "cause" anyone to use heroin, but their celebrity valorized opiate use among impressionable youth who were arriving at the centers of beat life, where they could find the drug knowledge they needed to change admiration into action.[7]

There were many newcomers in Greenwich Village in the early 1960s who were eager to learn about the beats, the new folk music scene, and alternative lifestyles that included drugs. Just as the jazz clubs in the Times Square area had attracted crowds of young people in the 1940s, coffeehouses and clubs featuring folk musicians lured the young to the Village in the early 1960s. Visitors traveled a ten-block circuit of a dozen clubs, from the Bitter End to Café Wha? to the Café Bizarre, and on weekends the Village streets were so crowded that police erected barricades to control people's movement.[8]

The coffeehouses, bars, and clubs served as drug marketplaces in addition to being musical and social venues, although marijuana was the drug most likely to be found. As one young woman explained, "I meet my friend, say in a coffeehouse or bar, and he'll shove a pack of cigarettes across the table, only there wouldn't be cigarettes in it—it's stuffed with pot." One social worker observed the scene at the Rienzi, a Village coffeehouse, noting the presence of several heroin addicts he knew from the neighborhood. He commented, "I had never heard of or been aware of involvement of neighborhood addicts with the 'beatnik' group." He was not sure if these addicts were dealing heroin or amphetamines to support their habits or were simply part of the social scene. He was also suspicious of the "A-trainers" (African Americans who took the A train from Harlem to the Village) who periodically disappeared into the bathrooms, then returned to sit with different groups of customers. As a reporter concluded, "In a half dozen bars on the Lower East Side, crude and dirty where Villagers and slummers mingle, marijuana and other drugs are sold."[9] The Village provided a social setting where drug users, experimenters, dealers, and visitors mixed and drug knowledge could be acquired.

Haight-Ashbury's history paralleled that of Greenwich Village. The Haight, like the Village, was a small, run-down, working-class neighborhood with a bohemian reputation. African Americans spilled over from the nearby Fillmore ghetto and joined working-class whites, labor activists, a few artists, and students from San Francisco State College, which was then located nearby. Journalist Hunter Thompson observed: "As recently as 1962, the

Haight-Ashbury was a drab, working-class district, slowly filling with Negroes and so plagued by crime and violence that residents formed vigilante patrols." No one would have predicted that the Haight would become the center for hippie life in the United States.[10]

The Haight only gradually assumed the role of San Francisco's bohemian center. North Beach had enjoyed that distinction as home to Lawrence Ferlinghetti's City Lights Bookstore and to expatriate New Yorkers who had come to San Francisco to participate in the burgeoning literary scene. Musicians, artists, poets, and refugees from other parts of America joined them, but as rents rose, increasing numbers of down-and-out beats relocated to the inexpensive Victorian houses that dotted Haight-Ashbury, which soon became the new hive of bohemian activity. Janis Joplin exemplifies the migratory pattern of many small-town residents who did not fit into mainstream America and who searched for alternatives. Joplin fled Port Arthur, Texas, first for the folk music community in Austin, then for North Beach in 1960, before settling in Haight-Ashbury. Joplin was on the cusp of the counterculture, attracted to the scene of the beats' triumph and folk music clubs and bars, but also on the verge of creating something entirely new. Her experimentation with different musical forms, her unbridled sexuality, and her drug use were the well-publicized versions of journeys eventually taken by many others. The influx of such newcomers to Haight-Ashbury was apparent in the changing retail scene, where one coffeehouse in 1965 turned suddenly into about thirty "hippie shops" a year later.[11]

Drug use cemented a sense of community among newcomers. In Haight-Ashbury, Ken Kesey's "Merry Pranksters" announced public "acid tests" to coincide with concerts and dances at a time when LSD was still legal in California. The pranksters rejected the careful, almost mystical use of LSD originally promoted by Timothy Leary and liberally spiked the punch provided to concert goers. The legendary Owsley Stanley, who had been an underground amphetamine producer, used his Berkeley lab to make pharmaceutical-grade LSD, which he distributed in colored tablets whose flawless production identified them as the genuine "Owsley." Drug consumption was featured at public festivals, such as the "Human Be In" in January 1967, where fifty thousand people gathered under paisley banners and marijuana-leaf flags to smoke marijuana, drop LSD, play instruments, dance, and have Allen Ginsberg lead Buddhist chants in order to raise their consciousness. Publicized by the mainstream press, these celebrations furthered the Haight's reputation as the national center for the counterculture. Called the "Hashbury" by Hunter Thompson, the Haight served as the capital "of what is rapidly becoming a drug culture." As Peter Coyote, actor, Digger, and member of the San Francisco Mime Troupe, recalled: "Individual freaks, isolated in heartland hometowns, were delighted to discover that there were thousands like them in San Francisco, who were prepared to embrace them as brothers and sisters; they wanted to be there too."[12] The trickle of migrants became a torrent as youths flocked to San Francisco for the "Summer of Love" in 1967.

Similar developments occurred in New York, where a discernible hippie presence could be found in Greenwich Village and a newly colonized East Village. As happened in San Francisco, high rents had driven newcomers out of Greenwich Village, and the seedier East Village absorbed the influx. The pioneers, "a scattering of beats and students," arrived in the early 1960s and established a certain camaraderie that was soon overwhelmed as young people by the thousands transformed ancient tenements into communes, crash pads, free stores, and shelters for runaways. A few years later the police estimated that a thousand twelve to eighteen-year-olds moved to New York City each month, and many, if not most, found their way to the East Village.[13]

Social disorganization, violence, and ethnic strife marked the East Village, making life there more difficult than in Greenwich Village. Hippies rejected the trappings of middle-class life and mixed uneasily with largely poor Puerto Ricans and African Americans, as well as the elderly populations of Ukrainians, Poles, and Jews. Young teens were particularly vulnerable. A social service report noted that runaways slept in abandoned buildings, in doorways, in phone booths, or on rooftops, supporting themselves through begging, street selling, dope dealing, petty thievery, and prostitution. "In the course of a typical year," the report concluded, "the average runaway or street youth is likely to have engaged in several thefts, to have taken many different drugs, to have contracted a serious disease, to have been arrested, mugged, and if female, raped." As one journalist concluded glumly, "If you wade in too deep, you may learn that the East Side undertow is no myth."[14] Heroin was more prevalent in the East Village, with its poor population clustered in public housing projects and decaying tenements, and observers believed that runaways and "weekenders" had begun experimenting with narcotics there.[15]

Despite these scattered reports, more systematic studies offered no evidence of heroin use among hippies and other middle-class whites as late as the mid-1960s. One survey of hippies in the East Village and Haight-Ashbury in 1966–67 found that fewer than 3 percent of them had ever tried heroin, a percentage that was lower than what had been found among the beats five years earlier.[16] Another study argued that two distinct drug-using subcultures had evolved in the United States. Whites lived in one, where they moved from marijuana to hallucinogens and amphetamines, while African Americans inhabited another, where the trajectory went from marijuana to heroin and cocaine. Even though youths of both races became involved in the underground marketplace, the consumption habits of their peers decided which drugs they used. Few whites were choosing to use heroin.[17]

National surveys and the media corroborated both the widespread use of drugs and the simultaneous avoidance of heroin.[18] The *New York Times* reported a twenty-state survey that revealed extensive amphetamine use on college campuses and found that many students did not even consider amphetamines a drug. LSD and hallucinogen use was rampant, the paper claimed, and most students smoked marijuana, which had become just "part of growing up." While the series was alarmist about the extent and types of drugs middle-class Americans ingested, it also reported that narcotics (opiates and cocaine) users "are largely slum dwellers, the hopeless and helpless who seek numbing oblivion."[19] In another report, Dr. Donald Louria, the president of the New York State Council on Drug Addiction, argued that heroin use was burgeoning, but not on high school and college campuses. "It is a problem of the areas of decay within our large cities," he stated. *Time* magazine proclaimed in 1969 that "pop drug" use—Dexedrine, methedrine, LSD, peyote, and especially marijuana—was increasing dramatically, but it noted reassuringly that heroin use was static.[20] And while President Richard Nixon declared in 1969 that drug abuse was a "growing menace," pointing to an alarming increase in drug arrests since 1960, heroin seemed to be what it always had been: primarily a plague on the urban poor.[21]

Then suddenly things changed. In 1970, *Time* flashed the headline "Heroin Hits the Young," while *Life* warned parents that heroin was leaving the ghetto and finding its way into small towns and middle-class homes.[22] The same Dr. Louria who had dismissed heroin as a problem in the nation's schools and colleges now predicted "Within a couple of years every high school and every college in the country will be inundated by heroin."[23] Other experts agreed, noting that "America's middle class is on the verge of experiencing the same upsurge that long ago was felt in slum neighborhoods."[24] Somehow the counterculture had gone radically wrong—pot and psychedelics had given way to a palpable sense of alienation and new choices of drugs.

White youth, the children of privilege, the kids who "counted," had apparently discovered heroin in a big way.

Both the media and knowledgeable observers, such as the physicians in the Haight-Ashbury Free Clinic, concluded essentially the same thing: middle-class white youths had begun using heroin. But their findings were not the same. Physicians at the Free Clinic had observed a trend that had been growing slowly over the previous few years in a specific location—the social setting of Haight-Ashbury—while the media extrapolated from that trend to predict a sudden upsurge in heroin use in communities where it had not been seen previously.

Despite the fear-mongering headlines, heroin was not spreading wildly across the nation. Heroin remained concentrated where it had traditionally been, in particular neighborhoods in the nation's largest cities.[25] Two things had changed, however. First, middle-class white youths were living among populations of heroin users in neighborhoods such as Haight-Ashbury, Greenwich Village, and the East Village, where they gained access both to drugs and to drug knowledge. Second, heroin use gradually rippled outward from these centers to nearby suburbs. Social setting determined how middle-class whites learned about heroin and where they began to use it, while geography dictated which suburbs experienced an increase in heroin use.

Why did some middle-class, psychedelic- and marijuana-using white youths suddenly start ingesting heroin around 1970? At the time, explanations focused on a three short-term causes. Some blamed President Richard Nixon's "Operation Intercept," which stemmed the flow of marijuana across the Mexican border in 1969. This argument held that drug users, unable to find marijuana, turned to more dangerous drugs, such as heroin, which remained in plentiful supply because it could be smuggled more readily due to its lack of bulk. In this scenario, the Nixon administration's drug policy backfired as a dangerous drug was substituted for a more harmless one. However, "Operation Intercept" started in the fall of 1969, after the increase in heroin use had already begun, and it lasted a mere twenty days, which was not long enough to have an impact on anything except Mexican-American relations. The argument also ignores the availability of other drugs and the fear that heroin inspired in many youths.[26]

A second argument, a slightly different version of the first, held that the Nixon administration deliberately allowed the substitution of heroin for marijuana. The reasoning went that if marijuana and hallucinogens had encouraged revolutionary thought and action, then heroin, which had proven effective in quieting the ghetto, was imported to foster a similar quiescence among America's restive white youth. For example, Dennis Thompson, the former drummer for the political Detroit band the MC 5, believed that "Nixon and the smart boys in the green room back in the brain trust sat down and said, 'Here's the easiest way to handle this damn thing.'"[27]

This argument suffers from the same objections as the first and the implausibility of the premise. Heroin became available in inner-city neighborhoods in the 1940s, after the restoration of international smuggling routes, and while heroin became more plentiful in the 1960s, it did not suddenly flood the ghettos (or the rest of the city) following the uprisings of the late 1960s. Its presence was independent of periods of both political activism and political apathy. The worst that can be said of the federal government is that drug policy consistently took a back seat to foreign policy during the Cold War. The Central Intelligence Agency, for example, was complicit in allowing Southeast Asian tribal groups to bring their opium crops to market during the war in Vietnam, but, however reprehensible, this was several steps removed from smuggling heroin into the United States.[28]

A third argument was more philosophical, suggesting that in their hopelessness over the seemingly unending war in Vietnam, the uprisings and brutal repression in American ghettos, and the splintering of the antiwar movement, young people turned to opiates as the ultimate nihilistic answer to their despair. This argument was more plausible than the others in linking heroin use to specific social conditions, without proposing an impossibly narrow time frame or a conspiracy theory of monstrous proportions. Opinion polls taken in the late 1960s revealed widespread alienation among youth from the institutions and ideologies of American society. Yet evidence that links alienation specifically to heroin use remains sparse. Few users, either in remarks at the time or in memoirs published subsequently, claimed that they began using heroin because of hopelessness. Most users described taking heroin as a desirable end in itself rather than as an escape from something else. While escapism seems like a reasonable hypothesis, the absence of direct evidence is a problem. Moreover, even if young people wanted to take heroin for this reason, they still had to find a social setting in which it was available.[29]

In the late 1960s, finding those social settings became easier. In the ecstatic, living-on-the-edge world of 1960s drug culture, participants celebrated an eternal present in which chemical intoxication was a vital ingredient. Even though heroin use itself remained relatively rare until the late 1960s, drug experimentation was so widespread that old shibboleths about drugs simply exploded. With medical and governmental warnings—especially about marijuana—exposed as ludicrous propaganda, youths wondered why warnings about heroin and more dangerous drugs should be heeded. (As an example of the power of misinformation, Jim Carroll, author of *The Basketball Diaries*, claimed that he began using drugs in 1964, thinking that heroin was "the non-addictive stuff" and that marijuana was addictive.)[30] Uppers, downers, marijuana, hash, LSD, peyote, and other drugs were the social lubricants of the counterculture. Those who wanted to go further and experiment with heroin found both drug knowledge and sources for heroin readily available in Greenwich Village, the East Village, Haight-Ashbury and similar locales. With thousands of young people moving to these areas, some increase in the number of heroin users was inevitable. At the same time, most youths regarded heroin as the king of drugs, terrifyingly powerful and alluring, the ultimate trip that anyone could take. Something else was needed to take that final step.

The use of amphetamines in this social setting provided the impetus—a chemical bridge—for experimenting with heroin. Amphetamines had been part of the drug scene since the late 1950s, and over time some amphetamine users, who were no longer satisfied with taking the drug orally, began to inject amphetamines intravenously. Not only had these individuals already become accustomed to drug injection, a technology that was otherwise a barrier to many potential heroin users, they also found that injecting heroin or barbiturates smoothed the way down from a speed run. For some proportion of youths in the Haight, the Village, and the East Village, speed and heroin were linked.

Amphetamines were a widely available part of American life and were far more commonly abused than opiates. Artists and their hangers-on experimented with amphetamines, as did the beats, and students received oral amphetamines from university health services to stay awake while cramming for exams. Soldiers and airmen received amphetamines to keep them alert while on patrol, and veterans returning from Korea and Japan, where amphetamine abuse was rampant from the end of World War II until the mid-1950s, continued their use stateside. Amphetamines were also used in medical practice as treatments for alcoholism, for obesity, and occasionally for heroin use. Some recreational drug users injected a combination of heroin and amphetamines, a poor man's speedball, when cocaine was still a rare and expensive commodity. Isolated amphetamine injectors posed no threat, but the upsurge in amphetamine use in 1967 and 1968 created a critical mass of people accustomed to the technology of intravenous drug use and potentially prepared to inject heroin.

In New York an amphetamine scene emerged in the early 1960s around Andy Warhol and the set of people associated with the Factory, as Warhol's film- and art-making studio was called. Ronnie Cutrone, a painter and former dancer with the Velvet Underground's Exploding Plastic Inevitable (which was a mix of performance art, film, and a concert), recalled that there was a sign warning "no drugs allowed" outside the elevator at the Factory. "Meanwhile everybody was shooting up [methedrine] on the staircase. Nobody actually took drugs in the Factory, except Andy." Ondine, a drag queen associated with Warhol, recalled that "high class" dealers would come to the Factory and sell amphetamines in a special deal for $300 a pound. Warhol surrounded himself with "A-heads," or "amphetamine heads," mostly gay men who dressed entirely in black, in a very campy style, who reveled in "a sort of severe kind of New York nighttime creative craziness." Another observer was less charitable, commenting. "These were insane people [who] wallowed in self-destruction."[31]

Warhol superstars, actors, models, and people with money often obtained their amphetamines from Park Avenue "vitamin doctors." These "Dr. Feelgoods" filled syringes with B-vitamins and amphetamines, and popped them into celebrity derrieres in return for a large fee. Joel Schumacher, a scriptwriter, recalled, "I went one night, got this shot, and it was the most wonderful shot in the world." First he went once a week, then twice, and "eventually I was going there every day, and then I was going two or three times a day," before starting to shoot up himself.[32] Class did not protect these users from the physiological effects of amphetamines, but it ensured access to pharmaceutical-grade drugs, and it protected them from arrest and hepatitis at least until they ventured into the illegal marketplace.

The same could not be said about the East Village hippies who were ingesting increasing amounts of speed. Bathtub chemists produced amphetamines for street sales, with the so-called "lumpen hippies," who were more throwaways than runaways from middle-class families, most likely to use and deal speed. Older hippies, fearful of the increasing rip-offs, paranoia, and street confrontations associated with amphetamine use, made posters and buttons that warned "speed kills." As one remarked, "Most speed freaks get to a point where they're seeing narks [narcotics detectives] in the trees with cameras and believe that the old lady next door has wired their pads." Physicians recognized that excessive amphetamine use induced "amphetamine psychosis," in which users exhibited signs of paranoia and an edgy aggressiveness that easily spilled over into violence. Amphetamines changed the tenor of street life as much as any single drug could.[33]

Amphetamines were even more entrenched in San Francisco than in New York. The beats and artists living in North Beach in the 1950s used amphetamines just like beats in New York, but so did a wider population. Many veterans settled in San Francisco after becoming habituated to the use of amphetamines while in the service. The problem of amphetamine abuse became so serious that in 1963 the California Attorney General restricted the sale of injectable amphetamine ampules in the state. Following that decision, the number of clandestine laboratories blossomed to meet the market demand, and by the mid-1960s a thriving underground marketplace existed.[34]

Amphetamine use merged into the hippie drug scene with the proliferation of inexpensive and impure LSD. As LSD ingestion spread during the Summer of Love, chemists produced batches laced with amphetamines because the combination induced a quicker rush. Naturally, as the use of LSD proliferated, so did users' acclimation to speed, and when LSD was of poor quality or not available, many users turned instead to amphetamines, which delivered an equally massive psychic jolt.[35]

Amphetamine use really took off in Haight-Ashbury in the fall of 1967. As in the East Village, those most susceptible seemed to be the "leftovers" of the Summer of Love, young people who supported themselves by begging, petty theft, and drug dealing. A division occurred in the hippie community between "heads," who were slightly older and more settled and had used drugs such as LSD for mind expansion, and "freaks," who were frequently younger newcomers and interested in only the pursuit of intense experience, such as the "flash" delivered by amphetamines. It was surprising how rapidly the Haight-Ashbury alternative community collapsed, as many heads fled for communes in rural northern California, and both mainstream and alternative merchants began closing their shops. A member of the Neighborhood Council commented that in the course of two short years "the Haight-Ashbury has become a violent teen-age slum."[36] The paranoid and violent speed culture changed the street scene in the Haight, much as it did in the East Village.

Amphetamine injection took a brutal toll on its users. "A-heads" shot up every two to four hours when on a speed run, which could last as long as ten or twelve days, during which time they went without food and sleep. The result of repeated speed binges was devastating. "I knew I was dying," recalled one user. "My tongue was shredded, my lips were cracked, the whole inside of my mouth was eaten out. My skin was itching all over, my fingernails were flaking off, and my hair and teeth seemed to be falling out." In addition to becoming malnourished, covered with skin lesions, and susceptible to disease, especially hepatitis, speed injectors experienced a devastating "crash" when their speed run inevitably ended. Handling the crash led to the relationship between amphetamines and heroin.[37]

"Speed freaks" eventually burned out as they could not physically maintain their self-destructive cycle.[38] Barbiturates offered one means of smoothing the way down from a speed run, and barbiturates did not have heroin's stigma. But barbiturates also brought a loss of muscle control, leaving its users drooling and staggering down the street, with their bodies lurching in every direction. As a result, some users found heroin preferable. One of the directors of the Haight-Ashbury Free Clinic concluded, "Heroin is now regarded as a 'mellow downer,' that is, it terminates the stimulative effects of speed, [and unlike barbiturates] allows one to function, and does not lead to loss of control." Some amphetamine users alternated between heroin and speed. One speed freak used barbiturates, Thorazine, or heroin to come down, but added, "heroin is really good for falling asleep when you're crashing." Others switched drugs periodically: one young woman reported, "I would do three days of speed, and then shoot heroin to come down, and then do more speed to get up," while an East Villager explained, "In the winter I switch to heroin so I won't catch pneumonia. In the spring I go back to speed." A staff member at Phoenix House, a therapeutic community in New York City, confirmed the new view of heroin. "A year ago, heroin was a dumb thing. Now junk's cool." Since the most serious speed users had experience with injecting drugs intravenously, injecting heroin came easily.[39]

The most systematic evidence for the emergence of white heroin use comes from San Francisco. The staff of the Haight-Ashbury Free Clinic published a number of papers based on an analysis of their patient population, which biased their sample in favor of more serious drug users rather than casual ones, and probably underestimated the extent of use. The physicians identified three groups of heroin users among those encountered at the clinic (Tables 4 and 5). "Old-style" users, a mix of whites and blacks, had begun their heroin use prior to 1963 and reflected the combination of the beat, white working-class, and African American populations who lived in the Haight prior to the hippie migration. They had the most serious heroin habits, as might be expected from their long history of use, they had comparatively less experience with LSD and amphetamines, which were the drugs of the hippie

TABLE 4. YEAR OF HEROIN INITIATION BY RACE

	1963 or earlier (N = 191)	1964–1966 (N = 149)	1967–1970 (N = 433)
White	67%	72%	81%
Black	22%	20%	14%
Hispanic	10%	6%	4%
Other	2%	2%	1%

Source: Sheppard, Gay, and Smith, "Changing Face of Heroin Addiction."

TABLE 5. YEAR OF HEROIN INITIATION BY GENDER

	1963 or earlier (N = 191)	1964–1966 (N = 149)	1967–1970 (N = 433)
Male	82%	81%	67%
Female	18%	19%	33%

Source: Sheppard, Gay, and Smith, "Changing Face of Heroin Addiction."

generation, and they had attempted withdrawal on a number of occasions. A small group of "transitional" users began taking heroin between 1964 and 1966. This group was transitional in the sense that it differed sociologically from the "old-style" users and signified the development of a new drug-using pattern, which commentators initially missed seeing. There were more whites and more "middle-class drop-outs" than among the "old-style" users, and they had a history of trying many types of drugs, especially LSD and amphetamines, before beginning heroin. The third group, "new-style" users, began taking heroin between 1967 and 1970, and the vast majority was white, a third was female, and they were largely middle class with histories of mixed drug use similar to those of the transitional users.[40] This was a significantly different population of users from the ones who had come before.

The San Francisco data show that middle-class whites participated in the rise of a new wave of heroin use in the mid- to late 1960s as they moved into a social setting characterized by heroin use. The transitional group, which probably learned about heroin from the beats, presaged a wider use of heroin among the whites following them to San Francisco. Their use of amphetamines is particularly significant, since over half had used the drug "heavily" prior to beginning heroin (Table 6). The transitional users merged with the newcomers, a much larger cohort of whites, who began taking heroin in the middle of the collapse of the hippie counterculture and deterioration of the

TABLE 6. YEAR OF HEROIN INITIATION BY DRUGS USED HEAVILY PRIOR TO HEROIN

	1963 or earlier (N = 191)	1964–1966 (N = 149)	1967–1970 (N = 433)
Marijuana	47%	63%	63%
LSD	17%	41%	41%
Amphetamines	32%	54%	46%
Barbiturates	24%	26%	25%

Source: Sheppard, Gay, and Smith, "Changing Face of Heroin Addiction."

Haight-Ashbury community. The transitional and new-style users reflected the polydrug-using habits of the counterculture, and their use of heroin became the basis for the Free Clinic's discovery of middle-class "junkies" in 1970.[41]

Because of San Francisco's place in the counterculture, the emergence of these heroin users is especially significant. Young people came to San Francisco from all over the country, making the Haight, according to one commentator, the hip equivalent of Fort Lauderdale, a prime destination for an alternative spring break "trip." While this may be an exaggeration, it was not much of one. One survey suggested the range and diversity of out-of-state visitors: only 12 percent came from the Bay Area, over a third came from just three cities (New York, Chicago, and Los Angeles), and the rest from elsewhere in the country.[42] More important, drug use in San Francisco created a ripple effect, as youths in other locations wanted to try what had been popular in San Francisco six to eighteen months earlier. As young people returned to communities across the country from their stay in the nation's drug capitals, they brought their drug experimentation home with them. According to observers at the Free Clinic, "The drug pattern of the Haight (and, simultaneously, of New York's East Village) seemed to spread in waves through American society."[43]

The proliferation of drug use differed depending on the drug, however. Marijuana, LSD, other hallucinogens, and amphetamines were either grown by backyard farmers or manufactured by bathroom chemists, and their use spread across American society, much as politicians and the media had forewarned. Adolescents in suburbs and smaller cities and towns had little trouble making connections to acquire these drugs. However, heroin, as an imported commodity, remained most available, purest, and least expensive in the centers through which it had been traditionally smuggled and distributed. Heroin centers such as New York and San Francisco became the source for heroin's spread to a wider middle-class clientele, but it was one living in nearby suburbs and towns.

Heroin traveled from central locations down the urban hierarchy to secondary and then tertiary marketplaces, such as those opened by youths in suburban communities. These enterprising youths seized on a market opportunity to supply eager peers and support their own heroin use, thereby broadening the circles in which heroin could be purchased. As in the postwar heroin boom, sites under adolescent control became places where interested youths could learn about and acquire drugs. High school students from Marin County traveled to the Haight, those in Nassau County went to the East Village, and those in Ann Arbor went to Detroit to acquire the heroin they could then sell to their less venturesome peers in local coffeehouses, basements, and school playgrounds.[44]

New York's suburbs were among the first to develop a heroin problem since New York remained the nation's center for heroin use. In one northern New Jersey community, 5 percent of the twelfth-grade males had tried heroin at least once in 1972, although only 1 percent of all respondents (ninth to twelfth graders) admitted to being current users, suggesting a pattern of occasional experimentation rather than consistent use.[45] An undercover informant, working for a suburban Connecticut police department, found a similar pattern. He recalled spending most of his time on "soft" drugs because "it was only a certain few that would try heroin because everyone knew that heroin was a nasty drug." Only one individual used much heroin, and "he would go to New Haven to cop it, [and] bring it back."[46]

A more disturbing portrait came from the Long Island newspaper, *Newsday*, which won a Pulitzer Prize for its coverage of the "heroin trail." The series documented the growth of the heroin trade on suburban Long Island and traced the drug back overseas to the poppy cultivators in Turkey. Reporters found that youths learned about drugs from one another at school. For example, one young man, Gil, told a reporter that he had snorted heroin for the first time as a fifteen-year-old in a car near Hempstead High School. He stated, "You'd go to the bathroom or to a car near school to cop. Guys carried stuff in their pockets or else they'd stash the stuff in the hedges near school." Occasionally a youth made a daily trip to the city, not to the East Village, but to Harlem, the nation's prime heroin market, where the drug was least expensive. Jack commented that he bought a quarter bag of heroin in Harlem for between $55 and $65, which was enough to make forty small bags. He shot half himself and sold the rest to cover his expenses. "In Hempstead, the same amount of heroin would cost . . . at least $115, and it would be even less potent," he claimed. One independent measure of the extent of heroin use in the Long Island area came from so-called overdose deaths: in 1972 there were twenty-five heroin overdoses on Long Island. Of these twenty-five, twenty were white, twenty-three were male, twenty-four were employed or students, seventeen died at home, and their average age was just under twenty-three. There were an additional twenty-two methadone-related deaths, with a profile very similar to that of the heroin users.[47] While the morgue provided information only about those who used heroin or metha-done fatally, the bodies are evidence of the growth of a population of subur-ban, white, middle-class heroin users, many of whom became known to authorities only through their deaths.

Although New York and San Francisco remained at the heart of the new wave of heroin use, heroin was not limited to these areas and their immediate hinterlands. Traditional heroin-using centers, such as Detroit, supplied her-oin users from nearby suburbs and from college towns such as Kalamazoo and Ann Arbor in the years after 1970.[48] Proximity to the city increased the likelihood of access to heroin and facilitated the growth of a local heroin marketplace. For example, two epidemiologists did a careful study of heroin use in Grosse Pointe, an exclusive suburb just over the Detroit city line. Grosse Pointe housed an estimated three hundred adolescent heroin users, or approximately 4 percent of a fifteen- to nineteen-year-old population of 7,471. This was about double the national rate, and was no doubt due to Grosse Pointe's geographic relationship to Detroit, where early heroin experi-menters bought their drugs. Slightly more than a third of the heroin users took the drug daily and were considered addicted, and these youths sold heroin to their peers in order to support their habits.

Heroin use in Grosse Pointe began around 1966–67, when two venture-some users initiated their habits in inner-city Detroit. These two users "turned on" additional adolescents, and over the following two years, heroin spread slowly through peer groups. Detroit remained the source for heroin, but by 1971 there were enough heroin users to support a local retail market: adolescents who did not have Detroit connections or were afraid of the inner city could go to a Grosse Pointe gas station, purchase heroin, get their gas tanks filled, and pay for both using their parents' credit cards.[49] Clearly, heroin had arrived in the white middle-class suburbs.

In the years between 1967 and 1972, young middle-class whites initiated heroin use for the first time in significant numbers. The growth of this heroin-using cohort occurred first in the social settings of Greenwich Village, the East Village, and Haight-Ashbury. It stemmed from widespread experimentation with drugs, especially the injection of amphetamines, it emerged out of the collapse of the hippie movement, and it then radiated outward to countercultural neighborhoods in other cities as well as to smaller college towns and suburbs.

The decline of the East Village and Haight-Ashbury in the 1970s into desolate, crime-ridden neighborhoods, the end of a cultural movement that celebrated and valorized drug use, experience with the costs of hard-drug use, and a temporary shortage of heroin following a treaty with Turkey and increased enforcement in Marseilles all contributed to a decline in heroin initiation, including among middle-class whites. Incidence of new heroin use peaked in 1972, and by mid-decade experts reported that the worst was over. Surveys of high school students revealed that no more than 3 percent had tried heroin, and only half of those who tried it used it more than twice.[50] Robert DuPont, appointed White House drug czar in 1973, claimed that a corner had been turned, and that there were signs of progress in the drug war.[51]

Unfortunately, he was wrong.

CHAPTER NINE

The War and the War at Home

PRESIDENT RICHARD NIXON eyed his prospects for reelection with some concern in early 1971. The Republican president had been swept into the White House after promising to solve the problem of crime in the streets and saying that he would extricate the United States from the quagmire in Vietnam. Not only had he not accomplished either objective, but the issues seemed to merge: veterans who had been addicted to heroin in Vietnam were coming home to uncertain prospects and an absence of treatment options. According to a bipartisan Congressional fact-finding team, approximately 10 percent of American enlisted men were addicted to the highly potent and readily available heroin that flooded South Vietnam, while two or three times that number used heroin at least occasionally. In some frontline units as many as half the men had used heroin. One military officer warned, "Tens of thousands of soldiers are going back as walking time bombs." If anything could unravel the presidency of a law and order, Cold War hawk, this was it.[1]

The question of how to handle addicted veterans had a controversial answer. Advisors to the president proposed that the federal government reverse fifty years of public policy and keep heroin users supplied with an opiate: methadone. Methadone was a long-lasting synthetic opiate that stabilized the addicted, readied them for employment, and kept them from having to commit crimes to support a habit. Methadone maintenance meant surrendering the ideal of abstinence, but it was a pragmatic policy that promised to solve the administration's problem with crime at home and addicted soldiers abroad.[2] Unlike the traditional abstinence programs in which over 90 percent of participants relapsed, methadone actually seemed to work for the majority of its users. The expansion of methadone maintenance promised Nixon everything he was looking for.

Ironically, most Vietnam veterans who had been addicted to heroin got off the drug without methadone or any other kind of intervention. A change in their social setting—simply coming home from Vietnam—was sufficient to get them to stop using heroin. If anything makes the case for the importance of social setting, for demand reduction, for attending to the communal rather than the individual aspects of drug abuse, it is the history of heroin use among American soldiers in Vietnam.

Wars have repeatedly been associated with increases in substance abuse among returning veterans, and Vietnam was no exception.[3] Early reports of drug use focused on marijuana, which many soldiers smoked by the late 1960s. Marijuana grew wild in Vietnam but had no users until American troops arrived. Then enterprising farmers began to cultivate marijuana for the GI market, and their product was particularly potent, with some servicemen reporting hallucinations and sensory distortions after smoking. Military authorities cracked down on marijuana consumption only to discover that they had a more serious problem on their hands: increasing numbers of GIs were using opiates. In some ways, authorities acknowledged, the campaign against marijuana had backfired. "We kept telling them how dangerous that [marijuana] was. They tried it, probably tried [it] at home first, and knew they weren't dying. We tell them how dangerous smoking scag [heroin] is and they don't believe it." Specialist Gabriel Lambiase made a similar point in a letter: "The men certainly can question the facts about cocaine and heroin when they see the Government evades the truth and launches a propaganda program designed to influence their opinions and scare them into blind acceptance."[4] With soldiers questioning their superiors about the purpose of the war, it was not surprising that they questioned them about drug use and its effects.

Opium and heroin had a long history of use in Vietnam, and soldiers had no trouble obtaining them. Under the French colonial administration, Vietnam had a government-controlled opium monopoly and therefore a tradition of opium smoking that soldiers visiting the brothels and gambling dens of Saigon encountered. While some soldiers smoked opium, heroin became more commonly used. Both reporters and the Defense Department began to count up heroin-related deaths among soldiers in Vietnam, which began to climb in 1970.[5]

The Southeast Asian "Golden Triangle" produced about 700 tons of opium annually, accounting for about half of the world's illicit production. Much of this was converted into purple heroin that the local expatriate Chinese population smoked, but the arrival of American troops presented a market opportunity. Manufacturers in Thailand began producing higher-grade, injectable white heroin in 1969, and American servicemen, Thai soldiers, the Royal Laotian Army, and South Vietnamese Air Force personnel smuggled it into South Vietnam. "Soul Alley" in Saigon, home to several hundred American deserters and off-limits to American soldiers, became the main distribution point for heroin. Soon the drug was available throughout Saigon and near most American bases. American soldiers from nearby Tansonnhut Air Base visited "Scag Alley" in the search for drugs. Cinder-block houses, open to the street and illuminated by bare bulbs, lined the alley, and inside American soldiers smoked "hits," cigarettes that contained tobacco laced with heroin. The soldiers were relatively safe since American military police could not enter a Vietnamese home unless accompanied by Vietnamese policemen, who were generally paid off by the "mama sans" who ran the drug retailing businesses. Children posted in the alley warned inhabitants in the unlikely case of a raid. An Air Force sergeant commented that "If the pigs are coming, we just throw away the hit, and we're clean." A Congressional study commission visited South Vietnam in 1970 and found that heroin was sold openly on the streets of Saigon. The study team itself was approached several times even though they were "accompanied by a uniformed member of the United States Army."[6]

Soldiers found heroin everywhere in Vietnam. A journalist traveling from Saigon to Longbinh, the largest military installation in South Vietnam, found more than a dozen roadside stands where peddlers offered heroin to passing troops. One, where Vietnamese children sold heroin "nearly every day of the week," stood directly across from the entrance to the headquarters of Lieutenant General Michael S. Davison, the commander at Longbinh. Heroin sales were not limited to big cities or the outskirts of military installations. A former military policeman recalled, "The scag was everywhere, even in the hospital where I had to go for a time with a bad leg." An investigation of drug use at Camp Crescenz, another American base, revealed that the Vietnamese maids who were employed to clean the barracks smuggled heroin into the compound in the food they brought with them or in their hair or elsewhere on their bodies. Representative Robert Steele, a Connecticut

Republican, estimated that "the soldier going to South Vietnam today runs a far greater risk of becoming a heroin addict than a combat casualty."[7]

Heroin in South Vietnam, because it was so close to the source, was over 90 percent heroin. Because of its purity, users did not have to inject it in order to get high: about half smoked it, usually mixed with tobacco, another 40 to 45 percent snorted it, and only between 5 and 10 percent resorted to injection. In fact, few users thought of themselves as junkies—that term was reserved for the injectors who presumably had less control over their habits.[8]

Soldiers used opiates for a variety of predictable reasons ranging from boredom to abject terror while in the jungle to a desperate desire to be released from military service. A former soldier, who was dropped behind enemy lines for days at a time on long-range reconnaissance patrols, used opium to stay calm. "I'd cut off a little slice of O and roll it in a little cigarette paper and stick it up my ass. It was even better than eating it because it bypasses the stomach and only takes three or four minutes to hit you. And it would . . . last all day like that." Patrols alternated between tedium and terror, and opium or heroin helped pass the time. "There were seven of us going out on ambush patrols—on patrol and smoking that stuff at the same time. Most of the time out there in the field there was nothing to do." Another GI said, "You see people getting blown up, you see your friends getting killed and you can't do nothing but heroin to help you forget it. . . . You take heroin to keep yourself straight, to keep yourself from going crazy." An army psychologist agreed, saying that heroin was a "terrific tranquilizer" that allowed soldiers to cope with the hassles of a year's tour in Vietnam and make the time pass more quickly. "It was boring until I started smoking skag," one soldier claimed. "Then I just couldn't believe how fast the time went." Another former GI, Dan Kellenbenz, had started using opiates to dull the lingering pain from some shrapnel wounds. The medics thought he was a malingerer and only gave him aspirin, but a fellow soldier offered him heroin, which not only enabled him to cope with the pain but also allowed him "to forget days gone by and not worry about when my time was coming."[9]

A soldier charged officially with using drugs received a prison sentence and a dishonorable discharge, but evidence suggests that some units tolerated drug use. One soldier claimed, "I walked point for six months and everyone knew I was a heroin addict." Dan Kellenbenz recalled, "An officer once told me that he knew I was using drugs, but as long as I kept on doing the job I was doing he didn't care what I did." However, in 1971 urine tests became mandatory for personnel leaving Vietnam as reports of drug use led the military to crack down. Failing a urine test twice and receiving a report from a commanding officer certifying that a soldier had made no attempt to withdraw qualified him for a "212," a dishonorable discharge that identified him as a habitual narcotics user. By the fall of 1971, between one thousand and two thousand soldiers were being dishonorably discharged each month because of their narcotics use. While these veterans lost access to military benefits and use of Veterans Administration (VA) hospitals, they earned a trip home in something other than a body bag.[10]

Drug use inevitably affected military discipline and preparedness. Some soldiers could not fulfill their duties, and one Marine corporal recalled having to cover up for his men and send half of them on sick call because they were too high to go into the field. A perimeter guard who nodded out on heroin placed his entire unit at risk, as did a soldier on patrol who had to respond rapidly to a firefight. As the war wore on and became increasingly unpopular, enlisted men became alienated from officers and "lifers," the noncommissioned officers who were making a career of the service. While heroin was not the only cause of disciplinary breakdowns, it certainly contributed as soldiers resisted the efforts of their superiors to control their drug use. Soldiers told an NBC News correspondent that officers let drug use slide because it wasn't cool to bust someone and then have to go out into the field: "they [officers] might not come back." Another soldier claimed that the officers were "afraid to get a frag [fragmentation grenade] thrown in the bed with them." Sergeant Robert Parkinson confirmed this in testimony before Congress: "These men had changed to the point of threatening senior sergeants and officers who attempted to prevent their use of drugs."[11]

The armed services responded in a piecemeal fashion to reports of heroin use. The Army had the most severe problem with heroin and was the first service to start a voluntary detoxification program. The Navy and Air Force had comparatively little use and developed fairly generous programs, while the Marines were the least sympathetic toward heroin users. Some Army units established "halfway houses" in which soldiers tapered off their heroin use over a two-week period with declining doses of methadone, although some units insisted that users go cold turkey. In order to encourage men to participate, the Army offered a one-time amnesty program under which they would not be prosecuted or dishonorably discharged if they volunteered for treatment. However, an unfortunate side effect of the Army program was that it did not benefit those who needed it the most. Soldiers who were addicted were unlikely to be able to succeed at a one-chance program, which was all the Army allowed, and were therefore more likely to try to conceal their habits. In contrast, the Navy announced a thirty-day amnesty program under which drug users who wished to kick the habit could turn themselves in without jeopardizing their careers. The Navy provided medical help during detoxification, offered psychiatric services, and for those personnel unable to stop their use, it guaranteed an honorable discharge from the service. The Marines had the harshest policy. As one Marine wrote to the *New York Times*, "The Corps considers drug-users weaklings to be gotten rid of as soon as possible. These people, once caught, will be jailed or discharged from duty with no attempt made to rehabilitate or help them." The Defense Department finally established a uniform policy and the Marines fell in line when ordered to do so, but the Corps still followed disciplinary procedures against any Marine who had a second positive urine test.[12]

The uniform policy established by the Defense Department had some loopholes, however. The policy required urinalysis tests from all servicemen prior to discharge, with a week of detoxification in Vietnam and three weeks of rehabilitation in the United States for those who failed. The DOD announced the policy sixty days in advance, which allowed servicemen the opportunity to prepare for the test. The FRAT (Free Radical Assay Technique) detected the presence of heroin only if it had been taken within three days of testing, so soldiers quit using several days prior to the scheduled test. Soldiers also claimed that drinking large quantities of beer diluted the urine sufficiently so as to foil the test. Some soldiers purchased clean urine that they substituted for their own. Reports indicated that only slightly more than 5 percent of the men tested positive for opiates; given evidence of widespread heroin use, this suggests that either soldiers stopped their opiate use several days before the test or they cheated.[13]

Addicted veterans returning to the United States found little help for their habits. In 1971, the VA had only five hospitals with a total of one hundred beds equipped to handle addicts. The military concentrated its efforts on detoxifying soldiers and readying them for discharge, but did not offer longer-term rehabilitative services, which, the Defense Department argued, were beyond its purview. No one knew what would happen when drug addicted veterans returned home to discover that a habit that cost five dollars a day in Vietnam now cost a hundred dollars a day. Moreover, these veterans were returning to towns all over the country, and "it is feared," the *New York*

Times reported, "heroin may soon invade towns in 'middle America' that hitherto have been almost free of it."[14]

In the face of charges that he was "sleeping through the problem," President Nixon asked Congress for $155 million to tackle the issue of drugs. (Congress eventually appropriated $1 billion for a variety of programs.) A new Special Action Office for Drug Abuse Prevention (SAODAP) was created in the White House, the Veterans Administration opened twenty-seven drug addiction centers in the nation's largest cities in the summer of 1971, and, most important, methadone maintenance became widely available as a drug treatment for the first time.[15]

The President's drug policy advisors had previously discussed methadone as part of a crime control strategy. The doubling of the nation's crime rate between 1960 and 1968 had been a major Republican campaign issue, and crime had shown no signs of abating during Nixon's presidency. The only good news came from cities such as New York, Chicago, and Washington, D.C., which had implemented methadone programs. Reports from these cities indicated that addicts in treatment had lower arrest rates and were not inclined to return to heroin use. It is possible that the Nixon administration would have supported methadone maintenance simply as a way of reducing the crime rate, but the discovery of addicted veterans clinched the case for methadone.[16]

It was a controversial choice, given methadone's history as an addictive drug. German scientists at I. G. Farben developed "amadone" as a morphine substitute in 1941, and the formula came to the United States as part of confiscated scientific information after the war. American scientists at Eli Lilly introduced "dolophine" into clinical trials in the United States, and the American Medical Association adopted the name methadone in 1947. Although it was an effective painkiller, methadone was addictive and its main use became helping addicts through withdrawal by substituting gradually diminishing doses of methadone for heroin. The discovery that methadone could be used to maintain (rather than withdraw) an addict in a nontherapeutic setting happened largely by accident.[17]

Scientist Vincent Dole and physician Marie Nyswander pioneered methadone maintenance in the United States. Dole became interested in the problem of addiction because he encountered so many heroin users in his daily commute from the New York Central train station in Harlem to his Rockefeller University offices in midtown Manhattan. Dole became the chair of the Health Research Council's Committee on Narcotics and began his initiation into the world of narcotics by consulting with experts. With the exception of Marie Nyswander, the experts did not impress him either with their knowledge or their sympathy for addicts.[18]

Marie Nyswander was a perfect colleague for Vincent Dole, and eventually became his wife as well as his research partner. After completing medical school and a surgical internship, Nyswander joined the Navy in 1945, a time when the Navy was not interested in having women surgeons. Posted to the U.S. Public Health Service Hospital at Lexington, Kentucky, Nyswander had her first encounters with addicts as well as the racism and disrespect with which they were treated. Nyswander eventually left Lexington in disgust and moved to New York, where she trained as a psychotherapist and opened a practice. She also volunteered to treat addicts in a storefront run by the East Harlem Protestant Parish; thus by the time she met Dole, she was well versed in working with addicts as well as in challenging gender, class, and racial boundaries.[19]

Dole and Nyswander questioned the central tenet that had guided addiction research, namely that abstinence should be the goal of treatment. They wanted to see if it were possible to maintain an addict on morphine, a practice for which the Federal Bureau of Narcotics had arrested clinicians in the past. Because he was a faculty member at a prestigious research university, with the backing of the president and university counsel, Dole was relatively immune to the FBN's threatening visits and harassment.

Dole began in 1963 with an observational study of two addicts, who received a quarter of a grain of morphine each four times a day. The main problem with the drug, as Dole recalled, was that it was so short acting. "In three or four hours the addict would be miserable and vomiting, needing another shot." Moreover, Dole had to keep increasing the doses because of rising tolerance, eventually giving each of them eight shots a day with a total of ten grains of morphine. Morphine became the focal point of their lives, and Nyswander remembered that they were "practically immobile." "Much of the time they sat passively, in bathrobes, in front of a television set. They didn't respond to any of the other activities offered them. They just sat there waiting for the next shot." It was clear that morphine (and heroin for the same reasons) posed too many problems to be useful for maintaining addicts.[20]

The same, however, could not be said for methadone. Dole and Nyswander initially used methadone as it had been used in Lexington—to withdraw patients from narcotics. Because their patients had been taking so much morphine, the doctors provided them with doses of methadone that far exceeded the usual ones in order to keep them comfortable during withdrawal. Over several days, they observed striking changes in the pair's appearance and behavior. According to Nyswander, "The older addict began to paint industriously and his paintings were good. The younger started urging us to let him get his high-school-equivalency diploma. We sent them both off to school, outside the hospital grounds, and they continued to live at the hospital. Neither of them—although both of them had every opportunity—copped heroin on the outside. From two slugabeds they turned into dynamos of activity." Methadone seemed to allow the patients to live more full lives and it had significant advantages: it was easily administered—it could be given orally once a day instead of being injected—it relieved drug cravings, and it prevented withdrawal symptoms for twenty-four to thirty-six hours. This was a research finding worth exploring.[21]

Dole and Nyswander began their methadone maintenance experiment in 1964 with a small group (eventually twenty-two) of long-term heroin addicts. First they stabilized their patients on high doses (originally 100 to 150 milligrams per day, but eventually reduced to 80 to 120 milligrams) of methadone. Once patients had been maintained on methadone for six weeks, they were encouraged to return home, find work or complete their schooling, and come to the clinic on an outpatient basis. By 1966 the pilot study had expanded to 128 patients; although fourteen were dropped for behavioral reasons, nearly two-thirds of the remainder were able to find and hold jobs. The researchers concluded that "patients who had spent the preceding 5 to 15 years in jail or as addicts on the street are now steadily employed, well dressed, in good health, responsible for families, and saving money. Heroin use has been stopped, except for intermittent experiments made by some patients in the early stages of treatment. No patient has become readdicted to heroin." Dole and Nyswander had substituted social rehabilitation, by which they meant assuming useful social roles, for abstinence as the goal of their drug treatment program.[22]

To understand the basis for their accomplishments, Dole and Nyswander began a "double blind" test with their patients in which physicians administered shots of morphine, dilaudid, heroin, and a saline solution to the methadone patients, with neither patient nor physician knowing what was administered. The shots had minimal effect, and Dole and Nyswander concluded that methadone formed a "blockade" that prevented the patient from feeling euphoria. Methadone worked because it eliminated the incentive for a user to return to heroin.[23]

The term "blockade" was somewhat misleading, however. Unlike opiate antagonists, which do block heroin's effects, methadone created a "cross tolerance," meaning that heroin's euphoric effect would not be felt under a certain dosage. However, it was possible to exceed that dosage, in which case a patient would get high from heroin. Dole conceded that he used the term blockade more for political purposes than with scientific precision. "We really chose the vivid term 'blockade' in the early days to help counter the criticism that we were merely switching addicts from one addictive substance to another."[24] Although the term produced a lasting controversy, it diverted criticism initially.

While the "blockade" concept was important for promoting methadone maintenance as public policy, the scientific basis of the program rested on Dole's metabolic theory. Dole rejected the prevailing wisdom that held that heroin users suffered from psychiatric disorders. Dole believed that addiction was a physical disorder in which prolonged exposure to narcotics caused irreversible cellular changes in the addict; only an opiate or a synthetic substitute could compensate for those changes. Methadone, as a long-lasting synthetic, satisfied the addict's physiological need for an opiate just as insulin satisfied a physiological need for a diabetic. Dole was thus able to justify keeping patients on methadone indefinitely.[25]

News of methadone's success ended any possibility of continuing to administer it in an experimental setting. City mayors, desperate for any measure to reverse the spiraling crime rate, eagerly seized on methadone as a "magic bullet." In New York City, Mayor John Lindsay accepted the resignation of his narcotics coordinator, Dr. Efren Ramirez, a staunch methadone opponent, and opened the city's first voluntary methadone clinic in 1969 in Brooklyn's Bedford-Stuyvesant neighborhood, which effectively converted methadone maintenance from a controlled experiment to a freely available therapy. At the same time, the City Council moved to supply methadone to any prisoner who requested it as an alternative to "cold turkey" withdrawal in the city jails. Illinois appointed Jerome Jaffe, a New York physician who would become the Nixon administration's first "drug czar," to run the Illinois Drug Abuse Program, which gave heroin users a choice of modalities, either therapeutic communities or methadone maintenance, to combat their addiction. By 1970, Jaffe had opened fifteen facilities with capacity for nine hundred patients and there was a long waiting list for admission. In Washington, D.C., Mayor Walter Washington supported physician Robert DuPont's request to begin a methadone program in 1969 after DuPont discovered that nearly half of the inmates in the District jail were heroin users. (It was also notable that three-quarters of the narcotics-using inmates had heard of methadone and viewed it favorably.) Since the District was the only local jurisdiction where the federal government could actually intervene to control crime, White House aides funneled money to DuPont to see if the methadone maintenance program could lower the crime rate.[26]

By all indications, the mayors were right about the usefulness of methadone in reducing crime. Research reports supported the early optimism about methadone turning addicts from criminals into productive citizens—or at least less active criminals. Dole claimed a 90 percent reduction in criminal convictions among program participants, and reports from other methadone programs were equally promising. While the FBI reported an 11 percent increase in crime nationally in 1970, crime in Washington, D.C., declined by 5.2 percent, which Robert DuPont linked to the expansion of the methadone program. New Yorkers also experienced their first decline in the crime rate in many years in 1972, and officials credited the expansion of treatment opportunities for addicts as one cause. Nationally, seventy-two of the largest cities reported a decline in crime in 1972, by which time methadone maintenance was available across the country. These statistics were hard to ignore, and political proponents of methadone gladly took credit.[27]

Despite the crime statistics, the expansion of methadone maintenance encountered medical, community, and political opposition. Some medical experts doubted the policy of substituting one addictive substance for another; it was like switching an alcoholic from Scotch to bourbon, some said. David Ausubel, a physician and narcotics expert, accused Dole and Nyswander of "openly giving addicts narcotics to gratify and perpetuate their addiction." Advocates of abstinence and therapeutic communities were among the harshest critics of methadone maintenance. Chester Stern, the director of the Synanon therapeutic community in Oakland, California, claimed, "Methadone is insidious. It's immoral. It treats the symptoms but not the disease." The former addicts who staffed therapeutic communities were particularly adamant that methadone maintenance only replaced one habit with another that was worse. With methadone, "you go into withdrawals so excruciating you damn near die," exclaimed one, maintaining that withdrawal from heroin was much easier. Another found withdrawal pains from methadone so severe that "the marrow of your bones screamed." Some

New Haven, Connecticut, methadone clinic, June 1973. Methadone users swallowed their doses in a cup of orange juice (hence the term "orange handcuffs") under the supervision of a nurse. *U.S. News and World Report* Magazine Collection, Library of Congress, LC-U9–27868-A and B 31A.

African American political leaders and journalists lambasted methadone as a form of chemical slavery. The word on the street was that methadone "melted your bones," "took your manhood," and was just "honky's way of keeping black men hooked." Floyd Hardwick of the United Front for a Drug Free Community, a Boston community group, echoed the sentiment, declaring that "methadone is a solution given to us by white, middle class America. It's a method of controlling third world peoples."[28]

The Bureau of Narcotics and Dangerous Drugs (BNDD, the successor to the FBN) predictably criticized the methadone programs, but from another point of view. The bureau maintained that while Dole and Nyswander were conducting a worthwhile research experiment (a stance contradicted by the bureau's harassment), any expansion of methadone maintenance was a retreat from sound public and medical policy and threatened to create a new black market for methadone.[29]

Many of these criticisms had merit. If one accepts the argument that heroin and crime were both produced by the social settings of inner-city communities, with their concentrated economic disadvantage and social marginality, then methadone treated a symptom and not the disease. To be sure, it lessened both individual and community suffering by allowing heroin users to stabilize their lives and substitute productive for criminal activity. However, in the end it was an individual and therapeutic response to a social and economic problem, and it still left the individual dependent on a chemical substance.

Despite the criticism, methadone maintenance expanded rapidly because of a confluence of interests. Mayors were willing to brave the criticism of some constituents because methadone promised lower crime rates. President Nixon was persuaded to try methadone as part of a treatment program because of the threat posed by addicted veterans. Physicians saw in methadone the possibility of turning addiction from a criminal justice problem into a medical one in which they could assert their traditional authority. Much of the public saw methadone as a solution to drug addiction, the third-ranked national problem (after the Vietnam War and the economy) according to public opinion polls. And users themselves flocked to the clinics, determined to get themselves into treatment. Although methadone maintenance did not receive the majority of the federal government's treatment funding, which went to abstinence and therapeutic communities, heroin users voted with their feet. Between 1969 and 1974 the number of methadone programs grew from 16 to 926 and the number of patients increased to 74,000, or approximately one-fifth of the nation's suspected addict population. Methadone, declared President Richard Nixon, was the "best available answer" to the problem of addiction.[30]

Methadone looked so good in part because the alternatives looked worse. Studies of patients released from Lexington and other hospital-based programs indicated that approximately 90 percent or more of those who completed treatment returned to heroin use, sometimes within hours of their release.[31] A review of the Manhattan State Hospital program, which treated males over the age of twenty-one, found a fairly typical pattern. About three-quarters of the patients signed out after only two weeks, and only 10 percent remained in the unit for the recommended minimum of twenty-five days. Interest in aftercare was minimal: "Patients who were given appointments as they left the hospital usually did not keep them. When asked to call, in most instances they failed to do so." Treatment programs helped heroin users get a handle on a habit that had spiraled out of control, or they satisfied the demands of family, a spouse, or a judge that a user get treatment, but they promised little permanent change once a patient returned to his or her usual social setting.[32]

One might expect that programs for adolescents would fare better than those for adults, but this was not the case. New York's Riverside Hospital was established for adolescents in 1952 during the height of the postwar heroin boom. A research team reviewed the case history of each patient admitted in 1955, and of these 247 adolescents, 11 were dead four years later and 89 had disappeared. Out of the 147 ex-patients interviewed, only 8 had not returned to heroin use after release, and these individuals maintained that they were never addicted in the first place. In the face of such an expensive and dismal failure, the city closed Riverside in 1961. As Vincent Dole observed, "Very few people could argue that the treatment of heroin addicts by so-called detoxification is a success." Rather, he said, the addict "lives a dismal cycle of increasing habit, detoxification, and increasing habit."[33]

Therapeutic communities, in which recovering users lived in a communal setting, religious communities that relied on evangelical faith to keep an addict straight, or a twelve-step program such as provided by Narcotics Anonymous, were alternatives to hospital programs. Each of these approaches worked, but only for a small number of addicts. Synanon was the first therapeutic community and served as the prototype for others, with some former Synanon residents going on to found their own houses. Charles Dederich established Synanon in Santa Monica, California, in 1958 in response to the refusal of Alcoholics Anonymous to work with drug addicts. The Synanon method of highly structured roles, hierarchical organization, group encounter sessions, individual confrontations, and reliance on former addicts as staff members became the model for therapeutic communities, including Daytop Village in New York, Gaudenzia House in Philadelphia, and Marathon House in Providence, among many others. The staffs of therapeutic communities, in contrast to Dole and Nyswander, did not believe that physical addiction was the problem. Instead, the addict's underlying personality disorder and a desire to withdraw emotionally from the world had to be corrected. The programs' rigid structure and the emphasis on honest, sometimes emotionally brutal, confrontation followed from this belief.[34]

Critics of these programs pointed to the authoritarian, almost messianic, nature of leadership, the reluctance to have clients "graduate" from the program, and, at least in Synanon, the increasing isolation of the program from the outside world and its eventual degeneration into violence and chaos. The therapeutic communities kept their residents away from drugs, but because so many people left, it was difficult to assess success. For example, at Daytop Village an average of twelve or thirteen people were admitted each month in the mid-1960s, but an average of twelve also left. One recent analysis concluded that as many as 95 percent of those admitted to Synanon left without completing the program, a figure comparable to that in other communities. These programs changed the social setting of heroin users, but only by enveloping them in an authoritarian institution. Success rates in these programs were about the same or a bit lower than those in hospital-based detoxification units.[35]

Faith-based programs existed in many cities and treated drug users through "cold turkey" withdrawal and a conversion experience. Teen Challenge, founded in Brooklyn by David Wilkerson, was one of the more significant among these programs if only because it attained national recognition and opened centers across the country. Wilkerson came to New York from rural Pennsylvania in 1958 to work with teenage gangs, but realized that heroin use was at least an equally important social problem. In the early 1960s, the organization opened a group home for delinquent and addicted boys, a facility for teenage girls, and a rural retreat in Pennsylvania that provided schooling, vocational training, and Bible study once youths spent about six weeks in the urban residences. Like the therapeutic communities, Teen Challenge located the origins of heroin addiction in the individual, but as a spiritual crisis rather than a psychological one. Instead of encounter groups, users went through a conversion process in which they were induced to experience abject despair and, as staff members prayed with them, spiritual light. Ex-addicts were absorbed into an authoritarian system that eventually incorporated graduates as missionaries to work with troubled youth in the Teen Challenge centers that were opening around the country. Thus, like the therapeutic communities, Teen Challenge replaced addiction with a lifelong, almost cultlike structure organized around recovery. According to Teen Challenge's unverified figures, about a third of those who entered the program were living "victoriously" and not using drugs or alcohol.[36]

Narcotics Anonymous, based on the sister program Alcoholics Anonymous, also provided a lifelong, religious, but nonresidential recovery program. The first meeting of what was at first called "Addicts Anonymous" occurred in the Public Health Service Hospital in Lexington in 1947, with the first noninstitutional meeting in Los Angeles. NA's program followed AA's Twelve Steps and asked users to recognize their powerlessness in the face of their addiction, to understand that they would always be addicts, and to place their fate in the hands of a higher power.[37] Members attended meetings as frequently as they thought necessary, and these meetings provided constant support and a network of recovering users who volunteered to help each other in times of crisis or during relapses. While these programs worked for some users, many cycled in and out, experiencing repeated failures in their effort to stay sober. None of these recovery programs could match the success rates reported by methadone maintenance.

Needless to say, methadone maintenance and the metabolic view of addiction threatened believers in abstinence. Therapeutic communities in particular depended on the difficulty of life as a street addict to make the demands of the community more palatable. The struggle to secure a daily supply of drugs, the necessity of avoiding arrest and incarceration, and the frequent degradation involved in being a street addict helped make addicts willing to endure the discipline and rigidity of the therapeutic community. "If these conditions were to change," stated one sympathetic analyst of a therapeutic community, "if heroin and other drugs of addiction were made legal and supplies became available at much lower prices—then the demand for admission to Daytop and the willingness to stay there could be expected to diminish greatly, possible vanishing altogether."[38] Supplying methadone to addicts threatened to cheapen the price of recovery and deprive residential communities of their clients. In addition, supporters of abstinence believed themselves to be in competition with methadone maintenance for funds. While the majority of federal funding flowed to abstinence programs, it was a reasonable fear that this would change if the majority of those seeking treatment chose to participate in methadone maintenance. But not only institutional interests were at stake.

Perhaps of equal importance, the groups were at odds philosophically in their views of addicts and the sources of addiction. In an address about therapeutic communities, the director of Daytop Village responded to a question about methadone maintenance. "I think methadone maintenance is a great idea," he said. "We should give money to bank robbers, women to rapists, and methadone to addicts."[39] Obviously if the source of addiction lay in a personality problem or a spiritual crisis, then supplying an addict with a drug was immoral and only masked the problem. That methadone treatment managed to retain many times more users than abstinence programs or therapeutic communities was irrelevant. Effectiveness of treatment was beside the point.

Ultimately, methadone's opponents questioned its efficacy. The original studies of methadone overstated its ability to transform the lives of addicts. Methadone users did not automatically become hard-working, law-abiding citizens. Rather, as they returned to the social setting of an unchanged inner city, they substituted other drugs for heroin. Proponents had oversold methadone's achievements.

The first group of methadone users was atypical, and thus conclusions based on their behavior turned out to be overly optimistic. The patients were older, "whiter," and more committed to recovery than a randomized selection of drug users would have been. Two-thirds were over thirty, twice the average age of users on the city's Narcotics Register, and this profile suggested a group of patients especially eager for recovery since they were close to the end of their street careers. There were also twice as many whites as African Americans in the group, when whites only accounted for about a quarter of the city's heroin users. Since whites generally were a more advantaged population, the distance to a "productive" way of life was shorter for them than for poor African American or Latino users. Since all applicants for the methadone program spent a long time on a waiting list before being admitted to one of the few treatment slots, those who persevered had high motivation and were therefore more likely to succeed. Moreover, the early methadone patients were aware that they were part of an experimental protocol that defied the established policies of the federal government. They felt protective of Dole and Nyswander and admired their maverick stance, and it was predictable that they would have better outcomes than a random selection of heroin users.[40]

Dole and Nyswander also made the mistake of overstating the program's successes in two areas: retention and the decline in criminal activity. Since retention declined over time, by publishing aggregate statistics that included old and newly admitted patients together, especially with the program expanding rapidly, the retention rate appeared to be much higher than it actually was. That nearly 60 percent of the patients admitted to the program still remained in treatment four years later was remarkable, but it was significantly lower than the 82 percent reported by Dole and Nyswander. Similarly, the decline in crime was exaggerated by including crimes related to drug possession and selling, which one might expect would decline. When arrests were examined by type, vice and narcotics arrests showed the largest decline, followed by crimes against property, while crimes against persons increased. The conclusion that methadone treatment reduced the crime rate had to be tempered by an analysis of which crimes were reduced and which were not, and methadone's causal role was not always clear. This left methadone treatment open to the charge that it was a "forlorn hope," when in actuality it was far more effective than any other form of treatment and suffered mostly from having been overpromoted.[41]

Although Dole and Nyswander never claimed that methadone blocked anything other than opiates, methadone patients' use of other drugs such as alcohol and cocaine contradicted expectations that they would become sober. Here again, the behavior of early patients, who were eager to get off the streets and assume productive roles in society, led to false optimism. Some of the later patients simply wanted to get their heroin habits under control while continuing to use other drugs. Instead of finding that between 50 and 85 percent of methadone users worked, attended school, or became homemakers, later studies reported that approximately two-thirds were supported on welfare. As one ethnographer commented, "the most typical drug scene on the streets today is two or more methadone users sitting on a stoop or standing on a street corner with pints of wine in paper bags panhandling for change to get more wine." The emergence of a "wine and welfare" subculture contradicted hopes that supplying methadone would transform heroin users into worker bees. The urban social settings that produced addiction could not be addressed by therapies that were aimed at individuals. There were no simple chemical solutions to complicated social problems.[42]

A black market in methadone developed over time as methadone programs expanded, just as the narcotics bureau had predicted. "Street methadone" circulated among heroin users and, instead of encouraging entry into treatment, allowed heroin users to modulate their use. The methadone came from pharmaceutical companies, where employees were able to steal supplies, from unscrupulous physicians who ran "pill mills" for anyone who could pay for treatment, or from clients who sold a portion of their maintenance doses. A *New York Times* investigation revealed that a reporter was able to walk into a clinic and, with no identification, no evidence of addiction, no track marks on his arms, and no history of attempted withdrawal and walk out with 560 milligrams of methadone in return for a $30 fee. Individual clients acted as entrepreneurial agents, selling portions of their take-home doses, or "spit backs" (in which a patient pretended to swallow the dose and then spit the methadone into a cup upon leaving the premises). Initially, buyers tended to be heroin users trying to self-regulate or reduce their habits, or those waiting to get on to a maintenance program, but over time methadone became a drug of entry for younger drug users. In 1973, deaths from methadone over-

Antidrug billboard, New Haven, Connecticut, June 1973. Even antidrug campaigns marked territory as belonging to a drug marketplace. *U.S. News and World Report* Magazine Collection, Library of Congress, LC-U9–27867-A 23.

doses exceeded deaths from heroin in New York City, indicating that the drug was circulating among novice users. The actions of methadone clients created major political problems for supporters of methadone treatment and helped undermine the program.[43]

Some of the newer methadone centers experimented with low-dose maintenance, which departed from the Dole-Nyswander protocols. On the one hand, they provided patients with less methadone, and thus there was less incentive to divert methadone to the black market since patients had to ration their supplies more carefully. On the other hand, while low doses were effective in preventing withdrawal symptoms, they also produced less cross-tolerance effect and therefore made it easier for patients to get high. Some methadone users purchased black market methadone because they found their maintenance levels too low and they experienced discomfort, if not withdrawal. "Gas station" programs allowed patients to "fill up," but without the therapy, vocational training, and emotional support that character-ized the early programs. Dole and Nyswander maintained that "a pharmacological cure is no more than a beginning," especially with street addicts who lacked educational, social, emotional, and employment-related skills—nor was methadone able to treat the user's social setting. Bargain-basement treatment offered no supports, and despite evidence that low-dose programs were less effective, the effects of federal legislation and declines in funding meant that more of these programs were established, again contributing to methadone maintenance's political problems.[44]

In response to reports of methadone abuses, the Food and Drug Administration created stricter federal guidelines for its distribution. A series of restrictions, beginning in 1972, mandated elaborate reporting standards, established abstinence as the ultimate goal for methadone users, set two years as the standard maintenance period, and limited the take-home doses given patients. Requiring that even long-term patients consume their daily orange juice and methadone in the presence of a nurse at a clinic created "orange handcuffs," a form of chemical probation that many patients resented and that made methadone maintenance seem more punitive than helpful.[45]

Over time methadone clinics became centers for drug distribution as well as magnets for hustlers and thus aroused community resentment. The clinic attracted entrepreneurs involved in all aspects of the drug trade. Buyers of illicit methadone waited nearby for possible sellers and produced a cup into which patients spat methadone. Others sold urine passed at home that could be heated in the clinic bathroom, or held in a balloon in a women's vagina, to those who might fail a urine test. Dealers of heroin, barbiturates, and cocaine knew that they would find customers at the local methadone clinic willing to barter their doses in order to get high. As Jerry Stahl recalled of his drug-using years, the best way to cop drugs was to show up at the methadone clinic "at six in the morning when the hard-core clientele is on hand to gulp its dose" and was getting ready to tend to the day's business.[46]

Methadone clinics also came to resemble fortresses, with bars on the windows and armed guards, to prevent thefts and disorderly conduct by patients or others. As the photographer and social critic Camilo Jose Vergara has argued, "A well-protected building that does not call attention to itself is considered the ideal location for a clinic in an inner-city community. . . . No attempt is made to mitigate the brutal look of their defenses." With the distribution of methadone concentrated in clinics, usually limited by neighborhood opposition to marginal areas with high concentrations of drug users, drug treatment returned users to the social settings that had produced their heroin use in the first place and further inscribed drug use upon the landscape of inner-city neighborhoods.[47]

Medical researchers, convinced that addiction was a chronic brain dis-

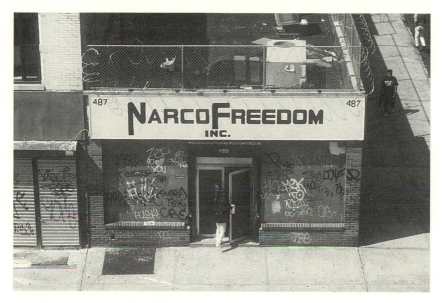

"Narcofreedom," used no doubt without irony, as the name of a methadone clinic, 147th Street and Willis Avenue, the Bronx. Community opposition limited these sites to neighborhoods with high levels of heroin use, which further inscribed drug use into the landscape. Photograph by Camilo Vergara, used with permission.

ease, spent their time looking for another magic bullet—something as effective as methadone but without the social baggage that methadone had accumulated. But as this research continued, something happened that confounded everyone.

The heroin-using soldiers who worried Richard Nixon and the American public so much stopped using heroin upon returning from Vietnam. Equally remarkably, most did it without the benefit of twelve-step programs, therapeutic communities (which were too regimented and too similar to the military for most ex-soldiers' tastes), or methadone maintenance. This conclusion was based on two samples of U.S. Army enlisted men (the group with the highest rate of heroin use) drawn from the approximately 13,760 soldiers who returned from Vietnam in September 1971. The first sample consisted of 470 soldiers drawn randomly from the returnee group. Interviewed between eight and twelve months after their return to the United States, the soldiers revealed several startling facts. First, the rate of heroin use was much higher than early reports or the urinalysis tests had indicated. Over 40 percent of the soldiers had tried heroin, opium, both, or another narcotic drug during

Methadone clinic, 789 Westchester Avenue, the Bronx. The building is designed to be secure against break-ins, and resembles an abandoned building with its graffiti and bricked-in windows. Photograph by Camilo Vergara, used with permission.

their tour in Vietnam, and half of them (20 percent of the sample) reported that they had been addicted. Second, although 10 percent reported using narcotics since their return, only 1 percent reported being addicted. Even if the entire 10 percent that used heroin since returning home were considered addicted (an unreasonable assumption), this still produced a remission rate that no program for addiction treatment in the United States could match. The second sample consisted of 495 men from the 1,400 returnees in September 1971 who had tested positive for narcotics use in Vietnam. In this group of more serious users, 33 percent reported taking heroin since their return, but only 7 percent were addicted at the time of their interviews. Thus, even in the group that was unable to heed the warning that they were going to be tested before leaving Vietnam and who were all presumably seriously addicted, about two-thirds stopped their use of narcotics entirely. And of those who did not, only a small percentage was addicted. A follow-up study done three years later concluded that alcohol, marijuana, and amphetamine abuse posed more serious problems than did heroin, which only 3 percent of the veterans used regularly (defined as more than once a week for a month or more).[48]

The most obvious explanation for these remission rates was that these were short-term users (a tour of duty in Vietnam lasted a year) who had been removed from the extremely stressful social setting that produced their heroin use. That is, their drug use was situational, and once they left behind the easy access to drugs, the intimate group with whom they had used heroin, and the stress of serving in Vietnam, there was little incentive for them to resume heroin use. Social setting was clearly more important than the physiological effects of the drug on the brain, even among the most heavily addicted users. Second, most heroin users had smoked heroin rather than injecting it. The small number of injectors apparently had a more difficult time stopping their use, suggesting the importance of the mode of ingestion. Finally, the heroin found in the United States was so impure and so expensive that that most of the returning soldiers realized they could never afford to be addicted here. As one veteran noted, "I had $900 in the bank and I spent it in eight days just to keep my sickness away. . . . There wasn't enough money, there wasn't enough dope to keep my habit going."[49] In the face of these conditions, most users simply stopped.

That so many Vietnam veterans were able to cease using heroin upon their return to the United States suggests that assumptions about the nature of addiction needed to be questioned. If those soldiers had been returned to Vietnam, it is likely that the vast majority would have resumed narcotics use. They would have been subject to the same stress and to the same social setting in which their heroin use had begun. Is it then surprising that dropouts from a therapeutic community or a detoxification program, who returned to the same social settings in which their heroin use began, would resume ingesting heroin? Or that the only effective treatment for heroin abuse under these conditions was methadone, which substituted a longer-acting, pure, and sta-bilizing synthetic opiate for a short-acting, impure, and destabilizing one? In the end, conditions for both addiction and treatment were shaped by social factors—the social setting of the inner city—where heroin use, drug trading, and methadone treatment were all concentrated. The solution to the problem of heroin addiction lay there, more than in the minds and bodies of individ-ual heroin users, and it was there that America's drug problem was about to become worse.

CHAPTER TEN

From the Golden Spike to the Glass Pipe

IN THE 1970S, the postwar system of centralized heroin distribution collapsed, which at first seemed like a triumph of antidrug policy. Long-term efforts to have Turkey limit opium production and to encourage French police to crack down on heroin-producing laboratories in southern France finally paid dividends in the 1970s. Estimates varied, but anywhere from two-thirds to 80 percent of the heroin arriving in the United States during the postwar period was Turkish in origin and was processed in France, and both the Lyndon Johnson and Richard Nixon administrations attempted to persuade Turkey to substitute other crops for opium. These efforts paid off in 1972 when Turkey agreed to ban opium cultivation in return for a $35 million payment for crop substitution. While the treaty did not have an immediate impact since heroin destined for U.S. shores was already in the pipeline, it promised future benefits. The unintended consequence was a transformation of the nation's drug market.

French police action against illicit heroin laboratories was felt immediately in the heroin marketplace. American administrations had lobbied French authorities to police its heroin-dealing underworld, but to no avail, because the French saw heroin addiction as an American problem and, perhaps more important, because members of the French secret services were involved in narcotics trafficking, which helped fund covert operations. But the situation changed in the late 1960s as heroin use increased in France, and French authorities reached an agreement in 1970 to cooperate more closely with the Bureau of Narcotics and Dangerous Drugs (the successor to the FBN). This paid off in a series of raids in 1972, eliminating three major heroin-processing laboratories in the Marseilles area, and disrupting the "French Connection" that had been delivering heroin to New York City since the 1950s.[1]

This combination of events created a heroin drought that hit East Coast cities most severely and started a heroin panic on the streets. Heroin users searched frantically for dope and then complained that when they could find it, the quality was terrible or that they had been "ripped off" and sold fake drugs. One user, Stella, recalled: "I felt like I was shooting flour, baking soda, it was cut so much," and Mick agreed, "You didn't know what you were putting in that cooker." The possibilities included quinine, ground-up sleeping pills, aspirin that had been pounded into dust, and Ajax cleanser. Two years of impossibly weak and very expensive heroin sent hardcore users scurrying to join methadone programs ("I was stayin' sick more than I was well"), and physicians reported a steep decline in hepatitis and other injection-related diseases as well as in overdose deaths.[2]

Success, however, was short-lived. By the mid-1970s, the East Coast's heroin drought was over, as was many users' brief flirtation with methadone. The demand of the East Coast market was simply too great for suppliers to ignore: "Mexican mud," the brown, tar-like heroin smuggled across the border in the Southwest, reached New York and replaced heroin from the Golden Crescent, as it had when World War II disrupted the international trade. In 1974, Mexican heroin, which had accounted for no more than 20 percent of the national market at the beginning of the decade, furnished over 70 percent (some accounts say as much as 90 percent) of the nation's heroin supply. As in the past, Mexican heroin formed a reserve, ready to meet demand when other sources disappeared. Asian sources provided the balance of the supply. Asian heroin arrived with returning servicemen, who opened smuggling routes from Southeast Asia, as traffickers around the world rushed to meet the demand created by the disruption in the French Connection.[3]

Smuggling from Mexico was more decentralized than smuggling from Europe, which made it more difficult to police. While officials identified a so-called "Mexican Connection"—the Herrera brothers of Durango, Mexico—that organized the export of Mexican heroin, they admitted that "the Herrera's [sic] . . . are simply the most popular and most visible of the heroin traffickers, and . . . there are many Mexican families, large and small, trafficking in heroin today . . . not to mention numerous 'independent' dealers." This army of smugglers organized many small runs across the border. "Mules" secreted heroin in cars with false side panels, in refitted gas tanks, or in drive shafts that had been cut open, stuffed with heroin packages and then welded back together ("Durango drive shafts"). The numerous small shipments meant that smugglers risked little on each trip while the number of trips increased to meet market demand.[4]

Distribution patterns changed with the new supply routes. Mexican heroin was smuggled overland into Chicago, a traditional destination of Mexican immigrants, and the city usurped New York's role as the national distributor of heroin. Trafficking followed the interstate highway system, sometimes referred to as the "heroin highway," that ran from Durango to Chicago; some traffickers transported both illegal immigrants and heroin on a regular basis along this route. Mexicans completely dominated the heroin market in Chicago (Reyes Herrera, who lived in Chicago, was in charge of the Herrera brothers' distribution network), and they sold the drug in wholesale lots for redistribution elsewhere in the country.[5]

Evidence for the success of the new smuggling enterprises came from the streets. Heroin purity, which had fallen to about 3 percent in New York during the drought (that is, a packet of heroin might consist of 97 percent adulterants), now began to climb while prices held steady or even dropped. (Some of this may have been due to the expansion of the methadone rolls, which reduced demand.) Mexican heroin contained fewer adulterants than its rivals, with packets running as high as 30 percent heroin. Latino dealers included more heroin per packet, most likely in order to establish market share for a product that users in the past had thought inferior because of its lower opiate content.[6]

The restoration of heroin supplies caused problems for all cities, but it could not have come at a worse time for New York. The police department was still reeling from the revelations of the Knapp Commission's investigation into police corruption. In response, the department placed severe restrictions on the average patrol officer's ability to make narcotics arrests and on the activities of plainclothes officers. Detectives could only enter bars and clubs if a superior officer directed them to do so and supervised their activities. While this limited the possibility of corruption, it also hampered officers' initiative. The Narcotics Division was reorganized and reduced in size by about a third, consequently producing about 20 percent fewer narcotics arrests. Then the city's fiscal crisis hit in 1977, resulting in five thousand police layoffs and cutbacks in other essential city services. (In response to New York's "fun city" advertising campaign, police handed out "Welcome to Fear City" flyers at transportation hubs.) The massive firings affected minority officers disproportionately as they had the least seniority, which harmed efforts to penetrate drug-selling networks. Officers were unavailable to appear in court as the city limited overtime pay, and laid-off officers refused to return to court to testify against defendants. Police resources and morale fell to a new low just as New York's heroin supplies were being replenished.[7]

New York's changing legal climate also affected the organization of the drug trade. The passage of the Rockefeller drug law in 1973, which presaged much tougher legislation nationwide, placed heroin selling in the same felony class as first- and second-degree murder and had consequences far beyond those Governor Rockefeller intended. Adults, in order to avoid the stringent mandatory minimum sentences imposed by the law, hired adolescents, who continued to be sent to juvenile court, to handle street-level sales. One youngster claimed, "I started cutting dope on the kitchen table of my family's apartment when I was 13. I was getting $150 a day, so I stopped going to school. The same man who had me cutting dope for him asked if I'd like to work the streets. In no time I was making $500 to $600 a day selling dope." Stories about fourteen-year-olds driving Cadillacs and shooting hoops for $500 a basket may have been apocryphal, but young people took over street level sales to an unprecedented degree. The Rockefeller law began the "juvenalization" of drug trading, which became even more apparent in the 1980s with the rise of the crack cocaine market. Heroin availability was the one thing the new law did not affect, and in some sections of New York, according to police, it was easier to buy heroin than "to pick up a loaf of bread."[8]

The mandatory sentences included in the Rockefeller law backfired in another way: they produced a logjam in the courts that ultimately resulted in fewer convictions. An analysis by the New York Bar Association revealed that more defendants insisted on going to trial than before the law was enacted. Faced with mandatory penalties if they pled guilty, defendants believed they risked very little by going before a jury, and as a result the whole criminal justice process slowed to a crawl. The courts and the jails became so overcrowded that by the end of the 1970s defendants were back on the streets within hours of arrest, and they could plan on delays and continuations of their cases that postponed any reckoning with justice almost indefinitely as the state system teetered on collapse.[9]

Housing abandonment, which had begun during the late 1960s and accelerated in the following decade, created a landscape that provided perfect shelter for the drug trade. Landlords walked away from their properties; neighborhoods in the South Bronx, Harlem, and the Lower East Side were particularly hard hit. One man returned to Harlem in 1977 after thirteen years in prison and was struck by the remarkable deterioration of his neighborhood. His mother's apartment was on Seventh Avenue, once one of the premier uptown streets on which to live, but as Teddy returned home he saw boarded-up stores and abandoned buildings. "Harlem wasn't Harlem any more," he concluded. Despite the fact that it was summertime, few people were out on the street: "It was almost like a ghost town." The vacant tenements and wrecked buildings offered hiding places for the drug trade. Looking out at the desolate landscape the morning after returning home, the first thing Teddy saw was "a guy out there selling dope."[10]

There were more "guys selling dope" from a variety of sources than ever before. The appearance of Mexican heroin in New York represented a democratization of wholesale drug dealing that was occurring across the nation. As long as Turkish heroin was shipped through New York, New York dominated the national market and the city's Italian and Jewish gangsters organized a centralized and hierarchical distribution system. With traditional European supply routes disrupted, African Americans, Cubans, and Puerto Ricans seized a market opportunity to introduce new sources of heroin from Mexico, Latin America, and Southeast Asia and to import large quantities of cocaine into the United States for the first time. Puerto Rican drug dealers from New York established links to Mexican American heroin traffickers in Chicago, and they were among the first to bring Mexican heroin into the city. African American gangsters forged alliances with Latinos and others to gain access to new supplies. The notorious African American heroin dealer Frank Matthews worked with Cubans to import cocaine and eventually heroin through Latin America and Jamaica, while Frank Lucas entered the heroin importing business by enlisting ex-servicemen to ship heroin home from Southeast Asia in the coffins of dead soldiers. As minority entrepreneurs established new heroin supply lines, they ended the traditional monopoly whites had on the wholesale heroin trade.[11]

Just as new sources of heroin appeared, an old one returned. Turkey decided to resume opium cultivation in 1974 as the Turkish government responded to political opposition from well-connected opium cultivators and to the failure of the United States to continue massive crop subsidies. While this did not have an immediate effect, it promised a surplus of high-quality heroin in the future. With Turkey resuming opium cultivation, new heroin supplies from Mexico, Latin America, and Southeast Asia available, new dealing networks established, and Latin American cocaine appearing on the market in larger quantities, the drug marketplace was transformed from a place of scarcity in 1972 to one offering a cornucopia of mind-altering substances five years later.

The appearance of open-air drug markets in New York testified to the decline of a controlled market. Open street sales occurred in several parts of the city, but Harlem and the Lower East Side were two of the largest marketplaces, where drug retailers competed for customers in an open fashion that shocked public officials. The area around 116th Street and Eighth Avenue in Harlem was like a bazaar, with dealers standing on the street corners calling out the names of their products. It was, in the words of Manhattan Borough President Percy Sutton, "just as though they were hawking fish from a fish wagon." Shouts of "Star Trek," "Jaws," and "Malcolm's Gold" filled the air, suggesting both the dealers' sense of humor and attention to popular culture in their efforts to gain customer loyalty to particular brands. A dealer explained that he labeled his drugs so that "the people would know who they were copping from. Like if I had red tape on my bags they'd know it was my dope and that my dope was good dope. So they'd come up and say, 'Got the RED TAPE?" As one law enforcement official explained, "They're doing everything but advertising on television."[12]

The Lower East Side surpassed even Harlem as a retail drug market in the 1970s, as its proximity to transportation routes and landscape of devastation stimulated ever larger numbers of drug users and traders. "Alphabetville," an area of approximately fifty square blocks located near the major tunnels and bridges into Manhattan, was in the words of the police "the retail drug capital of the world." Over three hundred abandoned buildings dotted the neighborhood and steerers flagged down motorists on the street, called out the names of their product, and directed buyers to buildings that had been transformed into heroin and cocaine retailing fortresses. Guard dogs, steel-reinforced doors, and lookouts posted on roofs defended the territory. Sometimes a buyer would place money into a pail that had been lowered from an upper story, which would be returned to the waiting customer with the appropriate order of drugs. At other spots, buyers waited on line along several flights of candle-lit stairs in abandoned buildings, and when they reached the right apartment, they handed their money through a slot in a steel door and received their drugs in return. Lookouts at the door watched for police and played red light, green light with departing customers, signaling if they should wait or if the coast was clear. Although precautions were taken, accounts from the period suggest the virtual absence of police. For example, in the morning users would get in line, as if waiting for their morning coffee and a doughnut at a local bakery: "You would see people lined up . . . in a line fifty feet deep—with people that sold the dope running up and down the line saying, 'Have your money ready, we'll be open in ten minutes.'"[13]

The open-air drug markets signaled the emergence of a third wave of heroin use in the United States that was formed by a combination of returning users and young initiators. Some increase in heroin use might have been expected, as new supplies meant that individuals who had taken refuge in methadone programs during the heroin drought were now able to obtain their preferred drug. Casual users returned to heroin after a period of abstinence because better supply meant that they would not be wasting their money on baking soda or risking their lives on some potentially toxic substitute being sold as heroin. And there were new initiators, as a report to New York Governor Hugh Carey made clear: by the early 1980s the number of heroin users had increased by 50 percent over what it had been a decade earlier.[14] The third wave of heroin users remained centralized in inner-city neighborhoods, but like the second wave of the 1960s, it included middle-class whites who moved to these neighborhoods, particularly the Lower East Side.[15] While this group formed an eddy among heroin users, they made up for their number with their cultural significance as the progenitors of punk music and culture.

The association among heroin, music, and place that appeared so often in American society in the decades after World War II reappeared with punk on the Lower East Side. The world of punk was shaped by the Lower East Side, with its portent of collapse, its hint of anarchy, its obvious misery in one of the nation's wealthiest cities, and its collection of burned-out buildings and open-air drug markets. Punk's roots were entangled with those of the Lower East Side, not because most of the musicians or its audience originated there (most were suburbanites or, like the Ramones, from the more suburban outer boroughs of New York City), but because it was the antithesis of the suburbs, the home of the clubs, the Ur source of punk culture, the site to which the suburbanites fled and punk musicians from around the nation flocked.[16] Its clubs and bars mixed musicians, fans, heroin users, and heroin sellers much in the same way that the jazz clubs of the 1940s and the Greenwich Village coffeehouses of the 1960s had, with the same result. That social setting, the heroin consumed in it, and the choices made by the largely white, middle-class youths who participated in the punk scene reverberated among alienated young people across the country. Those who wished to flirt with the dark side headed for the Lower East Side.

Three clubs in particular were the incubators of American punk music and culture. The venerable Max's Kansas City, CBGB, and the Mudd Club fostered the careers of punk musicians and underground artists, and functioned secondarily as sites for the sale and consumption of drugs. The clubs existed for those who consumed life at night, and they established alcohol, cocaine, heroin, and Quaaludes as an integral part of punk music making and lifestyle.[17]

Max's Kansas City missed the first stirrings of punk music, but it provided a link between Andy Warhol and the Velvet Underground and punk. Warhol and the Velvets pioneered the style of cross-dressing, sado-masochism, and drug use developed by punk musicians, and Max's served as the hub of social life for Warhol's superstars, models, musicians, and artists, who overlapped with the beginnings of punk. The famous back room at Max's was reserved for the hip, and sex and drug use were all part of it: Warhol star Edie Sedgwick could be found "sitting there with her head down, nodding at the table with Jim Morrison," the heroin-using lead singer for the Doors.[18] Max's turned into a punk club after it was sold in 1975, a natural evolution in keeping with its genealogy as the social center for the lower Manhattan bohemian set.

CBGB-OMFUG—Country, Blue Grass and Blues and Other Music for Uplifting Gormandizers—a name that did not reflect the music for which it became known, was the first and most famous of the original punk clubs. Hilly Kristal opened the club in 1973 on the Bowery, a street better known for drunks and flophouses. CBGB consisted of a long, narrow room with the bar at one end and the stage in the middle, and it reeked from stale beer and the constantly clogged toilets.[19]

Although the building in which the bar was located also housed a twenty-five-cents-a-night flophouse, by the 1970s heroin was taking over from alcohol even on the Bowery. One neighborhood observer commented on the proliferation of abandoned buildings that had been turned into heroin shooting galleries. It was a "dangerous place" for white suburban kids to hang out, but he added, the area "also had the cheapest apartments in the city—which made it a haven for starving rock musicians, many of whom began congregating at CBGB." David Byrne of the Talking Heads recalled that many of the musicians shared loft spaces near one another, and that Allen Ginsburg and William Burroughs lived nearby "and their attitudes toward life and art were part of the mystique of the area." Each morning outside of CBGB "there were empty envelopes marked with the logos of the various 'brands' [of heroin] all over the sidewalk." CBGB had been a neighborhood biker bar, and Kristal was searching for a new identity and audience for it. Punk musicians provided both while finding in CBGB one of the few available venues in which they could perform for an audience.[20]

The Mudd Club, which opened in 1979, served as the third major center for punk music. Filmmakers, painters, performance artists, graffitists, and musicians mingled there, and it attracted uptown elites out for a night of bohemian slumming. Like Max's and CBGB's, the Mudd Club was also a place to score drugs. "It very quickly became a drug club," recalled Carmel Johnson-Schmidt, an early regular. "A lot of down drugs were being used—heroin, Quaaludes."[21] The "down" drugs—heroin and depressants such as Quaaludes—fit both the social setting of the Lower East Side and the mood reflected in punk music and culture.

Punk style was fashioned out of the detritus of modern society: torn t-shirts and ripped jeans, fastened together with safety pins, assemblages of old styles reimagined, Nazi regalia, iron crosses, bondage gear, dog collars, and leather straps, which represented the plundering of the modern world's dark recesses. Punk style was designed to shock and disturb, and it succeeded. Steve Mass, who went on to found the Mudd Club, thought at first that punks "looked like some underground species that had survived a nuclear holocaust," while Deborah Spungen, the mother of soon-to-be-murdered Sex Pistols groupie Nancy Spungen, thought they resembled "futuristic Nazi stormtroopers."[22] Punk style accessorized the twentieth century's worst nightmares, and it fit right into the nightmarish landscape of lower Manhattan.

Punk music, like punk style, expressed a fundamental nihilism. The British punk group the Sex Pistols announced modernity's collapse in "God Save the Queen." Issued in time for the official celebration of Queen Elizabeth II's Silver Jubilee, the song was banned from British airwaves because of its seditious equation of the Queen's rule with a "fascist regime." However subversive the song seemed to British authorities, its broader cultural significance lay in its proclamation (and repeated refrain) that there was no future, "no future for you," which resonated with youth on both sides of the Atlantic and which captured the essence of punk culture.[23]

American punk music, while less overtly political than its British counterpart, espoused similar nihilistic themes in songs such as Television's "Blank Generation." Regular performances of punk music began at CBGB with

Television, a group that featured Richard Hell (Richard Meyers) and Tom Verlaine (Tom Miller), who met in a reform school in Delaware and moved to New York to find their way in the art scene. Together they formed the Neon Boys, which morphed into Television; it was Television for whom Richard Hell wrote one of his best-known songs, "Blank Generation."

"Blank Generation" captures punk's post-hippie, nihilistic worldview ("I belong to the blank generation and/I can take it or leave it each time"), and the lyrics (as well as the diaries of the lyricist) suggest heroin's attraction for punk artists and their followers. The song echoes the cry of an aimless generation that is indifferent to its future, or believed it had no future at all. In reflecting on the source of his music in his "heroin notebook," Hell wrote that he had decided to give up playing rock and roll. "I was killing myself with drugs and despair and cheap arrogance. All my songs came from hopelessness and that doesn't supply much fuel." "Blank Generation" reflected that hopelessness as well as a broader cultural malaise found in the United States in the late 1970s (proclaimed on national television by President Jimmy Carter).[24]

For members of a blank generation, heroin was the perfect drug. It offered a glorious oblivion, what Anne Marlowe called an erasure of time, in which only the present counted and the eventual cost of heroin use was irrelevant. Carmel Johnson-Schmidt recalled: "There seemed to be a definite fear of the future. People gave up on planning things. It was all for that moment, that night." Heroin supplied a sense of urgency for an aimless life, a reason to get up in the morning, dictated by the need to score, and that immediacy was enough. Richard Hell, in a comment similar to ones found in memoirs by other middle-class users suffering from boredom and existential angst, wrote: "Heroin allows—insists—that all your theoretical problems are reduced to/replaced by a simple question of logistics: how to cop today. Every day there's always some way to get that sixty dollars and someone to give it to." Heroin, even if it did not offer meaning, at least provided a way of organizing a life.[25]

Heroin had the twin allures of danger ("the danger was part of the thrill") and of being the drug used by punk heroes such as William Burroughs and Lou Reed. "I went through a period of brotherhood with the pageant of historical addicts," Hell wrote. Flirting with addiction, while experiencing the thrill of scoring and using, made heroin attractive. Anne Marlowe writes of "choosing" addiction ("once you realize addiction is out there, you have to try it"), of chasing after it and testing the limits of will while still trying to avoid becoming a junkie. Choosing heroin was part of organizing an alternative way of life, one inhabited only by a special few: Richard Hell described heroin in much the same way that aspiring jazz artists did in the 1940s, as offering a means of entrée into a sacred circle that had knowledge denied to ordinary people. Heroin was an essential part of a nihilistic bohemianism, of living underground, of choosing to be marginal, all of which were integral to punk culture and the social setting of the Lower East Side.[26]

Not surprisingly, heroin contributed as much to the ultimate collapse of the punk scene as to its rise. There were a number of reasons for the decline of punk external to drug use: punk style became commodified quickly, with photo spreads in *Vogue* and pre-torn shirts sold in Bloomingdale's, so that by the early 1980s the sense of being avant-garde had already passed. Art galleries opened that were devoted to graffitists and punk artists, tourists found CBGB and other punk hangouts, and commercialization promised to change the character of the Lower East Side. Loft living was becoming chic and capital was being reinvested in areas that had long been denied funds; the arrival of artists and an art market signaled the first stirrings of gentrification. As the Lower East Side changed and punk flamed out, so did many of its brightest lights. Observers attributed their demise to heroin. "Heroin addiction had taken the heaviest toll. A few artists continued to celebrate the junk lifestyle, but it was increasingly viewed as a downwardly mobile dead-end." The appearance of HIV/AIDS proved to be the ultimate dead end for heroin injectors and finally diminished some of bohemia's romance with heroin.[27] As had occurred with previous waves of heroin use, this one crested and receded, and by the mid-1980s had left behind a group of steady users around whom future waves could form, as more casual users moved on.

Even if bohemians were less inclined to experiment with heroin, they and other Americans did not suddenly become abstemious. The third wave of heroin initiation included experimentation with cocaine, which gradually eclipsed heroin in importance. A report in the *New York Times* concluded, "Supplies of heroin and cocaine have grown so plentiful in the New York City area that drug experts see a dissolving of the traditional lines between people who use the two drugs as well as people who sell them."[28] Not only in New York, but also in cities across the country, cocaine and crack assumed increased salience in the drug marketplace of the 1980s.

Cocaine had long been a rich person's drug, but this changed as drug entrepreneurs transported cocaine along with heroin from the Caribbean and Latin America into the United States. Over time rival Colombian cartels produced too much cocaine, and oversupply and competition drove down the price in the American market. As a result, ordinary heroin users injected a mix of heroin and cocaine (speedballs), a drug cocktail that had once been limited to high-end drug users such as successful rock musicians and movie stars. Others too found cocaine suddenly affordable: African Americans and whites, middle class and poor, countercultural gurus and Wall Street capitalists, Hollywood stars, and even White House aides thought cocaine was an enjoyable drug, which they believed to be nonaddictive. Bejeweled coke spoons and diamond-encrusted razor blades were the accoutrements of the stars, but cocaine use spread across the class structure. It became part of American recreational life more than any other illegal drug except for marijuana, reaching a high point in 1980 when nearly 20 percent of eighteen- to twenty-five-year-olds reported that they had tried cocaine in the previous year. Despite the increase in cocaine use, medical experts did not believe there was much potential for an addiction problem, since most users sniffed the drug occasionally. However, physicians warned that a change in the means of ingestion might prove more problematical. This caution proved accurate as the venturesome experimented with freebasing, a volatile process of mixing cocaine with another chemical, usually highly flammable ether, heating it, and then reducing the residue to a crystallized alkaline form that could be smoked, generally with a water pipe. These home chemistry experiments could literally go up in flames, but freebasing produced such a powerful and nearly instantaneous high that some users were willing to take the risk. Experts believed that if freebase were to be more widely available, then the nature of the cocaine problem would change dramatically.[29]

Crack cocaine became the means for that change. The genius of crack cocaine was that it was a prepackaged form of freebase that delivered the punch without the problem of potential self-immolation, and did so at a fraction of the cost of powdered cocaine.

Crack turned cocaine into a real mass-market commodity, what one scholar has called the "fast food of drugs," and its use spiked, especially in poor communities, between 1982 and 1984. In creating crack, dealers were responding to the demand for smokable cocaine, but in the process they solved the problem caused by oversupply. By mixing cocaine with water and baking soda (rather than ether) and heating the mixture until the water evaporated, dealers produced a hard, rock-like substance called crack from the sound that it made when heated. Crack had the advantage of being still more affordable and yet more potent than powdered cocaine and easier to consume than freebase. Dealers made their money by selling crack in smaller units ("rocks"), usually in five- or ten-dollar vials, that brought it into the price range of the poor. Since it was smoked, crack produced an intense, but short-lived, high that left a user thirsting for more. Crack was more insidious than snorted or even injected cocaine, and dealers could count on repeat business that more than made up for the decline in unit pricing.

Prolonged consumption of crack had far more deleterious consequences for users and communities than other forms of ingesting cocaine (or, for that matter, snorting or injecting heroin). Addicts went on binges that lasted several days, depriving themselves of food or rest until the lack of funds or physical exhaustion ended the cycle. Women, always subject to sexual abuse on the street, suffered the worst forms of degradation as "strawberries," or crack whores, who traded sex for rocks in crack houses. Violence was a problem both because of the drug's effects (crack was a stimulant and excessive use led to paranoia and hallucinations) and because of dealers' intense competition for market share. Rival "posses" of young men battling over the control of lucrative drug corners drove homicide rates to dizzying new heights during the 1980s as the market spun out of anyone's control.[30]

Perhaps the most significant event was the emergence of the drug trade as a major employer, a form of bootstrap capitalism, in which entrepreneurs exploited themselves and their neighbors as crack use rippled through inner-city neighborhoods. The open-air heroin markets of the 1970s with their posses of adolescent sellers had been building toward this moment, but crack cocaine opened even more opportunities. In an era of massive deindustrialization, crack dealers offered the opportunity for employment by opening retail spots that each employed crews of a half dozen or more teenagers who worked in shifts around the clock under the supervision of an older crew boss. A good location, such as near a public housing complex, might support several drug retailing spots in a single city block. Analyses of drug workers' earnings show that these were underground (and dangerous) versions of "McJobs," with only the higher-ups earning any real money while workers frequently spent their wages on their own drug consumption. The consequences of working in the drug trade included dropping out of school, acquiring an arrest record, perhaps becoming habituated to drug use, and finding oneself ever more distant from legitimate society.[31]

Heroin remained a part of this new marketplace (and its "return" was announced somewhat misleadingly several times by the media). Long-time heroin users continued to buy heroin, and some previous heroin users returned to the drug even if they continued to smoke crack or ingest cocaine. Because crack cocaine burned out its users, some crack smokers began taking heroin as a relief from crack's overstimulation. The appearance of additional supplies of heroin from Southwest Asia, chiefly Afghanistan and Pakistan, and from Colombia, where cocaine exporters readily adapted to the changing tastes of the American market, meant greater purity and continued lower prices for heroin.[32]

Purity mattered because it changed the form of ingestion. New users sniffed or smoked heroin ("chased the dragon") instead of injecting it, escaping both the danger and the stigma of intravenous drug use in an era of HIV and AIDS. By the mid-1990s, "heroin chic" models and depressed Seattle musicians graced the covers of entertainment magazines and filled national news outlets with stories of their addiction. Because they were white and middle-class, the media paid attention, announcing that heroin was back.[33] Of course in the poorest neighborhoods in the nation's largest cities, it had never left.

Despite fluctuations in the market and in public attention, the classical period of heroin use in the United States ended in the mid-1980s. The rise of crack cocaine and the collapse of the centralized heroin distribution system organized by New York signaled the arrival of a new era. The prevalence of polydrug use and the spread of cocaine in its different variations reduced heroin to only one of several drugs available to be abused, while the transportation routes opened by African Americans and Latinos provided many different entry points into the American market. While the "golden age" of heroin had ended, the glass pipe ensured that inner-city drug markets continued to flourish.

CONCLUSION

Heroin Markets Redux

I BEGAN THIS project with several questions but few convictions. I wanted to understand what was urban about heroin, what explained the demographic transitions in heroin use, how heroin affected the communities in which its use was concentrated, and how the heroin market worked. I had no particular policy agenda in mind.

In the course of my research, I discovered that the market linked the answers to my questions. The market explained both the creation of neighborhoods that concentrated economic and social marginality, which continuously produced heroin use, and the distribution of heroin by a hierarchy of cities organized by New York. New York's geographic and entrepreneurial advantages meant that it became the most important marketing center for heroin in the United States even before World War II. Because New York was home to pharmaceutical companies that made heroin legally, it also became the first city in which heroin, rather than morphine, was the primary drug of abuse. These historic factors concentrated a heroin-using population in New York City so that much of the drug imported into the United States was used there, and because heroin was cheaper and purer in New York than elsewhere in the country, heroin users moved to the city. Through these self-reinforcing processes, New York City became the urban center that directed the heroin market both nationally and internationally.

At the same time, the migration of African Americans and Puerto Ricans to segregated Northern city neighborhoods in the decades after World War II provided an opportunity for market expansion. Young men in particular expressed their resistance to the color line in the postwar city by adopting a "cool cat" persona in which heroin was the embodiment of a disdainful detachment from the world of working people. In the jazz and after-hours clubs of the postwar city, heroin users, hustlers, musicians, and young people shared a style that evolved around heroin, and its use gradually seeped into nearby neighborhoods.

The concentration of heroin users over time not only marked particular neighborhoods as heroin retail centers, but also ensured that drug knowledge would be available to youths residing there, which helped replenish the supply of both drug users and sellers. While only a minority of youths began taking heroin and community organizations worked tirelessly to find treatment opportunities and prevent young people from starting, heroin users drove up crime rates and made life for the majority of the area's population increasingly difficult. The accelerating abandonment of inner-city neighborhoods beginning in the late 1960s ensured the creation of landscapes that facilitated the drug trade. Treatment options for addicts remained few and largely ineffective until the advent of methadone, but even this was controversial. Methadone maintenance was predicated on the assumption that large numbers of clients would remain on methadone for years, perhaps for the rest of their lives, while the "orange handcuffs" tethered them to clinics that were usually located in poor neighborhoods and that etched a process of addiction, treatment, and recovery further into the urban landscape.

As young whites came to share a sense of alienation from American life, and more important, moved into city neighborhoods with a history of drug experimentation, they too began to use heroin, especially once they realized that much of what they had learned about drugs, especially marijuana, was either inaccurate or propaganda. Antidrug campaigns were usually highly misleading both in terms of the information they disseminated and, when they discussed heroin, in focusing on middle-class white youths even in the face of evidence that they were a small minority of users. The moral panics that followed from these campaigns (as well as from governmental investigations into heroin use) resulted in the passage of ever more draconian legislation that succeeded in incarcerating heroin users while leaving both the major traffickers and the actual sources of heroin use untouched. By focusing on users rather than on the production of use, American drug policy has been a self-perpetuating failure.

Much has changed in the past thirty years. The cultural forms associated with heroin; the ways in which heroin is ingested; the class, racial, and gender composition of heroin users; the growing importance of cities other than

New York in the distribution of drugs; the emergence of new countries as the sources for them; and the appearance of drugs such as OxyContin and methamphetamines, which affect rural areas in a way that heroin use never did and which are a reflection of these areas' increasing marginalization in a globalized and urbanized world. Two essential things, however, have remained the same: heroin is still a desired drug, and heroin markets are still located in poor communities. Demand remains at the root of the drug trade, and as long as that demand is unabated, market forces will create a supply, and the geography of disadvantage means that supply will meet demand in the inner-city marketplace.

When I began this project, I had few convictions about public policy regarding heroin. Should heroin use be legalized? I could see compelling arguments on both sides of the issue. Was methadone an appropriate form of treatment? It seemed to be effective, but I also understood the objection that long-term methadone maintenance was not a solution to drug use per se, and that tolerating drug use particularly in minority populations ran the risk of saying that being narcotized was acceptable as long as it only affected poor people. Should the state compel its citizens to be drug-free or was this an unwarranted interference with an individual's right to bodily control as long as no one else was harmed? The libertarian stance sounded appealing philosophically, but the potential social costs of this position seemed unclear. And how should I assess the war on drugs? In the international arena, our policy has tried to eliminate the production of opium, while in the United States it has tried to control the individual drug user. Neither facet of the war on drugs has worked particularly well, as opium production continues to spread and mass incarceration does little to deter drug use. As a historian I am hesitant to venture deeply into public-policy waters, at least in part because it is humbling to see how often policy-makers' actions have had unintended and sometimes disastrous consequences. Nonetheless, working on this topic has led me to some conclusions about policy.

Let's start with the international focus of the war on drugs. For ten dollars I can buy a bag of approximately 70 percent pure heroin at a number of drug-selling spots in North Philadelphia's "Badlands."[1] In the mid-1960s, that ten-dollar bag might have been 5 to 10 percent heroin, with the balance made up of different adulterants. After forty years of a war on drugs that has focused on controlling the foreign sources of supply, heroin has become cheaper, purer, and available from a larger number of countries than before.

Supply control is simply not an effective policy. As I have argued, there are too many marginal areas and too much political instability in the world to expect international protocols to limit opium production. Shifts in opium growing from the Golden Crescent to the Golden Triangle—and more recently to Latin America and back to Afghanistan—suggest the futility of pursuing a supply-side policy. Again and again different producers have entered the world market in response to the economic opportunity offered by consumers in the United States (and increasingly in Europe as well).

Americans consume vast amounts of licit and illicit drugs, and the organizing power of this market is visible throughout remote areas of the globe where peasant farmers see their illicit crops as the only opportunity to participate in a market economy. Political conflict, poverty, and a legacy of colonialism and economic underdevelopment—marginality—have left these areas without effective states and have sometimes opened the door for warlords or guerillas to use illicit commodities to fund civil war. One long-term goal for American policy should be the economic, political, and social integration of these otherwise marginal regions of the world. Simply put, peace and prosperity are inherently good and are clearly in everyone's best interest, even if these are distant and somewhat utopian objectives. However, the only real solution to the drug problem lies at home—in changing the market by reducing the demand for drugs.

The concept of marginality is key to understanding the size and shape of the domestic heroin market. Cities have concentrated large populations of marginalized people in central locations, and therefore have long been the organizers of the drug trade. Although patterns of rural and small-town heroin use have persisted and heroin retains a certain allure to the disaffected middle class, I am convinced that any attempt to solve the drug problem in America must begin in the inner city.

The most important task is to change the social setting of those marginalized peoples most prone to sell and use drugs. The best evidence for the importance of social setting is the low relapse rate of heroin-using Vietnam veterans once they returned to the United States. If they could stop using the potent heroin found in Southeast Asia upon a change in their social setting, it is evidence that social setting is at least as important as the operation of opiate receptors in the brain, and that solutions to the problem of drug use are to be found as much in society as in the science of addiction studies. The question is: how does one change the social setting in which most users reside?

This is no easy answer to this question, and before I attempt to address it, I would like to consider the implications of this study for some of our current drug policies, particularly in regard to opiates. The social costs of our domestic war on drugs have been considerable: in the early twentieth century, opium smokers turned to the more dangerous morphine and heroin when the importation of smoking opium was outlawed, while marijuana smokers following the passage of prohibitory legislation created a subculture conducive to the spread of heroin in the postwar years. Laws against carrying drug paraphernalia led to the creation of shooting galleries, which fostered unsafe injection practices, and harsh penalties for drug sales led dealers to use adolescents in the street trade. Prohibitory legislation has repeatedly backfired in ways unanticipated by its framers, and yet the response to failure has been to do more of the same. Again and again legislators have taken advantage of moral panics to support harsher penalties for drug infractions, to shift the balance in public policy further toward enforcement, and to militarize sections of American cities in a war on drugs. Advocates of the war on drugs might argue that without the enormous expenditures of resources, both financial and human, the situation might be worse and inexpensive heroin could be available on every corner in the city. This is not a persuasive argument. The purity and price of the drug indicate that the market is saturated, and a handful of central places, such as Philadelphia's Badlands and similar locales in other American cities, dominate the spatial organization of the heroin market, as they always have. While the sources of the heroin and the faces of the users and sellers have changed, and New York no longer dominates the trade, the billions of dollars spent on the war against drugs have not made much difference on the domestic market. But they have resulted in a mass incarceration of American citizens.

In 1974, near the beginning of the modern war on drugs, there were 216,000 inmates in federal and state prisons in the United States, with an additional quarter of a million in local jails. Since the early 1970s, inspired by New York State's Rockefeller drug legislation, state and federal authorities have adopted increasingly punitive measures. By 2002, the number of state and federal prisoners had reached more than 1.3 million, the total population incarcerated had exceeded 2 million, and, according to the American Bar Association, the United States had the dubious distinction of incarcerating a higher percentage of its population than any other country in the world. The average length of time spent in prison increased from eighteen months to five years even though the majority of people entering prison in the 1980s and

1990s were nonviolent offenders. The annual cost of this mass incarceration is approximately $40 billion.[2]

Our policy of incarcerating drug offenders has disproportionately affected African Americans and Latinos. Some have argued that this is evidence of racial bias in the creation of antinarcotics legislation and in the criminal justice system. While it would be foolish to discount prejudicial handling in the criminal justice system, the incarceration numbers are best explained as a reflection of where drug markets are located. Police focus their resources on market transactions, which, as we have seen, are spatially concentrated in inner-city neighborhoods, rather than on consumption, which is more spatially dispersed and likely to occur in private. Since drug sales do not produce a criminal complainant, only the active intervention of police as undercover agents in the transaction can result in a disruption of the market. In addition, police sweep drug corners in order to assert control, however temporarily, over public space that has been commandeered for the drug trade. Inevitably local sellers and users, often the identical parties, are going to be disproportionately represented in arrests as police concentrate on controlling the marketplace.

Critics of the drug laws often mention that possession of crack cocaine, used more heavily by poor people, is treated more harshly under law than possession of powdered cocaine, which is presumably favored by middle-class whites. These assumptions about use may be well founded, but it is worth remembering that crack has a more immediate and powerful impact on the brain than cocaine that is snorted or injected, which is a reasonable basis for making public policy. That said, the penalties are disproportionate, and more important, legislation against crack cocaine was enacted in one of our panics over drugs—it followed the usual trajectory of mandating longer sentences for dealers and catching mostly low-level dealer-users. The real problem is not in legislation regarding a specific drug but in the overall direction of American drug policy, which is targeted against the users themselves rather than the social setting that produces drug use.

If the war on drugs has failed, unfortunately the policies most frequently posed as alternatives have other, sometimes more serious, problems. Some commentators have taken a libertarian position that what one ingests is a matter of personal choice and the state should not regulate the market. As public policy, this invites a potential social disaster. Advocates of deregulating drugs argue that the black market would be eliminated and that crime rates would drop, but both of these propositions are debatable. More important, access to drugs has correlated positively with their use, thus in an unregulated market, it is likely that access to drugs would increase. It seems like a truism to say that drug use requires access, but it is worth noting that health professionals have had among the highest rates of narcotics use for the simple reason that they have better access to narcotics than any other group. Similarly, as I have noted repeatedly, the act of living near a drug-selling zone puts someone, particularly an adolescent, at a higher risk of using drugs. Access may not equal drug use, but it is a fundamental precondition. It follows that some form of regulation should remain at the heart of social policy.

The argument that deregulation would lower crime rates is suspect. Even in an unregulated market with lower drug prices, drug users would still need to raise income; to the degree that drug users are uneducated, unskilled, and underemployed, they would continue to turn to illegal enterprise. In addition, as Chapter 7 indicates (and most studies concur), criminal involvement begins during adolescence and prior to drug use. Both drug use and crime are symptomatic of ailing, marginalized urban communities, and their causation is interrelated. There is no reason to believe that simply deregulating drug markets without addressing more deep-rooted problems would lower crime rates.

As soon as a market is regulated, it invites the creation of a black market. To the degree that certain groups, such as minors, would continue to be prohibited from using opiates, and that drug sales would be taxed in order to cover the social costs of drug abuse, there would be built-in incentives to continue a black market.

Nor would the legalization of opiates (that is, regulated distribution such as would occur under medical supervision) offer a practical solution to drug dependency. It would not solve the black market issue since only registered and presumably addicted users would have access to supplies, leaving others to procure drugs illegally. Moreover, as seen in the Dole-Nyswander experiment with clinically administered morphine, heroin and morphine are short-acting drugs, users build up tolerance over time, requiring more frequent injections, and users would need to be in proximity to their supply at all hours of the day, curtailing their opportunities to work or have a choice of residence. Efforts to limit doses or to provide a take-home supply would invite the creation of a black market. The history of methadone indicates the problems with a legally supplied narcotic, with diversion and use of other drugs occurring in all but the most carefully controlled clinical settings.

Nonetheless, these trade-offs are worthwhile with methadone, a long-acting and inexpensive drug that allows motivated former heroin users to hold jobs and maintain families. Legalized heroin and morphine do not promise similar benefits.

Harm reduction is a modest policy that makes sense. Some individuals will resist all efforts to prevent them from using drugs, therefore minimizing the harmful effects of drug taking is as important as continuing to limit access to drugs. Needle exchanges, for example, inhibit the transmission of HIV and hepatitis from one user to another, and most political jurisdictions have finally recognized their public health value. Surely policies that prevent the transmission of deadly diseases and provide for a chemical dependency (such as methadone) that allows users to work and lead relatively "normal" lives are preferable to policies that promote the reverse. In general, treating drug abuse as more of a public health than a criminal justice matter is a step in the right direction. (It is worth recalling that in President Nixon's initial war on drugs, slightly more than half of the budget was allocated to treatment while in subsequent administrations the treatment proportion has fallen to about one-third.)[3] Reducing penalties for drug possession, sending nonviolent drug offenders to drug courts, and establishing mandatory treatment plans, in the context of expanding treatment more generally are all appropriate steps to take. However, we should recognize that harm reduction and treatment are only dealing with symptoms. The real problem is the social setting of the inner city that produces drug abuse.

Perhaps the most difficult and important issue to face is that drug trafficking has become the free market's answer to deindustrialization, and any antidrug policy must come to terms with the market. This is not the place to discuss globalization and the export of manufacturing jobs to other locations; suffice it to say that the benefits of globalization are distributed unevenly, with urban manufacturing zones stripped of the assets and jobs that once sustained working-class communities. No drug policy will be successful without confronting the fact that the drug economy is a form of economic enterprise that has evolved over time and has become increasingly prominent as other sources of employment have disappeared. Poor people have always been resourceful in using barter and pooling money from jobs, welfare, and the underground economy in order to survive, but the drug economy provides employment on a larger scale than traditional ghetto hustles. If we are dissatisfied with the form of economic organization supplied by the market, then we must be prepared to intervene and offer alternatives.

There is a relationship between work and social discipline that inhibits deviance. Historians of violence have long argued that industrialization reduced the high levels of violence that characterized the preindustrial era by keeping workers steadily at their tasks and limiting access to alcohol. Studies of controlled heroin use have emphasized the importance of routine, such as that imposed by regular work, in keeping drug use from spiraling out of control.[4] Conversely, as we have seen, musicians, artists, the very wealthy, and, of course, the very poor are either exempted from the daily discipline of work, are employed irregularly, or are in positions that valorize drug and alcohol use, and all of these groups are susceptible to uncontrolled drug consumption. Regular work is the antidote to unbridled excess, but what happens, to use William Julius Wilson's phrase, when work disappears?[5] Should municipal, state, and federal governments serve as employers of last resort?

To me the answer is an unequivocal yes. This would require a reversal of current social policy, it would take a number of years to effect substantive change, and it would have to be combined with the individually oriented criminal justice reforms and harm reduction policies outlined above in order to reduce the demand for drugs. But let me make an argument in its favor. Virtually anyone who has driven on a highway, seen crumbling, overcrowded inner-city public schools, used public transportation, visited the emergency room in an urban hospital, or witnessed housing costs in downtown markets price out working families can recognize the need for improving public infrastructure, making human capital investments, and creating publicly supported housing. A combination of public and private ventures could address these needs and supply incentives for work and family formation, which have historically reduced crime, deviant behavior, and violence. Transforming the inner-city landscape, creating jobs, and investing in education are not particularly radical proposals and are well within our capacity to accomplish. If targeted appropriately, they would change the social setting of the urban poor.

The alternative is to do more of what we have been doing, to incarcerate rather than employ, to punish rather than educate, to spend enormous sums of money dealing with the consequences of drug abuse rather than preventing it. In the absence of change, the social setting of concentrated poverty and social marginality will continue to produce drug users and sellers as it has over the past seventy years. I cannot see how this is acceptable.

NOTES

INTRODUCTION

1. Stewart Alsop, "The Smell of Death," *Newsweek*, February 1, 1971; "The City Disease," *Newsweek*, February 28, 1972; and "The Road to Hell," *Newsweek*, March 6, 1972.

2. Richard M. Nixon, "Special Message to the Congress on Control of Narcotics and Dangerous Drugs," July 14, 1969, *Public Papers of the Presidents of the United States, Richard Nixon 1969* (Washington, D.C.: U.S. Government Printing Office, 1971), pp. 513–18.

3. "Remarks About an Intensified Program for Drug Abuse Prevention and Control" and "Special Message to the Congress on Drug Abuse Prevention and Control," June 17, 1971, *Public Papers, Richard Nixon 1971*, pp. 738–49; "Remarks During a Visit to New York City to Review Drug Abuse Law Enforcement Activities," March 20, 1972, *Public Papers, Richard Nixon 1972*, pp. 449–50.

4. Howard S. Becker, "Becoming a Marijuana User," in idem, *Outsiders: Studies in the Sociology of Deviance* (New York: The Free Press, 1963).

5. Norman E. Zinberg, *Drug, Set, and Setting: The Basis for Controlled Intoxicant Use* (New Haven: Yale University Press, 1984).

6. David F. Musto, *The American Disease: Origins of Narcotic Control,* 2nd edition (New York: Oxford University Press, 1987); David F. Musto and Pamela Korsmeyer, *The Quest for Drug Control: Politics and Federal Policy in a Period of Increasing Substance Abuse, 1963–1981* (New Haven: Yale University Press, 2002); William B. McAllister, *Drug Diplomacy in the Twentieth Century: An International History* (London: Routledge, 2001); Alfred W. McCoy, *The Politics of Heroin: CIA Complicity in the Global Drug Trade,* rev. ed. (New York: Lawrence Hill Books, 1991); William O. Walker III, *Drug Control in the Americas* (Albuquerque: University of New Mexico Press, 1981); Martin Booth, *Opium: A History* (New York: St. Martin's Press, 1996); Kathryn Meyer and Terry Parssinen, *Webs of Smoke: Smugglers, Warlords, Spies, and the History of the International Drug Trade* (Lanham, Md.: Rowman and Littlefield, 1998).

7. David T. Courtwright, *Dark Paradise: Opiate Addiction in America before 1940* (Cambridge: Harvard University Press, 1982); Caroline Jean Acker, *Creating the American*

Junkie: Addiction Research in the Classic Era of Narcotic Control (Baltimore: Johns Hopkins University Press, 2002); Joseph F. Spillane, *Cocaine: From Medical Marvel to Modern Menace in the United States, 1884–1920* (Baltimore: Johns Hopkins University Press, 2000).

8. Rod A. Janzen, *The Rise and Fall of Synanon: A California Utopia* (Baltimore: Johns Hopkins University Press, 2001); John C. McWilliams, *The Protectors: Harry J. Anslinger and the Federal Bureau of Narcotics, 1930–1962* (Cranberry, N.J.: Associated University Presses, 1990); Nancy Duff Campbell, *Using Women: Gender, Drug Policy, and Social Justice* (New York: Routledge, 2000); Jill Jonnes, *Hep-Cats, Narcs, and Pipe Dreams: A History of America's Romance with Illegal Drugs* (New York: Scribner's, 1996); H. Wayne Morgan, *Drugs in America: A Social History, 1800–1980* (Syracuse: Syracuse University Press, 1981).

9. Isidor Chein, *Road to H: Narcotics, Delinquency, and Social Policy* (New York: Basic Books, 1964); Harold Finestone, "Cats, Kicks, and Color," *Social Problems* 5 (July 1957): 3–13; Richard A. Cloward and Lloyd Ohlin, *Delinquency and Opportunity: A Theory of Delinquent Gangs* (New York: Free Press, 1959); P. H. Hughes, *Behind the Wall of Respect: Community Experiments in Heroin Addiction Control* (Chicago: University of Chicago Press, 1977). For a more recent restatement of this work, Elliott Currie, *Reckoning: Drugs, the Cities, and the American Future* (New York: Hill and Wang, 1993).

10. Stanley Cohen, *Folk Devils and Moral Panics: The Creation of the Mods and Rockers* (New York: St. Martin's Press, 1980).

CHAPTER I. NEW YORK AND THE GLOBAL MARKET

1. I am not positing a strict central place model here, only noting the importance of urban hierarchies for understanding the distribution of illegal goods and services both within and among cities. For a summary of central place theory, see Leslie J. King, *Central Place Theory* (Beverly Hills, Calif.: Sage, 1984).

2. Martin Booth, *Opium: A History* (New York: St. Martin's Press, 1996), pp. 1–14; Newsday, *The Opium Trail* (New York: New American Library, 1974), pp. 12–15; Alvin Moscow, *Merchants of Heroin: An In-Depth Portrayal of Business in the Underworld* (New York: Dial Press, 1968), pp. 20–24.

3. Carl A. Trocki, *Opium, Empire and the Global Political Economy: A Study of the Asian Opium Trade, 1750–1950* (London: Routledge, 1999), pp. 35–37; John M. Jennings, *The Opium Empire: Japanese Imperialism and Drug Trafficking in Asia, 1895–1945* (Westport, Conn.: Praeger, 1997), pp. 18–19; William O. Walker III, *Opium and Foreign Policy: The Anglo-American Search for Order in Asia, 1912–1954* (Chapel Hill: University of North Carolina Press, 1991), pp. 3–9; Zheng Yangwen, *The Social Life of Opium in China* (Cambridge: Cambridge University Press, 2005); Booth, *Opium*, pp. 144–46; David T. Courtwright, *Forces of Habit: Drugs and the Making of the Modern World* (Cambridge: Harvard University Press, 2001).

4. Trocki, *Opium Empire*, pp. 142–49, 156; Courtwright, *Forces of Habit*, pp. 35–36; David T. Courtwright, *Violent Land: Single Men and Social Disorder from the Frontier to*

the Inner City (Cambridge: Harvard University Press, 1996), pp. 165–68; Ivan Light, "From Vice District to Tourist Attraction: The Moral Career of American Chinatowns," *Pacific Historical Review* 43, no. 8 (1974): 367–94; Ivan Light, "The Ethnic Vice Industry, 1880–1944," *American Sociological Review* 42 (June 1977): 464–79; Ramon D. Chacon, "The Beginning of Racial Segregation: The Chinese in West Fresno and Chinatown's Role as a Red Light District, 1870s–1920s," *Southern California Quarterly* 70, no. 4 (1988): 371–98.

5. Quoted in David T. Courtwright, *Dark Paradise: Opiate Addiction in America Before 1940* (Cambridge: Harvard University Press, 1982), p. 77.

6. Catherine Carstairs, *Jailed For Possession: Illegal Drug Use, Regulation, and Power in Canada, 1920–1960* (Toronto: University of Toronto Press, 2006), chapter 1.

7. Courtwright, *Dark Paradise*, p. 110.

8. Courtwright, *Dark Paradise*, chapters 2 and 3.

9. Interviews with Charlie and Jerry, "Addicts Who Survived" Collection, Oral History Center, Columbia University.

10. Courtwright, *Dark Paradise*, pp. 57–58, 78–88; David F. Musto, *The American Disease: Origins of Narcotic Control*, expanded edition (New York: Oxford University Press, 1987).

11. Leroy Street, *I Was a Drug Addict* (New York: Random House, 1953).

12. Harold Traver, "Opium to Heroin: Restrictive Opium Legislation and the Rise of Heroin Consumption in Hong Kong," *Journal of Policy History* 4, no. 3 (1992): 307–24; Frank Dikotter, Lars Laamann, and Zhou Xun, *Narcotic Culture: A History of Drugs in China* (Chicago: University of Chicago Press, 2004).

13. Carstairs, *Jailed for Possession*, chapter 2.

14. Courtwright, *Dark Paradise*, pp. 11–14.

15. Courtwright, *Dark Paradise*, pp. 87–88, 98–99.

16. Alan A. Block, "European Drug Traffic and Traffickers Between the Wars: The Policy of Suppression and Its Consequences," *Journal of Social History* 23 (Winter 1989): 315–37.

17. Courtwright, *Dark Paradise*, pp. 105–8.

18. Newsday, *Opium Trail*, pp. 12–14; Moscow, *Merchants of Heroin*, pp. 60–63, 112–16.

19. Harry J. Anslinger and Will Oursler, *The Murderers: The Story of the Narcotic Gangs* (New York: Farrar, Straus and Cudahy, 1961), pp. 46–47, 56–59; U.S. Congress, Senate, *Hearings Before the Permanent Subcommittee on Investigations of the Committee on Government Operations*, 88th Congress, 1st and 2nd sessions, *Organized Crime and Illicit Traffic in Narcotics*, Pts. 1–5 (Washington, D.C.: U.S. Government Printing Office, 1963, 1964), p. 896; letter from Charles Siragusa to Harry J. Anslinger, October 2, 1953, and letter from Paul Knight to Charles Siragusa, October 5, 1953, folder "Smuggling, 1933–1957," file 1935, Box 25, Accession number 170–75–17, Record Group 170, National Archives (NA).

20. U.S. Congress, Senate, Committee on the Judiciary, *Hearings Before the Subcom-*

mittee to Investigate Juvenile Delinquency, 87th Congress, 2nd session (Washington, D.C.: U.S. Government Printing Office, 1963), pp. 3139–40.

21. *Organized Crime and Illicit Traffic in Narcotics*, p. 759; New York (City), Temporary Commission on Narcotics Addiction, "Report to the Mayor of the City of New York," (November 1965), p. 1; Courtwright, *Dark Paradise*, p. 169.

22. *Organized Crime and Illicit Traffic in Narcotics*, pp. 920–23.

23. Mark Harrison Moore, *Buy and Bust: The Effective Regulation of an Illicit Market in Heroin* (Lexington, Mass.: D. C. Heath, 1977), discusses this on a retail level but the same principles apply for wholesale distribution.

24. *Organized Crime and Illicit Traffic in Narcotics*, p. 937.

25. *Organized Crime and Illicit Traffic in Narcotics*, p. 932.

26. U.S. Congress, Senate, *Hearings before a Special Committee to Investigate Organized Crime in Interstate Commerce*, 82nd Congress, 1st session, *Investigation of Organized Crime in Interstate Commerce: Part 14, Narcotics* (Washington, D.C.: U.S. Government Printing Office, 1951), p. 416 (hereafter *Investigation of Organized Crime in Interstate Commerce*), and *Organized Crime and Illicit Traffic in Narcotics*, p. 448.

27. *Organized Crime and Illicit Traffic in Narcotics*, pp. 788, 924; Memorandum Report by Benjamin Fitzgerald, September 4, 1958, folder "Complaints against officers," file 1515–3, Box 1, Accession number 170–75–17, Record Group 170, NA.

28. *Organized Crime and Illicit Traffic in Narcotics*, pp. 913, 915.

29. *Organized Crime and Illicit Traffic in Narcotics*, pp. 915, 927; interview with Dusty, "Addicts Who Survived" Collection, Oral History Center, Columbia University.

30. David Simon and Edward Burns argue that the marketplace for heroin was finite and access was limited; clearly this is nostalgia. David Simon and Edward Burns, *The Corner: A Year in the Life of an Inner City Neighborhood* (New York: Broadway Books, 1997), pp. 61–63.

31. *Investigation of Organized Crime in Interstate Commerce*, pp. 23, 26, 34, 48, 59, 86, 205; Michael Zwerin, *The Silent Sound of Needles* (Englewood Cliffs, N.J.: Prentice-Hall, 1969), p. 114.

32. *Organized Crime and Illicit Traffic in Narcotics*, pp. 631–37, 722, 877, 898; Evert Clark and Nicholas Horrock, *Contrabandista!* (New York: Praeger, 1973).

33. Jean-Pierre Charbonneau, *The Canadian Connection: An Expose on the Mafia in Canada and its International Ramifications* (Ottawa: Optimum, 1976).

34. Luiz R. S. Simmons and Abdul A. Said, "The Politics of Addiction," in *Drugs, Politics, and Diplomacy: The International Connection*, ed. Luiz R. S. Simmons and Abdul A. Said (Beverly Hills, Calif.: Sage, 1974), p. 12.

CHAPTER 2. JAZZ JOINTS AND JUNK

1. Meyer Berger, "Tea for a Viper," *New Yorker* (March 12, 1938), pp. 36–48.

2. Letter from Dr. George Baehr to Dr. James A. Miller, President, New York Academy of Medicine, September 13, 1938, File: Marihuana. 1938–1940, Public Health Ar-

chives, New York Academy of Medicine (NYAM). John C. McWilliams, *The Protectors: Harry J. Anslinger and the Federal Bureau of Narcotics, 1930–1962* (Newark: University of Delaware Press, 1990), pp. 54–55.

3. William D. Armstrong and John Parascandola, "American Concern over Marijuana in the 1930's," *Pharmacy in History* 14 (1972): 25–35; Jill Jonnes, *Hep-Cats, Narcs, and Pipe Dreams: A History of America's Romance with Illegal Drugs* (New York: Scribner's, 1996), pp. 121–23; McWilliams, *The Protectors*, pp. 48–54, 99–100; Charles Winick, "How High the Moon—Jazz and Drugs," *Antioch Review* 21 (1961): 5–68.

4. Milton "Mezz" Mezzrow and Bernard Wolfe, *Really the Blues* (New York: Random House, 1946), pp. 207–8.

5. Mezzrow, *Really the Blues*, p. 73; Eric Nisenson, *Blue: The Murder of Jazz* (New York: St. Martin's Press, 1997), p. 72.

6. Mayor LaGuardia's Committee on Marihuana, *The Marihuana Problem in the City of New York* (Lancaster, Pa.: Jacques Cattell Press, 1944), pp. 30–51, 80–81.

7. Committee on Marijuana, *Marihuana Problem*, pp. 213–14.

8. Clifford Geertz, *The Interpretation of Cultures: Selected Essays* (New York: Basic Books, 1973).

9. Olive J. Cregan, untitled report, no date, pp. 1–2, File: Marihuana. 1938–1940, NYAM.

10. Committee on Marijuana, *Marihuana Problem*, pp. 10–11; Cregan, untitled report, pp. 3–8, 12, 14–15, NYAM.

11. Cregan, untitled report, pp. 9–11, NYAM.

12. Olive J. Cregan, "Statements from School Principals," n.d., File: Marihuana, 1938–1940, NYAM.

13. David T. Courtwright, "The Road to H: The First Sixty Years of Heroin in America," paper presented at "One Hundred Years of Heroin," Yale University Medical School, New Haven, Conn., September 18–20, 1998.

14. Testimony before Attorney General Nathaniel Goldstein, New York State Narcotics Investigation, 1951–1952, typescript, pp. 59–60, New York State Library, Albany, N.Y.; *NYT*, June 18, 1951, p. 1.

15. John C. Ball, "Two Patterns of Opiate Addiction," in John C. Ball and Carl D. Chambers, eds., *The Epidemiology of Opiate Addiction in the United States* (Springfield, Ill.: Charles C. Thomas, 1970), pp. 81–94.

16. Red Rodney, quoted in Ira Gitler, *Swing to Bop: An Oral History of the Transition in Jazz in the 1940s* (New York: Oxford University Press, 1985), p. 282; Charles Winick, "The Use of Drugs by Jazz Musicians," *Social Problems* 7 (Winter 1959–60): 240–53.

17. I believe that drug users inhabited a subculture similar to the gay subculture described by George Chauncey that was visible to cognoscenti but not to others. See George Chauncey, Jr., "The Policed: Gay Men's Strategies of Everyday Resistance," in William R. Taylor, ed., *Inventing Times Square: Commerce and Culture at the Crossroads of the World* (Baltimore: Johns Hopkins University Press, 1996), pp. 315–28.

18. Timothy J. Gilfoyle, "Policing of Sexuality," in *Inventing Times Square*, pp. 297–

314; Morton Minsky and Milt Machlin, *Minsky's Burlesque* (New York: Arbor House, 1986), pp. 185–86, 280–91; "Vice in New York," *Fortune*, July 1939, reprinted in Milton Crane, ed., *Sins of New York* (New York: Boni and Gaer, 1947), pp. 269–78.

19. Jack Kerouac, *On the Road* (New York: Penguin, 1976), p. 131.

20. Herbert Huncke, *Guilty of Everything: The Autobiography of Herbert Huncke* (New York: Paragon House, 1990), pp. 51, 54, 59, 97–98.

21. Jonnes, *Hep-Cats*, pp. 122–25; Arnold Shaw, *52nd Street: The Street of Jazz* (New York: Da Capo Press, 1977), pp. 252–54. Feather is quoted in Shaw, p. 277.

22. Jonnes, *Hep-Cats*, pp. 130–36; interview with Ann, "Addicts Who Survived" Collection, Oral History Center, Columbia University; David Courtwright, Herman Joseph, and Don Des Jarlais, *Addicts Who Survived: An Oral History of Narcotic Addiction in America, 1923–1965* (Knoxville: University of Tennessee Press, 1989), chapter 3.

23. Scott DeVeaux, *The Birth of Bebop* (Berkeley: University of California Press, 1997), pp. 123–29; Bill Crow, *From Birdland to Broadway: Scenes from a Jazz Life* (New York: Oxford University Press, 1992), pp. 7–8.

24. John White, *Billie Holiday: Her Life and Times* (New York: Universe Books, 1987), pp. 75–76; Dizzy Gillespie with Al Fraser, *To Be, or not . . . to Bop: Memoirs* (New York: Da Capo Press, 1979), p. 210.

25. Wilder Hobson, "Fifty-Second Street," in Frederic Ramsey, Jr., and Charles Edward Smith, eds., *Jazzmen* (New York: Harcourt, Brace, 1939), pp. 249–53; Robert Sylvester, *No Cover Charge: A Backward Look at the Night Clubs* (New York: Dial Press, 1956), pp. 72–73; Arnold Shaw, *52nd Street*, pp. 10–12, 20–21, 170, 280; Ross Russell, *Bird Lives! The High Life and Hard Times of Charlie "Yardbird" Parker* (London: Quartet Books, 1976), p. 163; Gilbert Sorrentino, "Remembrances of Bop in New York, 1945–1950," *Kulchur* 3 (Summer 1963): 70–82.

26. Shaw, *52nd Street*, pp. xiii, 194–95, 296; Minsky and Machlin, *Minsky's Burlesque*, p. 144; A. B. Spellman, *Four Lives in the Bebop Business* (New York: Limelight Editions, 1985), p. 24; Sylvester, *No Cover Charge*, pp. 45, 58, 88–89, 284; Paul Chevigney, *Gigs: Jazz and the Cabaret Laws in New York City* (New York: Routledge, 1991), pp. 42–43, 57–59.

27. Leonard Feather quoted in Shaw, *52nd Street*, p. 277, Bobby Timmons quoted in J. C. Thomas, *Chasin' the Trane: The Music and the Mystique of John Coltrane* (Garden City, N.Y.: Doubleday, 1975), p. 62; Jackie McLean quoted in Spellman, *Four Lives in the Bebop Business*, p. 193.

28. Norman E. Zinberg, *Drug, Set, and Setting: The Basis for Controlled Intoxicant Use* (New Haven, Conn.: Yale University Press, 1984); Miles Davis with Quincy Troupe, *Miles: The Autobiography* (New York: Touchstone, 1989), p. 72; Hampton Hawes with Don Asker, *Raise Up Off Me: A Portrait of Hampton Hawes* (New York: Thunder's Mouth Press, 2001), p. 30. Taylor quoted in Nat Hentoff, *The Jazz Life* (New York: Da Capo Press, 1975), p. 87; Winick, "Use of Drugs by Jazz Musicians," p. 250. On gifts from fans and dealers, Art and Laurie Pepper, *Straight Life: The Story of Art Pepper* (New York: Da Capo Press, 1994), pp. 189, 260.

29. Robert George Reisner, "I Remember Bird," in Robert George Reisner, ed., *Bird: The Legend of Charlie Parker* (New York: Da Capo Press, 1977), pp. 25–26; Spellman, *Four Lives in the Bebop Business*, p. 132, 193; Billy Taylor in Nat Shapiro and Nat Hentoff, eds., *Hear Me Talkin' to Ya: The Story of Jazz as Told by the Men Who Made It* (New York: Dover, 1966), p. 378; Chevigney, *Gigs*, p. 44; Howard S. Becker, "The Culture of a Deviant Group: The Dance Musician," in Becker, *Outsiders: Studies in the Sociology of Deviance* (New York: Free Press, 1963), especially pp. 85–100.

30. Gillespie, *To Be*, pp. 140, 149, 186–87, 302; Nisenson, *Blue*, p. 108; Eric Lott, "Double V, Double-Time: Bebop's Politics of Style," *Callaloo* 11 (1988): 597–605; for a revisionist view, see DeVeaux, *The Birth of Bebop*.

31. Spellman, *Four Lives in the Bebop Business*, p. 193; Davis, *Miles: The Autobiography*, p. 129; Hentoff, *Jazz Life*, pp. 81, 88–89; Harold Finestone, "Cats, Kicks, and Color," in Howard S. Becker, ed., *The Other Side: Perspectives on Deviance* (New York: Free Press, 1967), 281–97.

32. Hawes, *Raise Up Off Me*, p. 12. This incident occurred in Los Angeles.

33. Hawes, *Raise Up Off Me*, p. 20; Rodney, Gordon, Rouse, and Mulligan are in Gitler, *Swing to Bop*, pp. 281, 283, 288–89; Russell, *Bird Lives*, p. 260; interview with arranger Marty Paich in Art and Laurie Pepper, *Straight Life*, p. 220; Winick, "Use of Drugs by Jazz Musicians," pp. 246–47.

34. Fuller is quoted in Gillespie, *To Be*, p. 257; Hawes, *Raise Up Off Me*, p. 8; Rodney is quoted in Gene Lees, *Cats of Any Color: Jazz Black and White* (New York: Oxford University Press, 1994), p. 103.

35. Interview with West Indian Tom, "Addicts Who Survived," Columbia University; Mulligan is quoted in Gitler, *Swing to Bop*, p. 287; Freeman quoted in Thomas, *Chasin' the Trane*, p. 62. Didier Deutsch, "Chet Baker and the Demons that Haunted Him," *Jazziz* (April–May 1989), pp. 10–13; Davis, *Miles: The Autobiography*, p. 96; Spellman, *Four Lives in the Bebop Business*, p. 193; Gillespie, *To Be*, p. 285; Gitler, *Swing to Bop*, pp. 174, 279; Hentoff, *Jazz Life*, pp. 85–88, 174, for other examples.

36. Susan J. Miller, *Never Let Me Down: A Memoir* (New York: Henry Holt, 1998), p. 6.

37. Florrie Fisher, *The Lonely Trip Back* (Garden City, N.Y.: Doubleday, 1971), pp. 56–58.

38. Brian Ward, *Just My Soul Responding: Rhythm and Blues, Black Consciousness, and Race Relations* (Berkeley: University of California Press, 1998), p. 10.

39. Sorrentino, "Remembrances of Bop," p. 70; Hentoff, *Jazz Life*, p. vii.

40. *NYT*, July 10, 1945, p. 1; November 5, 1945, p. 21.

41. Davis, *Miles: The Autobiography*, p. 108; Watkins quoted in Sylvester, *No Cover Charge*, pp. 82, 285–86; Gillespie, *To Be*, p. 257; Reisner, *Bird*, p. 150; McShane and Gitler, *Swing to Bop*, p. 285; Herman; *Downbeat*, November 17, 1950, p. 10; August 24, 1951, p. 10; *Metronome*, August, 1945, p. 7; August, 1947, pp. 12–13; August, 1951, p. 34; September, 1951, p. 34; October, 1951, p. 34.

42. Taylor quoted in Shapiro and Hentoff, *Hear Me Talkin' to Ya*, p. 367; Interview

with Whitehead, "Addicts Who Survived," Columbia University; Maclean quoted in Spellman, *Four Lives in the Bebop Business*, pp. 194–96; *NYT*, June 15, 1951, p. 15.

43. Shaw, *52nd Street*, p. 172; Sylvester, *No Cover Charge*, pp. 274–78; Marc Eliot, *Down 42nd Street: Sex, Money, and Politics at the Crossroads of the World* (New York: Rebel Road, 2001), pp. 96–98.

44. Testimony before Attorney General Nathaniel Goldstein, pp. 417–18, 419, 456–57; Winick, "Use of Drugs by Jazz Musicians," p. 245; Crow, *Birdland to Broadway*, p. 5; Shaw, *52nd Street*, p. 120; Huncke, *Guilty of Everything*, p. 110.

45. Testimony before Attorney General Nathaniel Goldstein, pp. 419, 440–42; *NYT*, June 13, 1951, p. 34.

46. Shaw, *52nd Street*, pp. 64–65, 213; Gitler, *Swing to Bop*, pp. 279–80; Crow, *Birdland to Broadway*, pp. 32–33; Interview with Stella, "Addicts Who Survived," Columbia University.

47. Testimony before Attorney General Nathaniel Goldstein, pp. 418–19, 420, 421–22.

CHAPTER 3. THE PLAGUE

1. Claude Brown, *Manchild in the Promised Land* (New York: Signet Books, 1965), p. 188.

2. Solomon Kobrin and Harold Finestone, "Drug Addiction Among Young Persons in Chicago: A Report of a Study of the Prevalence, Incidence, Distribution and Character of Drug Use and Addiction in Chicago During the Years 1947–53," in James F. Short, Jr., ed., *Gang Delinquency and Delinquent Subcultures* (New York: Harper and Row, 1968), pp. 110–30.

3. Statement from Thomas Warren Gordon, folder 2, 1948–1950, box 37, file 1080 (Juvenile Offenders), Accession number 170–74–12, Record Group 170, National Archives. All references are from the same folder, box, file, accession number and record group, so I will list only the titles and dates of materials, followed by NA.

4. Statements from Hugh Dean Dabney and Edward Davis, NA.

5. Letter from R. W. Artis to H. L. Anslinger, February 15, 1949, NA.

6. Letter from Narcotic Agent Albert Aman to District Supervisor Frank Sojat, May 3, 1948, NA.

7. Statements from Hugh Dean Dabney, George Anderson, and Reynolds Wintersmith, NA.

8. Statements from Grover Hatcher and Charles Durgens, NA.

9. "Surplus Property," *Time* (October 21, 1946), p. 86.

10. Statement from James Herman Logan, NA.

11. Statements from Edward Davis and Grover Hatcher, NA.

12. Quoted in Kobrin and Finestone, "Drug Addiction Among Young Persons in Chicago," p. 128.

13. Letter from Narcotic Agent Albert Aman to District Supervisor Frank Sojat, May 3, 1948; letter from Narcotic Agent Albert Aman to District Supervisor Frank Sojat, May 19, 1948; letter from R. W. Artis to H. L. Anslinger, May 28, 1948, NA.

14. See below and *St. Louis Star Times*, February 9, 1950.

15. Letter from R. W. Artis to H. L. Anslinger, February 15, 1949, NA.

16. *Report of the Mayor's Committee for the Rehabilitation of Narcotic Addicts* (Detroit: City of Detroit, 1953), p. 38; Isidor Chein, Donald L. Gerard, Robert S. Lee, and Eva Rosenfeld, *The Road to H: Narcotics, Delinquency, and Social Policy* (New York: Basic Books, 1964), pp. 10, 39–40, 52; United States Congress, Senate, *Illicit Narcotics Traffic (Chicago, Ill.) Hearings Before the Subcommittee on Improvements in the Federal Criminal Code of the Committee on the Judiciary*, 84th Congress, 1st session (Washington, D.C.: U.S. Government Printing Office, 1956), pt. 9, pp. 4246–47; idem, pt. 10, pp. 4489–91; Kobrin and Finestone, "Drug Addiction Among Young Persons in Chicago," p. 114.

17. Dharuba is quoted in *Look for Me in the Whirlwind: The Collective Autobiography of the New York 21* (New York: Random House, 1971), p. 69; Harold Finestone, "Cats, Kicks, and Color," in Howard S. Becker, ed., *The Other Side: Perspectives on Deviance*, (New York: Free Press, 1964), pp. 281–97.

18. David Courtwright, Herman Joseph, and Don Des Jarlais, *Addicts Who Survived: An Oral History of Narcotic Use in America, 1923–1965* (Knoxville: University of Tennessee Press, 1989), pp. 49, 150, 195.

19. Jill Jonnes, *Hep-Cats, Narcs, and Pipe Dreams: A History of America's Romance with Illegal Drugs* (New York: Scribner, 1996), pp. 241–43, for similar appraisals by Baltimore addicts.

20. Brown, *Manchild*, pp. 187–88.

21. Jervis Anderson, *This Was Harlem: A Cultural Portrait* (New York: Farrar, Straus, Giroux, 1982); Jonnes, *Hep-Cats, Narcs, and Pipe Dreams*, pp. 241–46; Central Avenue Sounds Editorial Committee, *Central Avenue Sounds: Jazz in Los Angeles* (Berkeley: University of California Press, 1998); Joseph Spillane, "The Making of an Underground Market: Drug Selling in Chicago, 1900–1940," *Journal of Social History* 32 (Fall 1998): 27–47.

22. Courtwright et al., *Addicts Who Survived*, p. 163; New York State Narcotics Investigation, testimony given before Attorney General Nathaniel Goldstein, typescript, New York State Library, Albany, N.Y., pp. 408–9, 414, 415–16; Anderson, *This Was Harlem*, p. 342.

23. *Report of the Mayor's Committee for the Rehabilitation of Narcotic Addicts* (Detroit: City of Detroit, 1953), p. 39; David T. Courtwright, *Dark Paradise: A History of Opiate Addiction in America* (Cambridge: Harvard University Press, 2001), pp. 149–51; Harry R. Hoffman, Irene C. Sherman, Fannie Krevitsky, and Forrestine Williams, "Teen-Age Drug Addicts Arraigned in the Narcotic Court of Chicago," *Journal of the American Medical Association* 149, no. 7 (June 14, 1952): 655–59.

24. *Report of the Mayor's Committee for the Rehabilitation of Narcotic Addicts*, pp. 150–53; author's calculations.

25. Artis to H. L. Anslinger, February 15, 1949, NA.

26. Letter from Narcotic Agent Ross Ellis to Joseph Bell, District Supervisor, June 16, 1950; statement of Mary Lou Schaefle, NA.

27. A. D. Carswell, Memorandum Report, Bureau of Narcotics, Minneapolis, April 15, 1950, NA.

28. George H. White, District Supervisor, "Memorandum for the Commissioner of Narcotics," January 26, 1951, NA.

29. George H. White, District Supervisor, "Memorandum for the Commissioner of Narcotics," January 26, 1951, NA.

30. George H. White, District Supervisor, "Memorandum for the Commissioner of Narcotics," January 26, 1951, NA.

31. "Narcotic Offenders under age 21 in 64 Principal Cities of the United States arranged alphabetically by states showing comparative concentrations, 1951–1952," folder 4, box 37, file 1080, NA; Chein et al., *Road to H*, pp. 32–33; *Report of the Mayor's Committee for the Rehabilitation of Narcotic Addicts*, p. 46; report from the Institute for Juvenile Research, Illinois Department of Public Welfare, summarized in California, Legislature, Senate, *Report of the Senate Interim Committee on Narcotics* (Sacramento: State of California, 1959), p. 124; on heroin use in California cities, California, Citizens' Advisory Committee to the Attorney General on Crime Prevention, *Narcotic Addiction* (Sacramento: State of California, 1954), p. 18; Julius Klein and Derek L. Phillips, "From Hard to Soft Drugs: Temporal and Substantive Changes in Drug Usage Among Gangs in a Working-Class Community," *Journal of Health and Social Behavior* 9 (June 1968): 139–45.

CHAPTER 4. THE PANIC OVER ADOLESCENT HEROIN USE

1. For a sensational account of comic books and their influence on adolescents, see Frederic Wertham, *Seduction of the Innocent* (New York: Rinehart, 1954).

2. Welfare Council of New York City, Committee on Narcotics, *Trapped!* (New York: Columbia University Press, 1951).

3. Mort Leav, *Holiday of Horrors*, Orbit Comics, *Most Wanted* series, no. 51 (St. Louis: Toytown Publications, 1952).

4. *Reefer Madness*, directed by Louis Gasnier, G. and H. Production, 1938.

5. Mayor LaGuardia's Committee on Marihuana, *The Marihuana Problem in the City of New York* (Lancaster, Pa.: Jacques Cattell Press, 1944).

6. Alfred R. Lindesmith, "The 'Dope Fiend' Mythology," *Journal of Criminal Law and Criminology* 31, no. 1 (May–June 1940): 199–208; Harry J. Anslinger and Will Oursler, *The Murderers: The Story of the Narcotic Gangs* (New York: Farrar, Straus and Cudahy, 1961), p. 38.

7. Joachim Joesten, *Dope, Inc.* (New York: Avon Books, 1953), p. 20; "Narcotics and Youth," *Newsweek* (January 20, 1950): 57–58.

8. Alwyn J. St. Charles, *The Narcotics Menace* (Los Angeles: Borden Publishing, 1952), pp. 81, 87; Dan Fowler, "Your Child May Be Hooked," *Look* (June 30, 1953): 92–95.

9. St. Charles, *Narcotics Menace*, p. 15; Herbert Brean, "A Short—and Horrible—Life," *Reader's Digest* (September 1951): 1–3, Harry J. Anslinger Papers, Pennsylvania Historical Collections and Labor Archives, Pattee Library, Penn State University (hereafter Anslinger Papers), box 7, file 1, Pamphlets on Drugs and Drug Addiction, 1951–57; Archie Lieberman, "9 Hours in Hell with a Dope Addict," *Pageant* 11, no. 12 (June 1956): 7–21.

10. Wenzell Brown, *Monkey on My Back* (New York: Greenberg Publishers, 1953),

p. 93; Fowler, "Your Child May Be Hooked," pp. 92–95. Lindesmith, "'Dope Fiend' Mythology," p. 205.

11. David Hulburd, *H Is for Heroin: A Teen-age Narcotic Tells Her Story* (New York: Popular Library, 1953), pp. 53–54.

12. "Narcotics and Youth," *Newsweek* (January 20, 1950): 57–58.

13. St. Charles, *Narcotics Menace*, p. 13.

14. James Gilbert, *A Cycle of Outrage: America's Reaction to the Juvenile Delinquent in the 1950s* (New York: Oxford University Press, 1986), chapter 4.

15. *New York World Telegram and Sun*, April 10, 1950, p. 1; April 15, 1950, p. 1; April 17, 1950, p. 1; April 18, 1950, p. 3; April 19, 1950, p. 1; April 20, 1950, p. 1; April 21, 1950, pp. 3, 30.

16. *NYT*, December 12, 1950, p. 36; April 6, 1951, p. 52.

17. New York State Narcotics Investigation, testimony given before Attorney General Nathaniel Goldstein, typescript, New York State Library, Albany, N.Y., pp. 92, 230, 262, 271, 282–83.

18. Isidor Chein, Donald L. Gerard, Robert S. Lee, and Eva Rosenfeld, *The Road to H: Narcotics, Delinquency, and Social Policy* (New York: Basic Books, 1964), p. 12.

19. *NYT*, January 6, 1951, p. 30, January 16, 1951, p. 33, June 14, 1951, p. 22; June 17, 1951, section IV, p. 2; Testimony before Attorney General Nathaniel Goldstein pp. 355–56, 422–23, 452–53.

20. Testimony before Attorney General Nathaniel Goldstein pp. 664–65; see pp. 91, 254, 880–81 for other accounts.

21. Testimony before Attorney General Nathaniel Goldstein pp. 875–76.

22. Testimony before Attorney General Nathaniel Goldstein pp. 781–85. The same point is made in Chein et al., *Road to H*, p. 12.

23. United States Congress, Senate, *Hearings before a Special Committee to Investigate Organized Crime in Interstate Commerce* 82nd Congress, 1st Session, Investigation of Organized Crime in Interstate Commerce, Part 14, *Narcotics* (Washington, D.C.: U.S. Government Printing Office, 1951), pp. 14–18. Hereafter *Investigation of Organized Crime*.

24. *Investigation of Organized Crime*, pp. 32–33, 193, 195.

25. *Investigation of Organized Crime*, pp. 41, 43, 48, 56.

26. Harold Finestone, "Cats, Kicks, and Color," in Howard S. Becker, ed., *The Other Side: Perspectives on Deviance* (New York: Free Press, 1964), pp. 281–97.

27. Chein et al., *The Road to H*, pp. 204–18, 224–25; Paul Zimmering, James Toolan, Renate Safrin, and S. Bernard Wortis, "Heroin Addiction in Adolescent Boys," *Journal of Nervous and Mental Disease* 114 (July 1951): 19–34; New York City Youth Board, *Reaching the Teen-age Addict: A Study of Street Club Work with a Group of Adolescent Users* (New York: New York City Youth Board, 1963). Mara L. Keire, "Dope Fiends and Degenerates: The Gendering of Addiction in the Early Twentieth Century," *Journal of Social History* 31 (Summer 1998): 809–22 for the association of drug use and effeminacy. Richard A. Cloward and Lloyd E. Ohlin, *Delinquency and Opportunity: A Theory of Delinquent Gangs* (Glencoe, Ill.: Free Press, 1960); the authors argue that drug-using groups were "retreatists," an analysis that follows directly from the psychological studies of the early 1950s.

28. Elaine Tyler May, *Homeward Bound: American Families in the Cold War Era* (New York: Basic Books, 1988), especially pp. 94–97.

29. Chein et al., *The Road to H*, p. 14; Charles Winick, "Physician Narcotic Addicts," in *The Other Side*, pp. 261–79.

30. Caroline Jean Acker, *Creating the American Junkie: Addiction Research in the Classic Era of Narcotic Control* (Baltimore: Johns Hopkins University Press, 2002), chapter 5.

31. Douglas Clark Kinder and William O. Walker III, "Stable Force in a Storm: Harry J. Anslinger and the United States Narcotic Foreign Policy, 1930–1962," *Journal of American History* 72, no. 4 (March 1986): 908–27; Lee Bernstein, *The Greatest Menace: Organized Crime in Cold War America* (Amherst: University of Massachusetts Press, 2002), chapter 6.

32. David Brion Davis, ed., *The Fear of Conspiracy: Images of Un-American Subversion from the Revolution to the Present* (Ithaca. N.Y.: Cornell University Press, 1971).

33. Bernstein, *Greatest Menace*, pp. 66–68.

34. Alfred W. McCoy, *The Politics of Heroin: CIA Complicity in the Global Drug Trade* (New York: Lawrence Hill Books, 1991), chapter 4; Kathryn Meyer and Terry Parssinen, *Webs of Smoke: Smugglers, Warlords, Spies and the History of International Drug Trade* (Lanham, Md.: Rowman & Littlefield, 1998), chapters 8 and 10.

35. "Anslinger Sees Dope Controlled," *The News Leader*, May 29, 1950, box 5, file 6 Scrapbook, 1948–1959, and Jack Anderson, "Castro Has a New Weapon, Dope," *Washington Post*, July 29, 1962, box 6, file 8 Scrapbook, 1962–1966, 1972, 1975. Anslinger's claims can be found in "The Smuggling of Narcotic Drugs from Communist China," Remarks of Commissioner Harry J. Anslinger, United States Representative on the United Nations Commission on Narcotic Drugs, 17th Session, May 8 to June 1, 1962, box 1, file 8, "Speeches by Harry Anslinger (1938–69), Anslinger Papers.

36. United States Congress, Senate, *Communist China and Illicit Narcotic Traffic: Hearings before the Subcommittee to Investigate the Administration of the Internal Security Act and Other Internal Security Laws of the Committee on the Judiciary*, 84th Congress, 1st Session (Washington, D.C.: U.S. Government Printing Office, 1955), pp. 4–5, 8; Richard L. G. Deverall, *Mao Tze-Tung: Stop this Dirty Opium Business! How Red China is Selling Opium and Heroin to Produce Revenue for China's War Machine* (Tokyo: Toyoh Printing and Book-binding Co., 1954).

37. Anslinger, quoted in John O'Kearney, "Opium Trade: Is China Responsible?" *Nation* (October 15, 1955), clipping in box 8, file 11 "Articles 1951–1969"; see also "The Illicit Narcotic Traffic in the Far East," box 7, file 7 "Selected Congressional Record Issues (1942–57)," Anslinger Papers; Anslinger, *The Murderers*, p. 226.

38. Anslinger used information supplied by the Nationalist Chinese in Taiwan, and their ambassador to the United States in turn promoted Anslinger's efforts. See Hollington K. Tong, Ambassador of the Republic of China to the United States, "Narcotics, Red China's Weapon," press release, March 12, 1958, box 7, file 6, "Law Enforcement Journals, Speeches, and Letters (1931–58)," Anslinger Papers.

39. "Red China Exports Opium to Make Dope Addicts of Our Boys in Asia!" *Saturday Evening Post* (January 9, 1954), box 8, file 11 "Articles, 1951–1969"; "Dope Flows From Red Sources," n.p. box 5, file 6 Scrapbook 1948–1959; Pierre J. Huss, "Mao—Big Time Dope Peddler," *New York Journal American,* October 22, 1961, box 6, file 8 Scrapbook 1960–1966, 1972, 1975, along with many other examples, Anslinger Papers. The *Nation* was one of the few periodicals that questioned Anslinger's evidence and rhetoric.

40. Bernstein, *Greatest Menace*, pp. 1–6; John C. McWilliams, *The Protectors: Harry J. Anslinger and the Federal Bureau of Narcotics, 1930–1962* (Cranbury N.J.: Associated University Press, 1990), pp. 144–46.

41. Salvatore Vizzini, Report to Bureau of Narcotics, September 30, 1959, folder 4 1959–April 1966, box 1, file 0970, accession 71–A–3555, Record Group 170, National Archives. Hereafter listed by folder, box, file, accession number, NA. Thomas Inglis, Office of the Chief of Naval Operations, Navy Department, "Memorandum on Charles Luciano," for J. Edgar Hoover, Director, Federal Bureau of Investigation (FBI), May 10, 1946, Luciano FBI file. John McWilliams supplied Luciano's FBI file.

42. *NYT,* February 27, 1947, p. 46; FBI, "Memorandum Salvatore Lucania with aliases," May 9, 1945; A. Rosen, Office Memorandum "Charles 'Lucky' Luciano Parole," to E. A. Tamm, April 18, 1946, Luciano FBI file; McWilliams, *The Protectors*, pp. 135–38.

43. FBI, "Miscellaneous Information Concerning Departure," May 5, 1946, Luciano FBI file; *Investigation of Organized Crime*, pt. 14, pp. 343–56; "Lucania's Criminal History in the United States," June 15, 1951, folder Luciano, box 4, file 0970, 71–A–3555, NA; Charles Siragusa, *The Trail of the Poppy: Behind the Mask of the Mafia* (Englewood Cliffs, N.J.: Prentice-Hall, 1966), pp. 83, 97.

44. "Summary from Italian [summary of a series that appeared in *L'Europeo* January 11, 18, and 25, 1959]"; FBI Memorandum, "Charles 'Lucky' Luciano," September 27, 1965. An FBI memorandum, "Charles 'Lucky' Luciano." September 17, 1965, concluded that allegations against Luciano were "overstatements," all in Luciano FBI file; Charles Siragusa, Memorandum to Outerbridge Horsey, U.S. Embassy, Rome, Italy, August 11, 1952, folder 4, Italy 1952, and "Interrogation of Jeremiah Harrington," folder 1, Italy through 1958, Box 1, file 0970, 71–A–3555, NA.

45. *NYT,* February 22, 1947, p. 1; October 2, 1948, p. 30; October 21, 1948, p. 54; December 4, 1948, p. 30; January 8, 1949, p. 1; May 29, 1949, p. 38; July 8, 1949, p. 4; February 9, 1950, p. 24; September 9, 1950, p. 31; March 1, 1951, p. 22; May 7, 1951, p. 38; June 10, 1951, p. 28; June 28, 1951, p. 1; July 15, 1951, p. 1; July 29, 1951, p. 1; August 5, 1951, p. 1; September 1, 1951, p. 7; December 21, 1951, p. 29; January 5, 1952, p. 28; March 9, 1952, p. 54; March 23, 1954, p. 5; November 20, 1954, p. 32; August 5, 1955, p. 40; April 6, 1956, p. 12; July 25, 1958, p. 20; July 31, 1958, p. 47; January 28, 1962, p. 66; February 3, 1962, p. 17.

46. Anslinger, *The Murderers*, p. 107.

47. Anslinger, *The Murderers*, pp. 99, 230; for a statement linking Red Chinese opium with Luciano, see *NYT*, August 17, 1951, p. 5.

48. McWilliams, *The Protectors*, pp. 108–16; Courtwright, *Dark Paradise*, p. 156.

49. McWilliams, *The Protectors*, pp. 109–10, 115.

CHAPTER 5. ETHNICITY AND THE MARKET

1. Testimony of Harry J. Anslinger, Commissioner, Federal Bureau of Narcotics, United States Senate, Committee on the Judiciary, *Hearings Before the Subcommittee on Improvements in the Federal Criminal Code of the Committee on the Judiciary on Illicit Narcotics Traffic*, 84th Congress, 1st Sess. (Washington, D.C.: U.S. Government Printing Office, 1955), p. 16. On arrests, see p. 3561.

2. Testimony of Captain Kenneth Irving, Los Angeles County Sheriff's Department, in *Illicit Narcotics Traffic*, p. 3680. For the alarmist view, see Citizens' Advisory Committee to the Attorney General on Crime Prevention, *Narcotic Addiction* (Sacramento: State of California, 1954), p. 18. On police harassment of patrons of black nightspots in the search for drug users, Anthony Macias, "Bringing Music to the People: Race, Urban Culture, and Municipal Politics in Postwar Los Angeles," in Raul Homero Villa and George J. Sanchez, eds., *Los Angeles and the Future of Urban Cultures* (Baltimore: Johns Hopkins University Press, 2005), pp. 195–219.

3. Joan W. Moore, *Homeboys: Gangs, Drugs, and Prison in the Barrios of Los Angeles* (Philadelphia: Temple University Press, 1978); Edward J. Escobar, *Race, Police, and the Making of a Political Identity: Mexican Americans and the Los Angeles Police Department, 1900–1945* (Berkeley: University of California Press, 1999).

4. Escobar, *Race, Police, and the Making of a Political Identity*, pp. 166–67, 178–84; George J. Sanchez, *Becoming Mexican American: Ethnicity, Culture and Identity in Chicano Los Angeles, 1900–1945* (New York: Oxford University Press, 1993), pp. 253–69; Ricardo Romo, *East Los Angeles: History of a Barrio* (Austin: University of Texas Press, 1983), pp. 7–12.

5. Moore, *Homeboys*, pp. 78–82; Bruce Bullington, *Heroin Use in the Barrio* (Lexington, Mass.: Lexington Books, 1977), pp. 43–44.

6. Eric Michael Schantz, "From the 'Mexicali Rose' to the Tijuana Brass: Vice Tours of the United States-Mexico Border, 1910–1965" (Ph.D. diss., University of California, Los Angeles, 2001); Eric Michael Schantz, "All Night at the Owl: The Social and Political Relations of Mexicali's Red-Light District, 1909–1925," in Edward Grant Wood, ed., *On the Border: Society and Culture Between the United States and Mexico* (Lanham, Md.: SR Books, 2004), pp. 91–143. Gabriela Recio, "Drugs and Alcohol: U.S. Prohibition and the Origins of the Drug Trade in Mexico, 1910–1930," *Journal of Latin American Studies* 34 (2002): 21–42, places the origins of heroin smuggling slightly earlier. On opium smuggling between Victoria and the U.S., David Chuenyan Lai, "Chinese Opium Trade and Manufacture in British Columbia, 1858–1908," *Journal of the West* 38, no. 3 (1999): 21–26.

7. Moore, *Homeboys*, pp. 83–84; Testimony of William H. Parker, Chief of Police, City of Los Angeles, in *Illicit Narcotics Traffic*, p. 3579; William S. Burroughs, *Junky* (New York: Penguin Books, 1977), p. 28.

8. Moore, *Homeboys*, pp. 36–39, 51, 83–85; for the contrast to gangs in the East, see Eric C. Schneider, *Vampires, Dragons, and Egyptian Kings: Youth Gangs in Postwar New York* (Princeton, N.J.: Princeton University Press, 1999).

9. Parker testimony, *Illicit Narcotics Traffic*, p. 3566; addict is quoted in Bullington, *Heroin Use in the Barrio*, pp. 44–45; Testimony of Lee E. Echols, Sheriff, Yuma County, Arizona, Before the Senate Subcommittee to Investigate Juvenile Delinquency, box 37, file 1080, Accession number 170–74–12, Record Group 170, National Archives (NA).

10. Raymond Chandler, *The Long Goodbye* (New York: Ballantine Books, 1971), p. 31.

11. "Statement of Michael Gullon," Investigator, Ventura County Sheriff's Department, Ventura, California, Before the Senate Subcommittee to Investigate Juvenile Delinquency, May 17, 1962, box 37, file 1080, Accession number 170–74–12, Record Group 170, NA.

12. Moore, *Homeboys*, pp. 88–92.

13. Bullington, *Heroin Use in the Barrio*, pp. 88–89; Moore, *Homeboys*, and Joan W. Moore, *Going Down to the Barrio: Homeboys and Homegirls in Change* (Philadelphia: Temple University Press, 1991).

14. "Rudolph Leyvas et al—Cal–5308," box 10, file 0350, "Conspiracy 1933–1968," Accession number 170–74–4, Record Group 170, NA.

15. Quoted in Bullington, *Heroin Use in the Barrio*, p. 99.

16. *Illicit Narcotics Traffic*, p. 3693; Bullington, *Heroin Use in the Barrio*, pp. 46–47.

17. Testimony of Bebe Phoenix, pp. 3700–3705; testimony of Rae Vader, Customs Agent in Charge, San Diego, California; testimony of W. L. Speer, investigator for the committee, *Illicit Narcotics Traffic*, pp. 3763–65.

18. Gullon Statement and Echols Testimony, box 37, file 1080, Accession number 170–74–12, Record Group 170, NA; Schantz, "All Night at the Owl," passim; Patrick N. McNamara, "Prostitution Along the U.S.-Mexican Border: A Survey," in Ellwyn R. Stoddard, ed., *Prostitution and Illicit Drug Traffic on the U.S.-Mexico Border* (El Paso, Tex.: Border-State University Consortium for Latin America, 1971), pp. 1–21; John A. Price, "International Border Screens and Smuggling," in *Prostitution and Illicit Drug Traffic*, pp. 22–42.

19. United States Senate, Committee of the Judiciary, *Interim Report of the Committee on the Judiciary on Juvenile Delinquency*, 84th Congress, 1st Session (Washington, D.C.: Government Printing Office, 1955), p. 38.

20. California Assembly, Interim Committee on the Judiciary, *Preliminary Report of the Subcommittee on Narcotics* (Sacramento: State of California, 1952), p. 28; *Interim Report of the Committee on the Judiciary*, p. 38; Schantz, "All Night at the Owl," pp. 115–21.

21. McCowan Testimony, *Illicit Narcotics Traffic*, pp. 3760–61.

22. Testimony of Ernest Roll, District Attorney, City of Los Angeles, in *Illicit Narcotics Traffic*, pp. 3626–29; Testimony of David R. Strubinger, Assistant Commissioner of Customs, in United States Senate, Committee of the Judiciary, *Juvenile Delinquency: Treatment and Rehabilitation of Juvenile Drug Addicts*, 84th Congress, 2nd Session (1956) Reprint Edition (New York: Greenwood Press, 1968), pp. 121–22; *Interim Report of the Committee on the Judiciary*, pp. 36–37.

23. Testimony of Richard L. McCowan, Customs Inspector, *Illicit Narcotics Traffic*,

p. 3761; California Assembly, Interim Committee on the Judiciary, *Preliminary Report*, p. 28; *Interim Report of the Committee on the Judiciary*, p. 38.

24. Josh Sides, *L.A. City Limits: African American Los Angeles from the Great Depression to the Present* (Berkeley: University of California Press, 2003), pp. 39–47.

25. Sides, *L.A. City Limits*, pp. 46–47; Edward Bunker, *Little Boy Blue* (New York: St. Martin's Press, 1981), p. 226.

26. "In re: Narcotic Agent Michael G. Picini-Court Appearance," June 1, 1951, box 1, file 1515–9, Accession number 170–75–17, Record Group 170, NA.

27. Testimony of Megan King, *Illicit Narcotics Traffic*, pp. 3738–50.

28. "Interview of Louis Fiano," August 24, 1961, Box 15, file 0550, Book 1, 1960 through Nov. 1961, Accession number 170–74–12, Record Group 170, NA.

29. Testimony of Col. Homer Garrison, Jr., Director, Department of Public Safety, Texas, p. 2362; testimony of Walter Naylor, Chief, Narcotic Division, Department of Public Safety, Texas, p. 3349; testimony of Agent Gentry, p. 3118; testimony of Thomas Odell Hicks, *Illicit Narcotics Traffic*, pp. 3041–49.

30. David Montejano, *Anglos and Mexicans in the Making of Texas, 1836–1986* (Austin: University of Texas Press, 1987).

31. Testimony of R. B. Laws, p. 2389; testimony of K.R. Herbert, Narcotics Division, Austin Police Department, p. 2394; unidentified witness, pp. 2428–29, *Illicit Narcotics Traffic*.

32. Lawrence John Redlinger and Jerry B. Bichel, "Ecological Variations in Heroin Abuse," *Sociological Quarterly* 11, no. 2 (Spring 1970): 219–29; testimony of Mary Ann Schofield, p. 2723; testimony of Juan Contreras, pp. 2489–2509; testimony of Roberto Hernandez, pp. 2509–23, *Illicit Narcotics Traffic*.

33. Richards testimony, p. 2552; testimony of J. F. Heard, Chief of Police, Houston, Texas, pp. 2694–95, 2700; testimony of Gladys Williams, pp. 2832–39; testimony of George Hall, pp. 2841–97, *Illicit Narcotics Traffic*.

34. Testimony of C. Anthony Friloux, Assistant U.S. Attorney, Southern District of Texas, in *Illicit Narcotics Traffic*, p. 2905.

35. John A. O'Donnell, *Narcotics Addicts in Kentucky* (Washington, D.C.: U.S. Government Printing Office, 1969); David T. Courtwright, *Dark Paradise: A History of Opiate Addiction in America* (Cambridge, Mass.: Harvard University Press, 2001), pp. 122–23, 145–46; Harper Lee, *To Kill a Mockingbird* (New York: Popular Library, 1962).

36. Testimony of Mary Ann Schofield, pp. 2721–22, *Illicit Narcotics Traffic*; O'Donnell, *Narcotics Addicts in Kentucky*, pp. 78–84; 96–98; 232–33.

37. Testimony of Perry Milton Turner, pp. 2371–81, *Illicit Narcotics Traffic*.

38. Exhibit 4, "An Analysis of the Trend and Distribution of Narcotic Offenses Known to the Police in San Francisco, 1945–54," pp. 4100–4101; Table B, "Contributions of Major Racial Groups to the total narcotic problem in San Francisco," p. 4103, *Illicit Narcotics Traffic*.

39. "Statement of Supervising Customs Agent, Martin G. Scott, Bureau of Customs, San Francisco," *Illicit Narcotics Traffic*, pp. 3946–49.

40. "George Poole et al—Cal–5347," box 10, file 0350, "Conspiracy, 1933–1968," Accession number 170–74–4, Record Group 170, NA.

41. Scott statement, *Illicit Narcotics Traffic*, pp. 3946–49.

42. David T. Courtwright, *Violent Land: Single Men and Social Disorder from the Frontier to the Inner City* (Cambridge, Mass.: Harvard University Press, 1996), pp. 165–68; Ivan Light, "From Vice District to Tourist Attraction: The Moral Career of American Chinatowns," *Pacific Historical Review* 43, no. 8 (1974): 367–94; Ivan Light, "The Ethnic Vice Industry, 1880–1944," *American Sociological Review* 42 (June 1977): 464–79; Ramon D. Chacon, "The Beginning of Racial Segregation: The Chinese in West Fresno and Chinatown's Role as a Red Light District, 1870s–1920s," *Southern California Quarterly* 70, no. 4 (1988): 371–98.

43. Citizens Advisory Committee, *Narcotic Addiction*, pp. 52–53; Brian J. Godfrey, *Neighborhoods in Transition: The Making of San Francisco's Ethnic and Nonconformist Communities* (Berkeley: University of California Press, 1988), pp. 67–69.

44. Testimony of June Evelyn Lindsay, p. 3877; testimony of Doris Celia de Leon, p. 3887, testimony of Bernard Sanchez, p. 3943, *Illicit Narcotics Traffic*.

45. Johnson stayed in Harlem's Theresa Hotel, an unlikely spot for a white dealer, and frequented a bar in Harlem's Sugar Hill. Dandridge's nickname suggests his racial identity.

46. "Information Furnished by Charles L. Johnson," box 7, file 0345, Organized Crime Special File, Book 1, Accession number 170–74–4, Record Group 170, NA.

CHAPTER 6. THE RISING TIDE

1. Joseph F. Morris, "The Narcotic Problem in Chicago," pp. 57–59, and Robert V. Murray, "Enforcement of the Narcotic and Drug Laws in the District of Columbia," pp. 59–61, in *Proceedings of the White House Conference on Narcotic and Drug Abuse*, September 27 and 28, 1962 (Washington, D.C.: U.S. Government Printing Office, 1962).

2. John Helmer, *Drugs and Minority Oppression* (New York: Seabury Press, 1975), table 5.5, p. 113; Garth L. Mangum and Stephen F. Seninger, *Coming of Age in the Ghetto: A Dilemma of Youth Unemployment* (Baltimore: Johns Hopkins University Press, 1978), pp. 14–15.

3. Mangum and Seninger, *Coming of Age in the Ghetto*, pp. 7, 10.

4. Bayrd Still, *Urban America: A History with Documents* (Boston: Little, Brown, 1974), Table 4.1, pp. 356–59; Kenneth T. Jackson, *Crabgrass Frontier: The Suburbanization of the United States* (New York: Oxford University Press, 1985), pp. 241–43; Lizabeth Cohen, *A Consumer's Republic: The Politics of Mass Consumption in Postwar America* (New York: Knopf, 2003), pp. 212–27.

5. The census changed categories, which makes direct comparisons difficult, but it is likely that the "non-white" population of 1960 was mostly African American, and therefore can be compared to "Negro" in 1970.

6. Helmer, *Drugs and Minority Oppression*, pp. 110–11.

7. Mangum and Seninger, *Coming of Age in the Ghetto*, pp. 18–19.

8. Richard R. Clayton and Harwin L. Voss, *Young Men and Drugs in Manhattan: A Causal Analysis* (Washington, D.C.: National Institute on Drug Abuse, 1981), p. 7; Lee N. Robins and George E. Murphy, "Drug Use in a Normal Population of Young Negro Men," *American Journal of Public Health* 57, no. 9 (September 1967): 1580–96.

9. Eric C. Schneider, *Vampires, Dragons, and Egyptian Kings: Youth Gangs in Postwar New York* (Princeton N.J.: Princeton University Press, 1999); Claude Brown, *Manchild in the Promised Land* (New York: Penguin Books, 1965), p. 153.

10. Isidor Chein, Donald L. Gerard, Robert S. Lee, and Eva Rosenfeld, *The Road to H: Narcotics, Delinquency, and Social Policy* (New York: Basic Books, 1964), pp. 179–88.

11. Anita S. Vogel and Mary Koval, *Youth in New York City: Out of School and Out-of-Work* (New York: New York City Youth Board, 1962), pp. 14, 17.

12. Mangum and Seninger, *Coming of Age in the Ghetto*, p. 27.

13. Helmer, *Drugs and Minority Oppression*, pp. 112–14.

14. Sudhir Alladi Venkatesh, *Off the Books: The Underground Economy of the Urban Poor* (Cambridge, Mass.: Harvard University Press, 2006). For the devastating impact of drug sales on the local community, see Philippe Bourgois, *In Search of Respect: Selling Crack in El Barrio* (Cambridge: Cambridge University Press, 1995), and Loic Wacquant, "Inside the Zone: The Social Art of the Hustler in the Black American Ghetto," *Theory, Culture and Society* 15 (1998): 1–36.

15. David N. Nurco, Norma Wegner, Howell Baum, and Abraham Makofsky, *A Case Study: Narcotic Addiction Over a Quarter of a Century in a Major American City, 1950–1977* (Washington, D.C.: National Institute on Drug Abuse, 1979), pp. 30–31; Edward Preble and John J. Casey, Jr., "Taking Care of Business: The Heroin User's Life on the Street," *International Journal of the Addictions* 4, no. 1 (1969): 1–24; Julius Hudson, "The Hustling Ethic," in Thomas Kochman, ed., *Rappin' and Stylin' Out: Communication in Urban Black America* (Urbana: University of Illinois Press, 1972), pp. 410–24.

16. *Chicago Defender*, June 8, 1935, p. 6; October 5, 1935, p. 9; February 8, 1936, p. 41; September 11, 1938, p. 18; *New Pittsburgh Courier*, April 24, 1965, p. 1; October 9, 1965, p. 1; Helen Lawrenson, *Stranger at the Party: A Memoir* (New York: Random House, 1972), chapter 9.

17. *NYT*, June 13, 1953, p. 7; July 10, 1968, p. 46; *Amsterdam News*, July 13 and July 20, 1968, p. 1.

18. Lawrenson, *Stranger at the Party*, p. 181.

19. Claude Brown, "Manchild in Harlem," *NYT Magazine*, Sept. 16, 1984, p. 38 ff.; Mark Jacobson, "The Return of Superfly," *New York Magazine* (August 14, 2000): 38–45; Frank Chapman, "People's Culture: Bumpy Still Lives in the Ghetto," *People's Weekly World*, 12, no. 16 (September 20, 1997): 17.

20. Lawrence W. Levine, *Black Culture and Black Consciousness: Afro-American Folk Thought from Slavery to Freedom* (New York: Oxford University Press, 1977), pp. 417–20.

21. Evert Clark and Nicholas Horrock, *Contrabandista!* (New York: Praeger, 1973), pp. 34–37, 39, 60–68.

22. Clark and Horrock, *Contrabandista!* pp. 79–93.

23. Venkatesh, *Off the Books*, chapter 6.

24. Robert M. Fogelson, *Big-City Police* (Cambridge, Mass.: Harvard University Press, 1977).

25. Leonard Shecter with William Phillips, *On the Pad: The Underworld and Its Corrupt Police, Confessions of a Cop on the Take* (New York: G. P. Putnam's Sons, 1973), pp. 168–69; James Lardner, *Crusader: The Hell-Raising Career of Detective David Durk* (New York: Random House, 1996).

26. *The Knapp Commission Report on Police Corruption* (New York: George Braziller, 1973), pp. 67–68.

27. Phillips, *On the Pad*, p. 115; *Fourteenth Annual Report of the Temporary Commission of Investigation of the State of New York to the Governor and the Legislature of the State of New York*, Legislative Doc. 92 (April 1972), pp. 197–99.

28. George Winslow, "Knapp Commission," in Kenneth Jackson, ed., *The Encyclopedia of New York City* (New Haven, Conn.: Yale University Press, 1995), p. 640.

29. Phillips, *On the Pad*, p. 88.

30. *Knapp Commission Report*, pp. 74–75; Phillips, *On the Pad*, p. 92; William L. Riordan, *Plunkitt of Tammany Hall: A Series of Very Plain Talks on Very Practical Politics* (New York: Dutton, 1963).

31. *Knapp Commission Report*, p. 4; Phillips, *On the Pad*, p. 88.

32. *Knapp Commission Report*, p. 92; Lardner, *Crusader*, quotes the conversation between Leuci and Codd on p. 134.

33. Lawrence W. Sherman, "Becoming Bent," in Frederick A. Elliston and Michael Feldberg, eds., *Moral Issues in Police Work* (Totowa, N.J.: Rowman and Allanheld, 1985), pp. 253–65.

34. Robert Leuci, *All the Centurions: A New York Cop Remembers His Years on the Street, 1961–1981* (New York: William Morrow, 2004), p. 173.

35. *Public Hearings of the Commission to Investigate Alleged Police Corruption, New York City* (Knapp Commission Hearings) October 18, 19, 21, 21, 26, 1971, typescript, Municipal Reference and Research Center, New York, p. 469. Leuci, *All the Centurions*, especially pp. 113–37.

36. Knapp Commission Hearings, p. 380.

37. Stephen Del Corso, Bill Erwin, and Michael Fooner, *Blue Domino* (New York: G. P. Putnam's Sons, 1978), p. 35; Robert Daley, *Prince of the City: The True Story of a Cop Who Knew Too Much* (Boston: Houghton Mifflin, 1978), p. 211; Peter K. Manning and Lawrence John Redlinger, "Working Bases for Corruption: Organizational Ambiguities and Narcotics Law Enforcement," in Arnold S. Trebach, ed., *Drugs, Crime, and Politics* (New York: Praeger, 1978), pp. 60–89.

38. *Knapp Commission Report*, p. 108; Lardner, *Crusader*, p. 136.

39. *Knapp Commission Report*, p. 94; David Durk with Arlene Durk and Ira Silverman, *The Pleasant Avenue Connection* (New York: Harper and Row, 1976), p. 37.

40. *Knapp Commission Report*, pp. 2, 56–57.

41. Phillips, *On the Pad*, p. 191.

42. *Knapp Commission Report*, pp. 110–11; *Fourteenth Annual Report of the Temporary Commission of Investigation*, p. 131.

43. Durk, *Pleasant Avenue Connection*, p. 36; Bill Davidson, *Collura: Actor with a Gun* (New York: Simon and Schuster, 1973), pp. 186–88; Donald Goddard, *Easy Money* (New York: Farrar, Straus and Giroux, 1978), pp. 243–44.

44. John C. McWilliams, *The Protectors: Harry J. Anslinger and the Federal Bureau of Narcotics, 1930–1962* (Cranberry, N.J.: Associated University Presses, 1990), pp. 40–42; 81–82.

45. Tom Tripodi with Joseph P. DeSario, *Crusade: Undercover Against the Mafia and KGB* (Washington, D.C.: Brassey's, 1993), pp. 19, 25–28; Testimony of Andrew S. Tartaglino, Chief Inspector, DEA, in U.S. Congress, Senate, *Federal Drug Enforcement*, Hearings Before the Permanent Subcommittee on Government Operations, 94th Congress, 1st Session (Washington, D.C.: U.S. Government Printing Office, 1975), p. 140.

46. Jill Jonnes, *Hep-Cats, Narcs and Pipe-Dreams: A History of America's Romance with Illegal Drugs* (New York: Scribner, 1996), pp. 191–97; Tripodi, *Undercover*, pp. 45, 155–63; Tartaglino testimony, *Federal Drug Enforcement*, pp. 140–43. For a different viewpoint, Donald Goddard, *Undercover: The Secret Lives of a Federal Agent* (New York: Times Books, 1988), p. 269.

CHAPTER 7. DEALING WITH DOPE

1. Robert F. Wagner, "Speech before the White House Conference on Narcotics," Washington, D.C., September 27, 1962, Folder: Narcotics 1962, box 213, Office of the Mayor Subject Files, Narcotics 1962–1965, Wagner Mayoral Papers, New York City Municipal Archives (NYCMA).

2. Statistics are from James Doig, "Crime, Police, and the Criminal Justice System," in Lyle C. Fitch and Annmarie Hauck Walsh, eds., *Agenda for a City: Issues Confronting New York*, (Beverly Hills, Calif.: Sage Publications, 1970), table 1, p. 252, and p. 257; Robert Snyder, "Crime," in Kenneth T. Jackson, ed., *Encyclopedia of New York City* (New Haven, Conn.: Yale University Press, 1995). On homicide, Eric H. Monkkonen, *Murder in New York City* (Berkeley: University of California Press, 2001), and Roger Lane, *Murder in America: A History* (Columbus: Ohio State University Press, 1997). As Lane notes, by the 1970s the proportion of homicides committed by strangers in the streets increased and the ability of police to clear the case by arrest declined. See p. 303. Vincent J. Cannato, *The Ungovernable City: John Lindsay and His Struggle to Save New York* (New York: Basic Books, 2001), especially pp. 525–34, blames Lindsay for failing to address crime.

3. "New Figures on Crime: Up, Up, Up," *New York Herald Tribune*, February 10, 1965; "Wagner's Fear: 'Underworld of Poor,'" *New York Herald Tribune*, February 19, 1965.

4. Jimmy Breslin and Dick Schaap, "The Lonely Crimes," *New York Herald Tribune*, October 25–29, 1965, p. 1.

5. Cannato, *Ungovernable City*, pp. 59–62; *New York Herald Tribune*, October 29, 1965, p. 21.

6. Doig, "Crime, Police, and the Criminal Justice System," Table 2, p. 254, and Table 3, p. 255; *NYT*, August 27, 1968, p. 1; November 6, 1968, p. 77; December 13, 1968, p. 1.

7. *NYT*, February 14, 1972, p. 1. Homicide rates for the Bronx were 2.20 and for Brooklyn 2.02. On crime in the garment district, see *NYT*, July 30, 1972, p. 17.

8. Federal Bureau of Narcotics, "Ten Leading Cities in Active Narcotic Addicts Reported in the United States," in United States Congress, Senate, *Organized Crime and Illicit Traffic in Narcotics: Hearings Before the Permanent Subcommittee on Investigations*, 88th Congress, 1st Session, 2 pts. (Washington, D.C.: U.S. Government Printing Office, 1963), part 1, p. 764; Mary Koval, *Opiate Use in New York City* (New York: New York State Narcotic Addiction Control Commission, [1969]), pp. 3–4; Dan Waldorf, *Careers in Dope* (Englewood Cliffs, N.J.: Prentice Hall, 1973). Waldorf's sample was 44 percent African American, 30 percent Puerto Rican, and 26 percent white (p. 6).

9. New York City was divided into thirty health districts, each of which included smaller "health areas."

10. Julius Hudson, "The Hustling Ethic," in Thomas Kochman, ed., *Rappin' and Stylin' Out: Communication in Urban Black America* (Urbana: University of Illinois Press, 1972), pp. 410–24; Paul J. Goldstein, "Getting Over: Economic Alternatives to Predatory Crime Among Street Drug Users," in James A. Inciardi, ed., *The Drug-Crime Connection* (Beverly Hills, Calif.: Sage Publications, 1981), pp. 67–84. Goldstein found (p. 70) that about half of users' daily income depended on "predatory crime."

11. James A. Inciardi, "Heroin Use and Street Crime," *Crime and Delinquency* 25 (July 1979): 335–46; John C. Ball, Lawrence Rosen, John A. Flueck, and David C. Nurco, "The Criminality of Heroin Addicts: When Addicted and When Off Opiates," in *The Drug-Crime Connection*, pp. 39–65; Duane C. McBride, "The Relationship Between the Type of Drug Use and Arrest Charge in an Arrested Population," in Research Triangle Institute, ed., *Drug Use and Crime: Report of the Panel on Drug Use and Criminal Behavior* (Springfield, Va.: U.S. Department of Commerce, National Technical Information Service, 1976), pp. 409–18; Harwin L. Voss, "Young Men, Drugs, and Crime," ibid., pp. 351–85; Carl D. Chambers, Sara W. Dean, and Michael F. Pletcher, "Criminal Involvements of Minority Group Members," in *The Drug-Crime Connection*, pp. 125–54; Bruce D. Johnson, Paul J. Goldstein, Edward Preble, James Schmeidler, Douglas S. Lipton, Barry Spunt, and Thomas Miller, *Taking Care of Business: The Economics of Crime by Heroin Abusers* (Lexington, Mass.: Lexington Books, 1985).

12. Patrick H. Hughes, *Behind the Wall of Respect: Community Experiments in Heroin Addiction Control* (Chicago: University of Chicago Press, 1977); George F. Rengert, *The Geography of Illegal Drugs* (Boulder, Colo.: Westview Press, 1996); Robert J. Bursik, Jr., and Harold G. Grasmick, *Neighborhoods and Crime: The Dimensions of Effective Community Control* (San Francisco: Jossey-Bass, 1993).

13. *NYT*, August 3, 1968, p. 24; Fred L. Cook, "There's Always a Crime Wave—

How Bad Is This One?" *NYT Magazine*, October 6, 1968, p. 38; *NYT*, June 3, 1969, p. 1; September 23, 1969, p. 1; Jonathan Reider, *Canarsie: The Jews and Italians of Brooklyn Against Liberalism* (Cambridge, Mass.: Harvard University Press, 1985), especially pp. 67–79. For a slightly earlier period, see Gerald Sorin, *The Nurturing Neighborhood: The Brownsville Boys Club and Jewish Community in Urban America, 1940–1990* (New York: New York University Press, 1990), chapter 6.

14. Cannato, *Ungovernable City*, pp. 397–439; Edward T. Rogowsky, Louis H. Gold, and David W. Abbott, "Police: The Civilian Review Board Controversy," in Jewel Bellush and Stephen M. David, eds., *Race and Politics in New York City* (New York: Praeger, 1971), pp. 78–80.

15. James Q. Wilson, *Thinking About Crime* (New York: Vintage Books, 1975), pp. 91–99; John E. Conklin, *Why Crime Rates Fell* (Boston: Pearson Education, 2003), chapter 4.

16. Jeffrey S. Adler, *First in Violence, Deepest in Dirt: Homicide in Chicago* (Cambridge, Mass.: Harvard University Press, 2006).

17. Lane, *Murder in America*; Roger Lane, "On the Social Meaning of Homicide Trends in America," in Ted Robert Gurr, ed., *Violence in America*, vol. 1: *The History of Crime* (Newbury Park, Calif.: Sage Publications, 1989), pp. 55–79; Roger Lane, *Roots of Violence in Black Philadelphia, 1860–1900* (Cambridge, Mass.: Harvard University Press, 1986); Ted Robert Gurr, "Historical Trends in Violent Crime: Europe and the United States," in *Violence in America*, 1: 21–54; David T. Courtwright, *Violent Land: Single Men and Social Disorder from the Frontier to the Inner City* (Cambridge, Mass.: Harvard University Press, 1996).

18. Courtwright, *Violent Land*, pp. 214–46; Eric C. Schneider, *Vampires, Dragons, and Egyptian Kings: Youth Gangs in Postwar New York* (Princeton, N.J.: Princeton University Press, 1999); Sudhir Alladi Venkatesh, *American Project: The Rise and Fall of a Modern Ghetto* (Cambridge, Mass.: Harvard University Press, 2000); William Julius Wilson, *When Work Disappears: The World of the New Urban Poor* (New York: Knopf, 1996); Katherine S. Newman, *No Shame in My Game: The Working Poor in the Inner City* (New York: Knopf and the Russell Sage Foundation, 1999).

19. Wilson, *Thinking About Crime*, pp. 71–86; Rieder, *Canarsie*, pp, 241–52; Michael W. Flamm, *Law and Order: Street Crime, Civil Unrest, and the Crisis of Liberalism in the 1960s* (New York: Columbia University Press, 2005). Flamm sees the crime issue as having more staying power than Wilson does.

20. *NYT*, September 23, 1969, p. 1; January 15, 1973, p. 1; January 16, 1973, p. 1; Jill Jonnes, *We're Still Here: The Rise, Fall, and Resurrection of the South Bronx* (Boston: Atlantic Monthly Press, 1986); Cannato, *Ungovernable City*.

21. Roger Sanjek, *The Future of Us All: Race and Neighborhood Politics in New York City* (Ithaca, N.Y.: Cornell University Press, 1998); Jane Jacobs, *The Death and Life of Great American Cities* (New York: Random House, 1961), pp. 121–27, 132–37; Robert J. Sampson, Stephen W. Raudenbush, and Felton Earls, "Neighborhoods and Violent Crime: A Multi-Level Study of Collective Efficacy," *Science* 277 (August 15, 1997): 918–24;

Ric Curtis, "Crack, Cocaine and Heroin: Drug Eras in Williamsburg, Brooklyn, 1960–2000," *Addiction Research and Theory* 11 (2003): 47–63; Bursik and Grasmick, *Neighborhoods and Crime*, pp. 24–45, 149–52; Ralph B. Taylor, *Breaking Away from Broken Windows: Baltimore Neighborhoods and the Nationwide Fight Against Crime, Grime, Fear, and Decline* (Boulder, Colo.: Westview Press, 2001). I am arguing that there are limits to the effectiveness of voluntarism.

22. Schneider, *Vampires, Dragons, and Egyptian Kings*, pp. 201–14; "Summary of a Proposal for an Adolescent Service Center Program," Folder: Proposals-3, box 20, Mobilization for Youth Papers, Rare Books and Archives, Columbia University (hereafter MFY Papers); Jeremy Larner and Ralph Tefferteller, *The Addict in the Street* (New York: Grove Press, 1964), p. 26.

23. "Proposal for a Fifth Year Detached Worker Program," Folder: Proposal-Fifth Year Detached Worker, box 20a, MFY Papers.

24. "Report of the MFY Coffee House Program," September 1962 to May 29, 1965, Folder: Operational Studies, box 19, MFY Papers; Beverly Luther, "Overview of Group Services," in Harold H. Weissman, ed., *Individual and Group Services in the Mobilization for Youth Experience* (New York: Association Press, 1969), pp. 112–13; Beverly Luther, "Programs for the Adolescent Addict," in *Individual and Group Services*, p. 138.

25. Edward Preble and John J. Casey, Jr., "Taking Care of Business—The Heroin User's Life on the Street," *International Journal of the Addictions* 4 (1969): 1–24.

26. Edward Preble, "Progress Report: Group and Community Approach to Dealing with Narcotic Use (the Block Approach), March 1, 1964 to February 28, 1965," Folder: MFY Program Units (Contract) Lower Eastside Narcotics Center, box 18, MFY Papers.

27. Jeffrey Chase, field notes, July–November 1964, Edward Preble Papers, in author's possession. Bruce Johnson gave me access to Edward Preble's papers.

28. Albert Fried, "The Attack on Mobilization," in Harold H. Weissman, ed., *Community Development in the Mobilization for Youth Experience* (New York: Association Press, 1969), pp. 137–62; Joseph H. Helfgot, *Professional Reforming: Mobilization for Youth and the Failure of Social Science* (Lexington, Mass.: Lexington Books, 1981); Herbert Krosney, *Beyond Welfare: Poverty in the Supercity* (New York: Holt, Rinehart, and Winston, 1966); Donald Knapp and Kenneth Polk, *Scouting the War on Poverty: Social Reform Politics in the Kennedy Administration* (Lexington, Mass.: Lexington Books, 1971).

29. Concerned Action Committee, Memorandum, n.d., Folder 5: Grand Street Settlement, box 80 UNH–SW 53, United Neighborhood Houses Collection, Social Welfare History Archives, University of Minnesota (SWHA).

30. Interfaith Adopt-A-Building, "A Portrait of the Lower East Side," June 1978, quoted in Christopher Mele, "The Process of Gentrification in Alphabet City," in Janet L. Abu-Lughod, ed., *From Urban Village to East Village: The Battle for New York's Lower East Side* (Cambridge, Mass.: Blackwell, 1994), p. 171.

31. Christopher Mele, "Neighborhood 'Burn-out': Puerto Ricans at the End of the Queue," pp. 125–40, and Neil Smith, Betsy Duncan, and Laura Reid, "From Disinvestment to Reinvestment: Mapping the Urban 'Frontier' in the Lower East Side," pp. 149–

67, in *From Urban Village to East Village*; Malve von Hassell, *Homesteading in New York City, 1978–1993* (Westport, Conn.: Bergin and Garvey, 1996), pp. 51–53.

32. David Durk with Arlene Durk and Ira Silverman, *The Pleasant Avenue Connection* (New York: Harper and Row, 1976); interview with Detective Ralph Salerno in David Courtwright, Herman Joseph, and Don Des Jarlais, eds., *Addicts Who Survived: An Oral History of Narcotic Use in America, 1923–1965* (Knoxville: University of Tennessee Press, 1989), pp. 201–5; U.S. Congress, Senate, *Organized Crime and Illicit Traffic in Narcotics: Hearings Before the Permanent Subcommittee on Investigations of the Committee on Government Operations,* 88th Congress, 1st Sess. (Washington, D.C.: U.S. Government Printing Office, 1963), pp. 912, 919–20; Robert Anthony Orsi, *The Madonna of 115th Street: Faith and Community in Italian Harlem, 1880–1950* (New Haven, Conn.: Yale University Press, 1985), pp. 102–4; Philippe Bourgois, *In Search of Respect: Selling Crack in El Barrio* (Cambridge: Cambridge University Press, 1995), chapter 2.

33. Dan Wakefield, *Island in the City: The World of Spanish Harlem* (Boston: Houghton Mifflin, 1959), pp. 105–7; East Harlem Protestant Parish Narcotics Committee, "Report Prepared at the Request of the Department of Health of New York City," May 1, 1961, box 18, and New York Council on Narcotics Addiction, "Statement of Aims for 1963," box 18, East Harlem Protestant Parish papers, Burke Library, Union Theological Seminary (EHPP papers); EHPP, "The Problem of Narcotics," May, 1956, Folder 5: Narcotics, 1951–57, box 9—series 1, administration, Union Settlement Papers, Rare Books and Archives, Columbia University.

34. Norman Eddy, "A Christian View of Addiction to Narcotics," February 1963, and Norman Eddy, "The Quest for Help by Addicted Individuals in the U.S.," September 24, 1962, Box 18, EHPP papers; EHPP, "To the Friends of Our Narcotics Committee," March 23, 1962, Folder: LENA, 1961–64, box 4, Ralph Tefferteller Papers, SWHA.

35. Interview with Norman Eddy, July 29, 1999.

36. Wakefield, *Island in the City*, pp. 105–6; New York Neighborhoods Council on Narcotics Addiction to the Honorable Mayor Robert F. Wagner, April 13, 1962, Folder: LENA, 1961–64, box 4, Ralph Tefferteller Papers, SWHA; Edwin Fancher, "The Origins and Early History of the New York Association on Narcotics Addiction, Inc.," copy supplied by Norman Eddy; interview with Edwin Fancher, October 20, 1999; George Metcalf, "Coping with Drugs," in author's possession; Seymour Ostrow, "Summary of the Metcalf Volker Bill," January 1963, File: Narcotics, box 33, U.S. Senate Campaign, Paul O'Dwyer Papers, NYCMA.

37. New York State, Temporary Commission of Investigation, "Narcotics Addiction in the State of New York," 1967, pamphlet collection of the New York Academy of Medicine; Fox Butterfield, *All God's Children: The Bosket Family and the American Tradition of Violence* (New York: Avon Books, 1995), p. 274; Michael Massing, *The Fix* (New York: Simon and Schuster, 1998), pp. 126–28; *NYT*, March 31, 1966, p. 1 and November 6, 1966, p. 1. The change in Rockefeller is apparent in his tenth State of the State message to the legislature; see *NYT*, January 4, 1968, p. 26, and Nelson A. Rockefeller, "War on Crime and Narcotics Addiction: A Campaign for Human Renewal" (Albany: State of

New York, 1966); Association of the Bar of the City of New York and the Drug Abuse Council, *The Nation's Toughest Drug Law: Evaluating the New York Experience, Final Report of the Joint Committee on New York Drug Law Evaluation* (Washington, D.C.: Drug Abuse Council, 1977).

38. Judith Calof, *A Study of Four Voluntary Treatment and Rehabilitation Programs for New York City's Narcotic Addicts*, part 1 (New York: Community Service Society of New York, 1967), pp. 5–17; *NYT*, July 10, 1966, p. 48.

39. *NYT*, October 13, 1968, p. 81; David and Sophy Burnham, "El Barrio's Worst Block Is Not All Bad," *NYT Magazine*, January 5, 1969, pp. 24 ff.

40. Interviews with Virginia S, William, Anselmo, Samuel, Edward, and Archie, Bernard Lander papers, in the author's possession. For the interviews that are not anonymous, I have used first names to identify respondents. Bernard Lander gave me access to his papers.

41. Ball et al., "The Criminality of Heroin Addicts"; Carl D. Chambers and Arthur D. Moffett, "Negro Opiate Addiction," in John C. Ball and Carl D. Chambers, eds., *The Epidemiology of Opiate Addiction in the United States* (Springfield, Ill.: Charles C. Thomas, 1970), pp. 178–201; Delbert S. Elliott and A. Rex Ageton, "The Relationship Between Drug Use and Crime Among Adolescents," in *Drug Use and Crime: Report of the Panel on Drug Use and Criminal Behavior*, pp. 297–321; Charles E. Faupel, *Shooting Dope: Career Patterns of Hard-Core Heroin Users* (Gainesville: University of Florida Press, 1991).

42. Interviews with Archie, Anselmo, anonymous male #2, Richard, Wilfredo, Luis, Nelson, Edward, Charles, Samuel, and Mike, Lander papers; Mercer L. Sullivan, *"Getting Paid": Youth Crime and Work in the Inner City* (Ithaca, N.Y.: Cornell University Press, 1989), pp. 114–15, 152–53.

43. Interviews with Virginia S, Pedro, and Charles, Lander papers.

44. Interview with Virginia S, Lander papers; Sudhir Alladi Venkatesh, *Off the Books: The Underground Economy of the Urban Poor* (Cambridge, Mass.: Harvard University Press, 2006).

45. Interviews with Nelson, Charles, anonymous male #1, anonymous male #2, anonymous male #4, Lander papers.

46. Interviews with Cecilia, Edward, Benjamin, Virginia S, Pascual, Virginia M, and Mike, Lander papers.

47. Marilynn S. Johnson, *Street Justice: A History of Police Violence in New York City* (Boston: Beacon Press, 2003), pp. 238–41; interviews with Wilfredo, Richard, Anselmo, Esther, McKinley, anonymous male #1, and anonymous male #3, Lander papers.

48. *NYT*, July 13, 1965, p. 35; "El Barrio's Worst Block," p. 25; interviews with Esther, Charles, and Virginia S, Lander papers.

49. Interviews with Esther, Benjamin, Marcellino, and Virginia M, Lander papers.

50. William Julius Wilson, *The Truly Disadvantaged: The Inner City, the Underclass, and Public Policy* (Chicago: University of Chicago Press, 1987) on the concentration of poverty.

51. Schneider, *Vampires, Dragons, and Egyptian Kings*, pp. 66–67; Samuel Lubell,

The Future of American Politics (New York: Harper and Row, 1951), pp. 93–97; Ronald H. Bayor, *Neighbors in Conflict: The Irish, Germans, Jews, and Italians of New York City, 1929–1941*, 2nd ed. (Urbana: University of Illinois Press, 1988), pp. 157–62.

52. Robert Jensen, *Devastation/Resurrection: The South Bronx* (Bronx, N.Y.: Bronx Museum of the Arts, 1979), pp. 39–44; Rodriquez quoted on p. 50; Jonnes, *We're Still Here*, pp. 117–26. On the impact of Robert Moses' construction projects, see Robert Caro, *The Power Broker* (New York: Vintage Books, 1975) and for a critique, Ray Bromley, "Not So Simple! Caro, Moses, and the Impact of the Cross-Bronx Expressway," *Bronx County Historical Society Journal* 35 (Spring 1998): 4–29.

53. Jonnes, *We're Still Here*, pp. 219–21; Johnson quoted pp. 290–91.

54. Interview with Sam Strassfield, Folder: Charlotte Street interviews, box 5, Charlotte Street, Jill Jonnes Papers, Special Collections, Lehman College Library; New York City Youth Board, *Juvenile Delinquency Profile: 1955 New York City* (New York: New York City Youth Board, 1956), table 2, pp. 23–24.

55. Isidor Chein, Donald L. Gerald, Robert S. Lee, and Eva Rosenfeld, *The Road to H: Narcotics, Delinquency, and Social Policy* (New York: Basic Books, 1964), pp. 39–40, 50–55, 69–70. While the study did not specify which ten health districts had the highest rates of heroin use, the South Bronx was the only reasonable location. In the city as a whole, the two leading social indicators that correlated with heroin use were the percentage of the population that was African American and the percentage of the population with income of $2,000 or less in 1949, while in the Bronx the percentage of the population that was Puerto Rican was also statistically significant.

56. New York State Narcotics Investigation, Testimony Given Before Attorney General Nathaniel Goldstein, typescript, New York State Library, Albany, N.Y., pp. 353–58, 373.

57. Interview with Neil Connolly, Folder: Father Neil A. Connolly, interview with Louis Gigante, Folder: Louis Gigante, interview with Mercedes Melendez, Folder: Mercedes Melendez, box 1, People, Jonnes Papers.

58. Connolly interview, Gigante interview, Jonnes Papers; interview with Ralph Porter, Folder: Charlotte Street interviews, interview with Charles and Bertha Lefkowitz, Folder: Charlotte Street interviews, box 5, Charlotte Street, Jonnes Papers; *NYT*, September 23, 1969, p. 34; September 24, 1969, p. 1; October 31, 1969, p. 38; Joseph P. Fitzpatrick, "Drugs and Puerto Ricans in New York City," in Ronald Glick and Joan Moore, eds., *Drugs in Hispanic Communities* (New Brunswick, N.J.: Rutgers University Press, 1990), pp. 103–26.

59. Interview with Robert Banome, Bronx Oral History Collection, Special Collections, Lehman College Library; Dennis Smith, *Report from Engine Co. 82* (New York: Pocket Books, 1973); *NYT*, January 15, 1973, p. 19; Jonnes, *We're Still Here*, pp. 231–35.

60. *NYT*, September 24, 1969, p. 30; September 26, 1969, p. 31; October 7, 1969, p. 49; January 15, 1973, p. 19; Jonnes, *We're Still Here*, pp. 182–98, 256–58; Fitzpatrick, "Drugs and Puerto Ricans in New York City," pp. 117–20.

61. Interview with William Smith, Jonnes Papers.

CHAPTER 8. HEROIN SUBURBANIZES

1. Anne C. Gay and George R. Gay, "Evolution of a Drug Culture in a Decade of Mendacity," in David E. Smith and George R. Gay, eds., *"It's So Good, Don't Even Try It Once": Heroin in Perspective* (Englewood Cliffs, N.J.: Prentice-Hall, 1972), p. 13.

2. Robert G. Newman, Margot Cates, Alex Tytun, and Bent Werbil, "Narcotics Addiction in New York City: Trends from 1968 to Mid-1973," *American Journal of Drug and Alcohol Abuse* 1, no. 1 (1974): 53–66; Bruce D. Johnson and Andrew Golub, "Generational Trends in Heroin Use and Injection in New York City," in David F. Musto, ed., *One Hundred Years of Heroin* (Westport, Conn.: Auburn House, 2002), pp. 91–128; Charles W. Sheppard, George R. Gay, and David E. Smith, "The Changing Face of Heroin Addiction in the Haight-Ashbury," Drug Enforcement Administration (DEA) Library, Vertical File (VF): Addiction—Incidence, 1960–1975.

3. Ned Polsky, *Hustlers, Beats, and Others* (Chicago: University of Chicago Press, 1985), pp. 162–71; Richard S. Campbell and Jeffrey B. Freeland, "The Hippie Turns Junkie: The Emergence of a Type," *International Journal of the Addictions* 9, no. 5 (1974): 719–30.

4. Charles Eaton and Masato Kawasaki, "Village Aid and Service Center: Preliminary Study of Caseload of Village Residents," May 1, 1963, Fales Library, New York University, Judson Memorial Church Archives, box 63, folder 1 (hereafter Judson Memorial Archives, NYU); "Outline of Research Project on Non-Tourist Teenagers in the Village Area" [no date, but early 1960s], box 63, folder 5, Fales Library, Judson Memorial Archives, NYU. Used by permission of Judson Memorial Church.

5. Polsky notes that a comparatively small number of the younger beats used heroin because it had lost its glamour with the older group.

6. R. R. Monroe and H. J. Drell, "Oral Use of Stimulants Obtained from Inhalers," *Journal of the American Medical Association* 135 (1947): 909–15; Diane di Prima, *Memoirs of a Beatnik* (San Francisco: Last Gasp, 1988), p. 126; Steven Watson, *The Birth of the Beat Generation: Visionaries, Rebels, and Hipsters, 1944–1960* (New York: Pantheon Books, 1995); Ted Morgan, *Literary Outlaw: The Life and Times of William S. Burroughs* (New York: Henry Holt, 1988), p. 123; Allen Ginsberg, "Howl," in *Collected Poems, 1947–1980* (New York: Harper & Row, 1984), p. 126.

7. "Terry Corsi," interviewed in Martin Torgoff, *Can't Find My Way Home: America in the Great Stoned Age, 1945–2000* (New York: Simon and Schuster, 2004), p. 184; interview with Jim Grauerholz, Burroughs's secretary, in Legs McNeil and Gillian McCain, *Please Kill Me: The Uncensored Oral History of Punk* (New York: Grove Press, 1996), pp. 381–82.

8. David Crosby and Carl Gottlieb, *Long Time Gone: The Autobiography of David Crosby* (New York: Doubleday, 1988), pp. 50–51; Alice Echols, *Scars of Sweet Paradise: The Live and Times of Janis Joplin* (New York: Metropolitan Books, 1999), pp. 50–51.

9. "Narcotics a Growing Problem of Affluent Youth," *NYT*, January 4, 1965, p. 1; Charles R. Eaton, "Interim Report on Drug Use Patterns," March 1964, box 63, folder 5, Fales Library, Judson Memorial Archives, NYU.

10. Hunter S. Thompson, "The 'Hashbury' Is the Capital of the Hippies," *NYT*, May 14, 1967, p. SM14; Sherri Cavan, *Hippies of the Haight* (St. Louis, Mo.: New Critics Press, 1972).

11. Alice Echols, "Hope and Hype in Sixties Haight Ashbury," in Alice Echols, ed., *Shaky Ground: The '60s and Its Aftershocks* (New York: Columbia University Press, 2002), pp. 17–50; Thompson, "The 'Hashbury.'"

12. Charles Perry, *The Haight-Ashbury: A History* (New York: Random House, 1984); Martin A. Lee and Bruce Shlain, *Acid Dreams: The Complete Social History of LSD: The CIA, the Sixties, and Beyond* (New York: Grove Press, 1985); Jay Stevens, *Storming Heaven: LSD and the American Dream* (New York: Atlantic Monthly Press, 1987); Thompson, "The 'Hashbury'"; Peter Coyote, *Sleeping Where I Fall: A Chronicle* (Washington, D.C.: Counterpoint, 1998), pp. 75–76.

13. Don McNeill, *Moving Through Here* (New York: Knopf, 1970), p. 22; Ronald Sukenick, *Down and In: Life in the Underground* (New York: William Morrow, 1987), p. 103; "New Way Center Fact Sheet," March 4, 1971, box 63, folder 24, Fales Library, Judson Memorial Archives, NYU.

14. Yuri Kapralov, *Once There Was a Village* (New York: St. Martin's Press, 1974), p. 12; Lewis Yablonsky, *The Hippie Trip* (New York: Western Publishing Company, 1968); "New Way Center: A Program for Troubled Youth," February 8, 1971, box 63, folder 24, Fales Library, Judson Memorial Archives, NYU; McNeill, *Moving Through Here*, p. 28; Joan Didion, *Slouching Toward Babylon* (New York: Farrar, Straus and Giroux, 1968), pp. 84–128.

15. Natalie Jaffe, "Program to Aid Village Youth found making Little Progress," undated *NYT* clipping, box 64, folder 7, Fales Library, Judson Memorial Archives, NYU.

16. Yablonsky, *Hippie Trip*, p. 346.

17. Bruce D. Johnson, *Marihuana Users and Drug Subcultures* (New York: John Wiley and Sons, 1973).

18. Richard H. Blum and Associates, *Drugs II: College and High School Observations* (San Francisco: Jossey-Bass, 1969); Ernest Hamburger, "Contrasting the Hippie and Junkie," *International Journal of the Addictions* 4, no. 1 (1969): 121–35; Richard C. Stephens, "The Hard Drug Scene," in Frank R. Scarpitti and Susan K. Datesman, eds., *Drugs and the Youth Culture* (Beverly Hills, Calif.: Sage Publications, 1980), pp. 59–79.

19. *NYT*, January 8, 1968, p. 1; January 9, 1968, p. 18; January 10, 1968, p. 26; January 11, 1968, p. 18; January 12, 1968, p. 30.

20. Donald S. Louria, "Cool Talk about Hot Drugs," *NYT*, August 6, 1967, pp. 188 ff.; *Time*, September 26, 1969, pp. 68–78; *NYT*, March 10, 1969, p. 1.

21. *NYT*, July 15, 1969, p. 18.

22. *Time*, March 16, 1970, pp. 2–7; "Life on Two Grams a Day," *Life* (February 20, 1970), pp. 24–32.

23. *NYT*, February 6, 1970, p. 39.

24. *NYT*, February 2, 1970, p. 24; February 16, 1970, p. 1; March 9, 1970, p. 29.

25. Jerry M. Wiener and James H. Egan, "Heroin Addiction in an Adolescent Population," *Journal of the American Academy of Child Psychiatry* 12, no. 1 (1973): 48–58.

26. Gay and Gay, "Evolution of a Drug Culture," p. 27; Edward M. Brecher and the Editors of Consumer Reports, *Licit and Illicit Drugs: The Consumers Union Report on Narcotics, Stimulants, Depressants, Inhalants, Hallucinogens, and Marijuana—including Caffeine, Nicotine, and Alcohol* (Boston: Little, Brown, 1972), pp. 434–50, explain why this interpretation cannot be correct.

27. Interview with Dennis Thompson in McNeil and McCain, *Please Kill Me*, p. 68.

28. Alfred W. McCoy, *The Politics of Heroin: CIA Complicity in the Global Drug Trade*, rev. ed. (New York: Lawrence Hill Books, 1991). After the original publication of McCoy's book in 1972, the Bureau of Narcotics and Dangerous Drugs investigated his charges and concluded, "He has done an outstanding job in reporting the historical development of the opium traffic in Southeast Asia and in bringing it up to date (circa early 1971)." John Warner, "Critique on *The Politics of Heroin in Southeast Asia* by Alfred W. McCoy," box 1, File: New York Joint Taskforce, Accession number 170–86–0163, Record Group 170, National Archives.

29. Sheppard et al., "Changing Face of Heroin Addiction in the Haight-Ashbury"; David E. Smith, George R. Gay, and Barry S. Ramer, "Adolescent Heroin Abuse in San Francisco," *Proceedings of the Third National Conference on Methadone Treatment, New York City, 1970* (Rockville, Md.: Public Health Services Publication, 1970), pp. 89–91.

30. Jim Carroll, *The Basketball Diaries* (New York: Penguin, 1978), p. 30.

31. Cutrone quoted in McNeil and McCain, *Please Kill Me*, p. 13; Jean Stein, *Edie: An American Biography* (New York: Knopf, 1982), pp. 163, 208, 269.

32. Stein, *Edie*, Schumacher quoted p. 260; interview with Cherry Vanilla, pp. 264–65; Coyote, *Sleeping Where I Fall*, pp. 161–62.

33. McNeil and McCain, *Please Kill Me*, pp. 21–22; McNeil, *Moving Through Here*, pp. 49–50; *NYT*, October 17, 1967, p. 1; June 21, 1970, p. 198 ff; Gail Sheehy, *Speed Is of the Essence* (New York: Pocket Books, 1971), p. 55. James V. Spotts and Carol A. Spotts, *Use and Abuse of Amphetamine and its Substitutes* (Rockville, Md.: National Institute on Drug Abuse, n.d.).

34. David E. Smith and John Luce, *Love Needs Care: A History of San Francisco's Haight-Ashbury Free Medical Clinic and its Pioneer Role in Treating Drug Abuse Problems* (Boston: Little, Brown, 1971), pp. 14–19; Lester Grinspoon and Peter Hedblom, *The Speed Culture: Amphetamine Use and Abuse in America* (Cambridge, Mass.: Harvard University Press, 1975), pp. 19, 24–25.

35. Nicholas von Hoffman, *We Are the People Our Parents Warned Us Against* (Chicago: Quadrangle Books, 1968), pp. 46–47; Stevens, *Storming Heaven*, pp. 336–44; Smith and Luce, *Love Needs Care*, pp. 170–71.

36. McNeil, *Moving Through Here*, p. 151; Smith and Luce, *Love Needs Care*, pp. 3–5; Fred Davis and Laura Munoz, "Heads and Freaks: Patterns and Meanings of Drug Use Among Hippies," *Journal of Health and Social Behavior* 9 (June 1968): 156–64; John Robert Howard, "The Flowering of the Hippie Movement," *Annals of the American Academy of Political and Social Science* 382 (March 1969): 43–55.

37. Smith and Luce, *Love Needs Care*, pp. 17–20; Brecher, *Licit and Illicit Drugs*, pp. 281–89; *NYT*, June 21, 1970, pp. 198ff.

38. Gay and Gay, "Evolution of a Drug Culture," pp. 26–27; James T. Carey and Jerry Mandel, "A San Francisco Bay Area 'Speed' Scene," *Journal of Health and Social Behavior* 9 (June 1968): 164–74.

39. *NYT*, June 21, 1970, pp. 198 ff; Harrison Pope, Jr., *Voices from the Drug Culture* (Boston: Beacon Press, 1971), p. 107; Roger C. Smith and D. Crim, "Compulsive Methamphetamine Abuse and Violence in Haight-Ashbury," DEA Library, VF Addiction-Crime, 1950–1975; Roger C. Smith, "The World of the Haight-Ashbury Speed Freak," *Journal of Psychedelic Drugs* 2 (1969): 20–24; McNeil and McCain, *Please Kill Me*, interview with Peter Jordan, p. 153. In one sample, 96 percent of the male and 85 percent of the female amphetamine injectors also injected a "hard narcotic" (heroin, morphine, Demerol), but it is not clear which use came first. Jan Howard and Phillip Borges, "Needle Sharing in the Haight: Some Social and Psychological Functions," *Journal of Health and Social Behavior* 11 (September 1970): 220–30.

40. Sheppard et al., "Changing Face of Heroin Addiction in the Haight-Ashbury"; George R. Gay, John A. Newmeyer, and John J. Winkler, "The Haight-Ashbury Free Medical Clinic," in Smith and Gay, *"It's So Good, Don't Even Try It Once,"* pp. 71–85.

41. John A. Newmeyer and George R. Gay, "Observations on the Changing Face of Heroin Addiction in a San Francisco Clinic Population," Proceedings of the 48th Congress of the International Anesthesia Research Society, pp. 717–22, DEA Library, VF: Addiction.

42. Smith and Luce, *Love Needs Care*, pp. 218–19.

43. Gay, Newmeyer, and Winkler, "The Haight-Ashbury Free Medical Clinic," pp. 82–83.

44. G. Thomas Gitchoff, *Kids, Cops, and Kilos: A Study of Contemporary Suburban Youth* (San Diego: Malter-Westerfield, 1969). Gitchoff estimated that it took six months for drugs popular in the Haight to make an appearance in "Pleasant Hill."

45. Marvin A. Lavenhar and Amiram Sheffet, "Recent Trends in Nonmedical Use of Drugs Reported by Students in Two Suburban New Jersey Communities," *Preventive Medicine* 2 (1973): 490–509.

46. David Courtwright, Herman Joseph, and Don Des Jarlais, interview with Peter Santangelo, "Addicts Who Survived" Collection, Oral History Center, Columbia University.

47. Editors and staff of *Newsday*, *The Heroin Trail* (New York: Signet Books, 1973), pp. 269, 281–82, 286, 303–5.

48. "Interview with Edward Prince," July 12, 1970, Box 4, Gwendolyn Midlo Hall Papers, Michigan Historical Collection, Bentley Historical Library, University of Michigan (Hall Papers); for Kalamazoo, interview with Janet Golden, September 21, 2004.

49. Robert Levengood, Paul Lowinger, and Kenneth Schoof, "Heroin Addiction in the Suburbs: An Epidemiological Study," DEA Library, VF Addiction—Incidence, 1960–1975.

50. John A. O'Donnell and Richard R. Clayton, "Determinants of Early Marijuana Use," in George M. Beschner and Alfred S. Friedman, eds., *Youth Drug Abuse: Problems, Issues and Treatment* (Lexington, Mass.: Lexington Books, 1979), p. 65; Clyde McCoy, Duane C. McBride, Brian R. Ruse, J. Bryan Page, and Richard R. Clayton, "Youth Opiate Use," in *Youth Drug Abuse*, pp. 353–75; Judith Green, "Overview of Adolescent Drug Use," in *Youth Drug Abuse*, pp. 17–44.

51. "Heroin Crisis Ending? Signs Point that Way," *Medical World News* 14, no. 15 (1973): 15–17; Robert L. DuPont and Mark H. Green, "The Decline of Heroin Addiction in the District of Columbia," DEA Library, VF Addiction—Incidence, 1960–1975.

CHAPTER 9. THE WAR AND THE WAR AT HOME

1. Richard R. Clayton, "Federal Drugs-Crime Research: Setting the Agenda," in James A. Inciardi, ed., *The Drugs-Crime Connection* (Beverly Hills, Calif.: Sage Publications, 1981), pp. 17–38; Lee N. Robins, *The Vietnam Drug User Returns* (Washington D.C.: Special Action Office for Drug Abuse Prevention, 1973); John J. Brody and Robert K. Boyer, *The U.S. Heroin Problem and Southeast Asia: Report of a Staff Survey Team of the Committee on Foreign Affairs, House of Representatives* (Washington, D.C.: U.S. Government Printing Office, 1973), p. 41; *NYT*, May 16, 1971, p. 1; David F. Musto and Pamela Korsmeyer, *The Quest for Drug Control: Politics and Federal Policy in a Period of Increasing Substance Abuse, 1963–1981* (New Haven, Conn.: Yale University Press, 2002), pp. 48–53.

2. Edward Jay Epstein, "The Krogh File—the Politics of 'Law and Order'," *Public Interest* 39 (Spring 1975): 99–124.

3. Byron Stinson, "The Army Disease," *American History Illustrated* 6 (1971): 10–17.

4. *NYT*, March 16, 1970, p. 24; March 21, 1970, p. 26; March 22, 1970, p. 19; March 25, 1970, p. 14; March 26, 1970, p. 14; March 29, 1970, p. 146; June 8, 1970, p. 36; July 23, 1970, p. 8; August 19, 1970, p. 16; August 21, 1970, p. 9; October 31, 1970, p. 3; November 20, 1970, p. 11; May 16, 1971, p. 1; January 5, 1971, p. 34; January 8, 1971, p. 6.

5. Carl A. Trocki, *Opium, Empire and the Global Political Economy: A Study of the Asian Opium Trade, 1750–1950* (London: Routledge, 1999), chapters 7 and 8; Alfred W. McCoy, *The Politics of Heroin: CIA Complicity in the Global Drug Trade* (New York: Lawrence Hill Books, 1991), chapter 5; Richard G. Du Rant, "Marijuana Use in Asia, Especially Vietnam, by the Military and Civilians," August 22, 1969, Vertical File (VF), "Armed Forces, 1969," Drug Enforcement Administration (DEA) Library, Arlington, Va.

6. NBC Evening News, January 24, 1971; CBS Evening News, January 6, 1971, Vanderbilt Television Archives (VTA); *NYT*, August 30, 1971, p. 1; Morgan F. Murphy and Robert H. Steele, *The World Heroin Problem: Report of Special Study Mission* (Washington, D.C.: U.S. Government Printing Office, 1971), pp. 18–29; *NYT*, May 17, 1971, p. 1; May 18, 1971, p. 10; Brody and Boyer, *U.S. Heroin Problem and Southeast Asia*, p. 1.

7. *NYT*, February 25, 1971, p. 39; May 16, 1971, p. 1; June 6, 1971, p. E1; September 12, 1971, p. 2; "The GI's Other Enemy: Heroin," *Newsweek* (May 24, 1971): 26–27.

8. Murphy and Steele, *World Heroin Problem*, p. 18; Larry H. Ingraham, "'The

Nam' and 'The World': Heroin Use by U.S. Army Enlisted Men Serving in Vietnam," *Psychiatry* 37 (May 1974): 114–28.

9. "Terry Corsi," interviewed in Martin Torgoff, *Can't Find My Way Home: America in the Great Stoned Age, 1945–2000* (New York: Simon and Schuster, 2004), p. 187; *NYT*, May 17, 1971, p. 1; Av Westin and Stephanie Shaffer, *Heroes and Heroin: The Shocking Story of Drug Addiction in the Military* (New York: Pocket Books, 1972), pp. 47, 83–84, 243; NBC Evening News, May 24, 1971, VTA.

10. Westin and Shaffer, *Heroes and Heroin*, p. 48; NYT, January 4, 1971, p. 1; December 19, 1971, p. 2; Ingraham, "'The Nam' and 'The World,'" p. 121; Norman E. Zinberg, "G.I.'s and O.J.'s in Vietnam," *NYT Magazine*, December 5, 1971, pp. 37ff.

11. Westin and Shaffer, *Heroes and Heroin*, pp. 59, 130; NBC Evening News, January 25, 1971, VTA; Ingraham, "'The Nam' and 'The World,'" p. 119; *NYT*, September 12, 1971, p. 2; September 15, 1971, p. 40; September 22, 1971, p. 10.

12. *NYT*, May 30, 1971, p. 1; May 30, 1971, p. 27; June 6, 1971, p. E1; June 23, 1971, p. 17; June 24, 1971, p. 4; June 30, 1971, p. 40; July 15, 1971, p. 1; August 5, 1971, p. 4; October 13, 1971, p. 5; M. Duncan Stanton, "Drugs, Vietnam, and the Vietnam Veteran: An Overview," *American Journal of Drug and Alcohol Abuse* 3, no. 4 (1976): 557–70; Norman E. Zinberg, "Heroin Use in Vietnam and the United States," *Archives of General Psychiatry* 26 (May 1972): 486–88.

13. *NYT*, September 5, 1971, p. 7; September 15, 1971, p. 40; September 22, 1971, p. 10; "They All Agree: _% [*sic*] of Viet G.I.s are Addicts," *Medical World News* 12 (September 3, 1971): 15–17. Eventually the services began randomized drug testing for all personnel in Vietnam, for those going on leave, and for those reenlisting.

14. Westin and Shaffer, *Heroes and Heroin*, pp. 94–95; Norman E. Zinberg, "Rehabilitation of Heroin Users in Vietnam," *Contemporary Drug Problems* 1 (1972): 263–94; *NYT*, June 16, 1971, p. 21; June 18, 1971, p. 1.

15. ABC Evening News, June 3, 1971, VTA; Musto and Korsmeyer, *The Quest for Drug Control*, pp. 87–98; Michael Massing, *The Fix* (New York: Simon and Schuster, 1998), pp. 107–12.

16. Massing, *The Fix*, pp. 97–112.

17. Arthur J. Giuliani to H. J. Anslinger, Commissioner of Narcotics, August 31, 1946; A. H. Fiske, Vice President, Eli Lilly and Company, to H. J. Anslinger, Commissioner of Narcotics, October 16, 1946; box 10, folder 0480–203, vol. 1; H. J. Anslinger, Commissioner of Narcotics, to Bibiano L. Neer, Collector of Internal Revenue for the Philippines, November 19, 1947, box 10, folder 0480–203, vol. 3; Allen Greenacre, "Methadone—Boon or Menace," *American Weekly*, July 3, 1949, box 10, folder 0480–203, vol. 4, all in Accession number 170–74–12, Record Group (RG) 170, National Archives.

18. "Conversation with Vincent Dole," *Addiction* 89 (January 1994): 23–30; interview with Vincent Dole in David Courtwright, Herman Joseph, and Don Des Jarlais, *Addicts Who Survived: An Oral History of Narcotics Use in America, 1923–1965* (Knoxville: University of Tennessee Press, 1989), pp. 331–43 (Dole interview).

19. David Courtwright, "Marie Nyswander," American National Biography Online,

http://www.anb.org, accessed June 8, 2005; David Courtwright, "The Prepared Mind: Marie Nyswander, Methadone Maintenance, and the Metabolic Theory of Addiction," *Addiction* 92 (March 1997): 257–65.

20. Nat Hentoff, *A Doctor Among the Addicts* (New York: Rand McNally, 1968), p. 113; Dole interview, p. 335.

21. "Conversation with Vincent Dole," pp. 23–24; Dole interview, p. 336; Hentoff, *Doctor Among the Patients*, pp. 113–14; J. Thomas Payte, "A Brief History of Methadone in the Treatment of Opioid Dependence: A Personal Perspective," *Journal of Psychoactive Drugs* 23 (April–June 1991): 103–7; Vincent P. Dole and Marie Nyswander, "A Medical Treatment for Diacetylmorphine (Heroin) Addiction: A Clinical Trial with Methadone Hydrochloride," *Journal of the American Medical Association* 193 (August 23, 1965): 646–50.

22. Vincent P. Dole, Marie E. Nyswander, and Mary Jeanne Kreek, "Narcotic Blockade," *Archives of Internal Medicine* 118 (October 1966): 304–9; Marie E. Nyswander, "The Methadone Treatment of Heroin Addiction," *Hospital Practice* 2 (April 1967), Reprint, VF, "Methadone, Dole-Nyswander," DEA Library.

23. Dole, Nyswander, and Kreek, "Narcotic Blockade," pp. 306–7.

24. "Methadone Maintenance: How Much, for Whom, for How Long?" *Medical World News* (March 17, 1972): 53–63, VF "Methadone-Newspapers," DEA Library.

25. Vincent P. Dole, "Heroin Addiction—an Epidemic Disease," part of the Harvey Lecture Series, VF "Methadone—Dole-Nyswander," DEA Library; "Why a Drug Addict's Habit May Not Stay Kicked," *Medical World News* (May 24, 1968), p. 58; Vincent P. Dole and Marie Nyswander, "Heroin Addiction—A Metabolic Disease," *Archives of Internal Medicine* 120 (July 1967): 19–24; *NYT*, April 23, 1968, p. 27; Andrew Moss, "Methadone's Rise and Fall," in Paul E. Rock, ed., *Drugs and Politics* (New Brunswick, N.J.: Transaction Books, 1977), pp. 135–53.

26. *NYT*, May 30, 1969, p. 1; June 9, 1969, p. 21; July 3, 1969, p. 28; August 28, 1969, p. 35; September 10, 1969, p. 57; September 16, 1969, p. 55; October 19, 1969, p. 55; March 29, 1970, p. 61; October 4, 1970, p. E 9; March 19, 1971, p. 23; September 30, 1971, p. 1; Massing, *The Fix*, pp. 86–96, 101–2; Nicholas J. Kozel, Barry S. Brown, and Robert DuPont, "A Study of Narcotics Addicted Offenders at the D.C. Jail," VF "Addiction Incidence, 1960–1975," DEA Library; *Washington Daily News*, April 2, 1970, VF "Methadone-Newspapers," DEA Library.

27. Vincent P. Dole, Marie E. Nyswander, and Alan Warner, "Successful Treatment of 750 Criminal Addicts," *Journal of the American Medical Association* 206 (December 16 1968): 2708–11; Robert L. DuPont and Richard N. Katon, "Development of a Heroin-Addiction Treatment Program: Effect on Urban Crime," *Journal of the American Medical Association* 216 (May 24, 1971): 1320–24; Urbane F. Bass, Velma A. Brock, and Robert DuPont, "Narcotic Use in an Inmate Population at Three Points in Time," *American Journal of Drug and Alcohol Abuse* 3 (1976): 375–86; Massing, *The Fix*, pp. 106, 124–25; *NYT*, March 13, 1972, p. 18; December 28, 1973, p. 26; ABC Evening News, June 3, 1971, VTA.

28. David P. Ausubel, "The Dole-Nyswander Treatment of Heroin Addiction," *Journal of the American Medical Association* 195 (March 14, 1966): 165–66; "Drug vs. Drug; Methadone Treatment for Heroin Addiction Sparks a Controversy," *Wall Street Journal,* September 9, 1969; "Methadone: Can It Get Them Off the Hook?" *New York Post,* October 18, 1969, VF "Methadone-Newspapers," DEA Library; Lewis Yablonsky, "Stoned on Methadone," *New Republic* (August 13, 1966): 14–16; *Bay State Banner,* December 7, 1972, p. 1; Sharon Stancliff, Julie Elana Myers, Stuart Steiner, and Ernest Drucker, "Beliefs About Methadone in an Inner-City Methadone Clinic," *Journal of Urban Health: Bulletin of the New York Academy of Medicine* 79 (December 2002): 571–78.

29. Gene R. Haislip, "Legal Control of the Use of Narcotic Drugs in the Treatment of Narcotic Drug Addiction," VF "Methadone Regulation, 1970–71," DEA Library.

30. Ron Miller, "Towards a Sociology of Methadone Maintenance," in Charles Winick, ed., *Sociological Aspects of Drug Dependence* (Cleveland, Ohio: CRC Press, 1974), pp. 169–98; Miller, "Methadone's Rise and Fall," p. 142; James V. DeLong, "The Methadone Habit," *New York Times Magazine,* March 16, 1975, pp. 16ff; CBS Evening News, June 15, 1971, VTA; Jerome H. Jaffe, "One Bite of the Apple: Establishing the Special Action Office for Drug Abuse Prevention," in David F. Musto, ed., *One Hundred Years of Heroin* (Westport, Conn.: Auburn House, 2002), pp. 43–53; ABC Evening News, June 3, 1971, VTA.

31. George E. Vaillant, "A 12-Year Follow-Up of New York Narcotic Addicts: III. Some Social and Psychiatric Characteristics," *Archives of General Psychiatry* 15 (March 1966): 599–609.

32. Harold Meiselas, "A Report of Some Early Clinical Experiences from the New York State Department of Mental Hygiene's Narcotic Research Unit," VF "Methadone-New York Programs," DEA Library.

33. Report from Ray E. Trussell to Herman Hilleboe, Commissioner of Health, State of New York Department of Health, May 15, 1959, supplied by David Courtwright, in author's possession; Dole is quoted in "Methadone vs. the Evils of Narcotics Addiction," *Medical Tribune,* March 26–27, 1966, VF "Methadone-Newspapers," DEA Library.

34. Rod Janzen, *The Rise and Fall of Synanon, A California Utopia* (Baltimore: Johns Hopkins University Press, 2001); Barry Sugarman, *Daytop Village: A Therapeutic Community* (New York: Holt, Rinehart and Winston, 1974).

35. Sugarman, *Daytop Village,* p. 7; Geoffrey R. Skoll, *Walk the Walk, Talk the Talk: An Ethnography of a Drug Abuse Treatment Facility* (Philadelphia: Temple University Press, 1992), p. 55; Janzen, *Rise and Fall of Synanon,* p. 55 on rates. On the decline of Synanon, see Janzen, chapter 8.

36. Judith Calof, *A Study of Four Voluntary Treatment and Rehabilitation Programs for New York City's Narcotic Addicts* (New York: Community Service Society of New York, 1967), pp. 28–37.

37. William L. White, "Trick or Treat? A Century of American Responses to Heroin Addiction," in *One Hundred Years of Heroin,* pp. 138–39; Narcotics Anonymous, *Who, What, How and Why?* http://www.na.org/ips/eng/IP1.htm, accessed June 16, 2005.

38. Sugarman, *Daytop Village*, p. 119.

39. Quoted in Herbert D. Kleber, "Methadone: The Drug, the Treatment, the Controversy," in *One Hundred Years of Heroin*, p. 150.

40. Edward Jay Epstein, "Methadone: The Forlorn Hope," *Public Interest* 36 (Summer 1974): 3–14; Nat Hentoff, "Profile: Marie Nyswander, Part 2," *New Yorker* (July 3, 1965): 32ff.

41. Robert G. Newman, Sylvia Bashkow, and Margot Cates, "Arrest Histories Before and After Admission to a Methadone Maintenance Treatment Program," *Contemporary Drug Problems* 2 (Fall 1973): 417–30; H. Joo Shin and Wayne A. Kerstetter, "The Illinois Experience: Arrest Rate Changes after Methadone-Centered Multi-Modality Treatment," *Journal of Research in Crime and Delinquency* 10 (1973): 163–76; Paula Holzman Kleinman and Irving F. Lukoff, "The Magic Fix: A Critical Analysis of Methadone Maintenance Treatment," *Social Problems* 25 (1977): 208–24; Epstein, "Methadone: The Forlorn Hope," pp. 8–11.

42. Edward Preble and Thomas Miller, "Methadone, Wine, and Welfare," in Robert S. Weppner, ed., *Street Ethnography: Selected Studies of Crime and Drug Use in Natural Settings* (Beverly Hills, Calif.: Sage Publications, 1977), pp. 229–48; Bernard Bihari, "Alcoholism in MMTP Patients: Etiological Factors and Treatment Approaches," in *Proceedings of the Fifth National Conference on Methadone Treatment, Washington, D.C., 1973*, vol. 1 (New York: National Association for the Prevention of Addiction to Narcotics, 1973), pp. 288–95; Irving H. Soloway, "Methadone and the Culture of Addiction," *Journal of Psychedelic Drugs* 6 (January–March 1974): 91–99.

43. *NYT*, April 18, 1971, p. 1; January 1, 1972, p. 1; July 24, 1974, p. 47; August 16, 1974, p. 1; CBS Evening News, September 25, 1972, VTA; "Methadone Cited in Rising Deaths," *International Narcotic Report* (August 1973), VF "Methadone New York Programs," DEA Library; Barry Spunt, Dana E. Hunt, Douglas S. Lipton, and Douglas S. Goldsmith, "Methadone Diversion: A New Look," *Journal of Drug Issues* 16 (Fall 1986): 569–83; Ethan Nadelmann and Jennifer McNeely, "Doing Methadone Right," *Public Interest* 123 (Spring 1996): 83–93; Adam Yarmolinsky and Constance M. Pechura, "Methadone Revisited," *Issues in Science and Technology* 12 (Spring 1996): 38–42; Peter G. Bourne, "Methadone Diversion," in *Proceedings of the Fifth National Conference on Methadone Treatment*, vol. 2, pp. 839–45; Michael H. Agar and Richard C. Stephens, "The Methadone Street Scene: The Addict's View," *Psychiatry* 38 (November 1975): 381–87.

44. David J. Bellis, *Heroin and the Politicians: The Failure of Public Policy to Control Addiction in America* (Westport, Conn.: Greenwood Press, 1981), p. 104; Preble and Miller, "Methadone, Wine, and Welfare," p. 242; Avram Goldstein, "Blind Controlled Dosage Comparisons with Methadone in 200 Patients," in *Proceedings of the Third National Conference on Methadone Treatment, New York, 1970* (Rockville, Md.: Public Health Services Publications, 1970), pp. 31–37; Moss, "Methadone's Rise and Fall," pp. 144–45; Vincent P. Dole and Marie E. Nyswander, "Rehabilitation of the Street Addict," *Archives of Environmental Health* 14 (March 1967): 477–80; Wayne Hall, Jeff Ward, and Richard P. Mattick, "The Effectiveness of Methadone Maintenance Treatment 1: Heroin Use and

Crime," in Jeff Ward, Richard P. Mattick, and Wayne Hall, eds., *Methadone Maintenance Treatment and Other Opioid Replacement Therapies* (Amsterdam: Harwood Academic Publishers, 1998), pp. 17–57.

45. Mary Carol Newmann, C. James Klett, and Richard Stillman, "Implementing a National Study of a New Maintenance Drug," *American Journal of Drug and Alcohol Abuse* 2 (1975): 289–300.

46. Soloway, "Methadone and the Culture of Addiction," p. 94; Jerry Stahl, *Permanent Midnight: A Memoir* (New York: Warner Books, 1995), p. 142; Seymour Tozman and Edwin DeJesus, "Portrait of a Pusher—'Mother,'" *Journal of Clinical Psychiatry* 39 (August 1978): 656–59.

47. Camilo Jose Vergara, *The New American Ghetto* (New Brunswick, N.J.: Rutgers University Press, 1997), pp. 168–70.

48. Lee N. Robins, Darlene H. Davis, and Donald W. Goodwin, "Drug Use by U.S. Army Enlisted Men in Vietnam: A Follow-Up on Their Return Home," *American Journal of Epidemiology* 99 (April 1974): 235–49; Lee N. Robins, John E. Helzer, and Darlene H. Davis, "Narcotic Use in Southeast Asia and Afterward," *Archives of General Psychiatry* 32 (1975): 955–61; Lee N. Robins, Darlene H. Davis, and David N. Nurco, "How Permanent Was Vietnam Drug Addiction?" *American Journal of Public Health Supplement* 64 (December 1974): 38–43; Lee N. Robins and John E. Helzer, "Drug Use among Vietnam Veterans—Three Years Later," *Medical World News* 16 (October 27, 1975): 44ff; Lee N. Robins, John E. Helzer, Michi Hesselbrock, and Eric Wish, "Vietnam Veterans Three Years After Vietnam: How Our Study Changed Our Views of Heroin," in Jeffrey A. Schaler, ed., *Drugs: Should We Legalize, Decriminalize or Deregulate?* (Amherst, N.Y.: Prometheus Books, 1998), pp. 249–65; CBS Evening News, April 23, 1973, VTA.

49. Zinberg, "Heroin Use in Vietnam and the United States," pp. 486–87, and "Rehabilitation of Heroin Users in Vietnam," pp. 267–70; Ingraham, "'The Nam' and 'The World,'" p. 117; Robins et al., "Narcotic Use in Southeast Asia and Afterward," p. 959; NBC Evening News, May 24, 1971, VTA.

CHAPTER 10. FROM THE GOLDEN SPIKE TO THE GLASS PIPE

1. David F. Musto and Pamela Korsmeyer, *The Quest for Drug Control: Politics and Federal Policy in a Period of Increasing Substance Abuse, 1963–1981* (New Haven, Conn.: Yale University Press, 2002), pp. 42–48, 171, 175; Alfred W. McCoy, *The Politics of Heroin: CIA Complicity in the Global Drug Trade* (Chicago: Lawrence Hill Books, 1991), pp. 67–71.

2. Mark H. Green, "The Resurgence of Heroin Abuse in the District of Columbia," Exhibit No. 11 in U.S. Congress, Senate, *Federal Drug Enforcement*, Hearings Before the Permanent Subcommittee on Government Operations, 94th Congress, 1st Session (Washington, D.C.: U.S. Government Printing Office, 1975), pp. 242–54; John S. Marr, Charles E. Cherubin, and Joseph Sapira, "Medical Indices of Narcotics Addiction: Rise and Fall in New York City, 1963–1977," *New York State Journal of Medicine* 79 (April 1979):

727–30; Michael Agar and Heather Schacht Reisinger, "A Tale of Two Policies: The French Connection, Methadone, and Heroin Epidemics," *Culture, Medicine and Psychiatry* 26 (2002): 371–96. Interviews with Stella, Mick, and Jim B, "Addicts Who Survived" Collection, Oral History Center, Columbia University.

3. Comptroller General's Report, Efforts to Stop Narcotics and Dangerous Drugs Coming From and Through Mexico and Central America, Attachment No. 6, in *Federal Drug Enforcement*, pp. 121–23; Agar and Reisinger, "A Tale of Two Policies," pp. 388–89.

4. Illinois, Legislative Investigating Committee, *Mexican Heroin: A Report to the Illinois General Assembly* (Chicago: State of Illinois, 1976), pp. 7, 14–17; Testimony of Thomas E. Bryant, President, Drug Abuse Council, in *Federal Drug Enforcement*, p. 81; James Q. Wilson, *The Investigators: Managing FBI and Narcotics Agents* (New York: Basic Books, 1978), pp. 150–51.

5. Legislative Investigating Committee, *Mexican Heroin*, pp. 42–44; *NYT*, January 9, 1978, p. 16.

6. *NYT*, December 8, 1975, p. 1.

7. *NYT*, June 28, 1975, p. 32; October 12, 1975, p. 1; December 8, 1975, p. 1; February 24, 1976, p. 39; July 26, 1976, p. 89; January 7, 1977, p. 1; Dan Greenburg, "The Ninth Precinct," *NYT Magazine*, January 21, 1979, p. 8; U.S. Congress, House of Representatives, Select Committee on Drug Abuse and Control, *Second Interim Report*, 95th Congress, 2nd Session (Washington, D.C.: U.S. Government Printing Office, 1977), p. 17; Jonathan Mahler, *Ladies and Gentlemen, The Bronx Is Burning: 1977, Baseball, Politics, and the Battle for the Soul of a City* (New York: Farrar, Straus and Giroux, 2005), pp. 6–9.

8. The Association of the Bar of the City of New York and the Drug Abuse Council, *The Nation's Toughest Drug Law: Evaluating the New York Experience* (Washington, D.C.: Drug Abuse Council, 1977); *NYT*, April 21, 1977, p. 53; Bob Herbert, "The Fleetwood Kids," *Penthouse* (August 1978): pp. 68ff; "Children in a Deadly Trade," *NYT*, May 1, 1977, Vertical File (VF): Illicit Traffic, 1976–1979; "Teens with More Money than They Can Spend," *Daily News*, June 13, 1974, VF: Mafia, Drug Enforcement Administration (DEA) Library, Arlington, Va.; Select Committee on Drug Abuse, *Second Interim Report*, p. 33.

9. New York City Bar Association, *The Nation's Toughest Drug Law*, pp. 17–18, 23–24; *Los Angeles Times*, January 8, 1984, VF: New York City, DEA Library; *NYT*, December 9, 1975, p. 85, June 26, 1977, p. 144.

10. *NYT*, August 21, 1976, p. 25; Teddy is quoted in David Courtwright, Herman Joseph, and Don Des Jarlais, eds., *Addicts Who Survived: An Oral History of Narcotic Use in America, 1923–1965* (Knoxville: University of Tennessee Press, 1989), p. 254.

11. *NYT*, December 8, 1975, p. 1; December 9, 1975, p. 85; December 19, 1978, p. 1; Fred Ferretti, "'Mister Untouchable,'" *NYT Magazine* June 5, 1977, pp. 15ff; Howard Blum, "A Heroin War Is Coming to Harlem," *Village Voice* 20 (November 3, 1975): 12–13; Testimony of Leroy Barnes, in U.S. President's Commission on Organized Crime, *Organized Crime and Heroin Trafficking*, Hearing V, February 20–21, 1985, VF Illicit Traffic-Leroy "Nicky" Barnes, DEA Library; U.S. Congress, House of Representatives, *Hear-*

ings on New York City Law Enforcement, Hearings before the Select Committee on Narcotics Abuse and Control, 94th Congress, 2nd session, November 19 and December 10, 1976 (Washington, D.C.: U.S. Government Printing Office, 1977), p. 46; Francis A. J. Ianni, *Black Mafia: Ethnic Succession in Organized Crime* (New York: Simon and Schuster, 1975); Rufus Schatzberg and Robert J. Kelly, *African American Organized Crime* (New Brunswick, N.J.: Rutgers University Press, 1996), pp. 107–39; Mark Jacobson, "The Return of Superfly," *New York* (August 14, 2000): 38–45.

12. *NYT*, December 8, 1975, p. 1; February 24, 1976, p. 39; January 25, 1977, p. 74; January 30, 1977, p. 1; *Hearings on New York City Law Enforcement*, pp. 26–27, 62; Paul Goldstein, Douglas Lipton, Edward Preble, Ira Sobel, Tom Miller, William Abbott, William Paige, and Franklin Soto, "The Marketing of Street Heroin in New York City," *Journal of Drug Issues* 14 (1984): 553–66.

13. *Los Angeles Times*, January 8, 1984, and *NYT*, February 19, 1984, VF: New York City, DEA Library; Susan Gordon Lydon, *Take the Long Way Home: Memoirs of a Survivor* (New York: Harper & Row, 1973), pp. 164–65; Richard Lloyd in Legs McNeil and Gillian McCain, *Please Kill Me: The Uncensored Oral History of Punk* (New York: Grove Press, 1996), pp. 209–10.

14. *NYT*, June 15, 1982, VF: New York City, DEA Library.

15. James A. Inciardi, Duane C. McBride, and Hilary L. Surratt, "The Heroin Street Addict: Profiling a National Population," in James A. Inciardi and Lana D. Harrison, eds., *Heroin in the Age of Crack-Cocaine* (Thousand Oaks, Calif.: Sage Publications, 1998), pp. 31–50.

16. Tricia Henry, *Break All Rules! Punk Rock and the Making of a Style* (Ann Arbor, Mich.: UMI Research Press, 1989); Thomas C. Shevory, "Bleached Resistance: The Politics of Grunge," *Popular Music and Society* 19 (2): 23–48; Bill Osgerby, " 'Chewing Out a Rhythm on my Bubble-Gum': The Teenage Aesthetic and Genealogies of American Punk," in Roger Sabin, ed., *Punk Rock: So What? The Cultural Legacy of Punk* (London: Routledge, 1999), pp. 154–69.

17. Clinton Heylin, *From the Velvets to the Voidoids: A Pre-Punk History for a Post-Punk World* (New York: Penguin Books, 1993), pp. 317–19; Steven Hager, *Art After Midnight: The East Village Scene* (New York: St. Martin's Press, 1986), pp. 51, 119; Richard Hell, *Artifact: Notebooks from Hell, 1974–1980* (New York: Hanuman Books, 1992), p. 62.

18. Yvonne Sewall-Ruskin, *High on Rebellion: Inside the Underground at Max's Kansas City* (New York: Thunder's Mouth Press, 1998); Ruby Lynn Reyner quoted on p. 132.

19. Hell, *Artifact*, p. 1; Dee Dee Ramone with Veronica Kofman, *Lobotomy: Surviving the Ramones* (New York: Thunder's Mouth Press, 2000), p. 78.

20. Stephen Colegrave and Chris Sullivan, *Punk: The Definitive Record of a Revolution* (New York: Thunder's Mouth Press, 2001), p. 64; Jon Savage, *England's Dreaming: Anarchy, Sex Pistols, Punk Rock and Beyond* (New York: St. Martin's Press, 1991), pp. 90–91; Steven Hager is quoted in Henry, *Break all Rules*, p. 53; Heylin, *From the Velvets to the Voidoids*, pp. 118–19; David Byrne, "Afterward," in Tamar Brazis, ed., *CBGB & OMFUG: Thirty Years from the Home of Underground Rock* (New York: Harry N. Abrams, 2005), n.p.

21. Hager, *Art After Midnight*, p. 51.

22. Mass quoted in Hager, *Art After Midnight*, p. 50; Deborah Spungen, *And I Don't Want to Live This Life* (New York: Villard Books, 1983), p. 263.

23. Dick Hebdige, *Subculture: The Meaning of Style* (London: Methuen, 1979); Greil Marcus, *Lipstick Traces: A Secret History of the Twentieth Century* (Cambridge, Mass.: Harvard University Press, 1989); Savage, *England's Dreaming*, pp. 351–56; Mark Sinker, "Concrete, so as to Self-destruct: The Etiquette of Punk, Its Habits, Rules, Values and Dilemmas," in *Punk Rock: So What?* pp. 120–39. Lyrics are at www.lyricsfreak.com, accessed June 19, 2006.

24. Heylin, *From the Velvets to the Voidoids*, pp. 93–95, 123; Bernard Gendron, *Between Montmartre and the Mudd Club: Popular Music and the Avant-Garde* (Chicago: University of Chicago Press, 2002), chapter 11; lyrics are at http://www.richardhell.com/lyrics2.html, accessed June 26, 2006, and reprinted under license from Alfred Publishing Company; heroin notebook, Fales Library, New York University, Richard Hell Papers, Box 10, folder 751 (Hell Papers); personal communication with Richard Hell, May 24, 2007.

25. Hager, *Art After Midnight*, p. 51; heroin notebook, Hell Papers, Box 10, folder 751; Ann Marlowe, *How to Stop Time: Heroin from A to Z* (New York: Basic Books, 1999), p. 57.

26. Sewell-Ruskin, *High on Rebellion*, p. 174; Marlowe, *How to Stop Time*, pp. 144–45, 188; McNeil and McCain, *Please Kill Me*, pp. 381–82; Untitled ms. "Before I tried it," Hell Papers, Box 4, Folder 96, and "Notes on Junk/Rock," Hell Papers, Box 4, Folder 106; Jill Jonnes, "Hip to Be High: Heroin and Popular Culture in the Twentieth Century," in David Musto, ed., *One Hundred Years of Heroin* (Westport, Conn.: Auburn House, 2002), pp. 227–36.

27. Henry, *Break All Rules!* p. 115; Hager, *Art After Midnight*, pp. 119, 131; Sharon Zukin, *Loft Living: Culture and Capital in Urban Change* (Baltimore: Johns Hopkins University Press, 1982); Linda Yablonsky, *The Story of Junk* (New York: Farrar, Straus and Giroux, 1997); Bruce D. Johnson and Andrew Golub, "Generational Trends in Heroin Use and Injection in New York City," in *One Hundred Years of Heroin*, pp. 91–128.

28. *NYT*, May 20, 1984, VF: New York City, DEA Library.

29. Jill Jonnes, *Hep-Cats, Narcs, and Pipe Dreams: A History of America's Romance with Illegal Drugs* (New York: Scribner, 1996), pp. 303–35, 367–74.

30. Jonnes, *Hep-Cats, Narcs, and Pipe Dreams*, p. 376; Bruce D. Johnson and Eloise Dunlap, "Final Report: Natural History of Crack Distribution/Abuse," submitted to the National Institute on Drug Abuse, 5 R01 DA05126–08, April, 1998, in the author's possession; James A. Inciardi, "The Crack Violence Connection Within a Population of Hard-Core Adolescent Offenders," in Mario De La Rosa, Elizabeth Y. Lambert, and Bernard Gropper, eds., *Drugs and Violence: Causes, Correlates, and Consequences* (Rockville, Md.: U.S. Department of Health and Human Services, 1990): 92–111, and Joan Moore, "Gangs, Drugs, and Violence," in *Drugs and Violence*, pp. 160–76; Terry Williams, *The Cocaine Kids: The Inside Story of a Teenage Drug Ring* (Reading, Mass.: Addison-Wesley, 1989);

Philippe Bourgois, *In Search of Respect: Selling Crack in El Barrio* (Cambridge: Cambridge University Press, 1995); Mitchell S. Ratner, ed., *Crack Pipe as Pimp: An Ethnographic Investigation of Sex-for-Crack Exchanges* (New York: Maxwell Macmillan International, 1993).

31. See Williams, *Cocaine Kids*, and Bourgois, *In Search of Respect*; Steven D. Levitt and Sudhir Alladi Venkatesh, "An Economic Analysis of a Drug-Selling Gang's Finances," *Quarterly Journal of Economics* (August 2000): 755-89.

32. Timothy W. Kinlock, Thomas E. Hanlon, and David N. Nurco, "Heroin Use in the United States: History and Present Developments," in *Heroin in the Age of Crack Cocaine*, pp. 1-30; U.S. Department of Justice, Drug Enforcement Administration, "Southwest Asian Heroin: Operation Cerberus," Intelligence Appraisal, January 1980, in "Terrorism and U.S. Policy, 1968-2002," TE00617, and National Narcotics Intelligence Consumers Committee, "The Supply of Drugs to the Illicit U.S. Market from Foreign and Domestic Sources in 1983," Afghanistan Collection, AF01520, National Security Archive, Washington, D.C.

33. "Heroin Alert: Rockers, Models and the New Drug Crisis—Are Teens at Risk?" *Newsweek* (August 26, 1996); George Kalogerakis, "Retox: It's Drugs Again," *New York* (May 1, 1995): 40-46; "Heroin Deaths Fuel Music Industry's Soul-Searching," *Los Angeles Times*, July 15, 1996, and "Musician's Death Creates Run on Suspected Heroin Brand," *NYT*, July 15, 1996, both in VF: Addiction-Music-Addicts, DEA Library; Dale D. Chitwood, Mary Comerford, and Norman L. Weatherby, "The Initiation of the Use of Heroin in the Age of Crack," in *Heroin in the Age of Crack Cocaine*, pp. 51-76.

CONCLUSION. HEROIN MARKETS REDUX

1. The Fifteenth Statewide Investigating Grand Jury, "Investigating Grand Jury Report No. 2," Supreme Court of Pennsylvania, 2001, in author's possession. My field notes from the Badlands confirm the information in the Grand Jury report.

2. American Bar Association, Justice Kennedy Commission, *Report with Recommendations to the ABA House of Delegates*, August, 2004, pp. 16-17; 23.

3. Michael Massing, *The Fix* (New York: Simon and Schuster, 1998).

4. Charles E. Faupel, *Shooting Dope: Career Patterns of Hard-Core Heroin Users* (Gainesville: University of Florida Press, 1991); Elliott Currie, *Reckoning: Drugs, the Cities, and the American Future* (New York: Hill and Wang, 1993), pp. 85-91, 253-59.

5. William Julius Wilson, *When Work Disappears: The World of the New Urban Poor* (New York: Knopf, 1996).

INDEX

Page numbers in italics refer to illustrations.

Pont on, 158; failure of, 198–201; inequities in enforcement, 201; legislation, 132, 185, 200; Nixon's initiation of, x, xiv, 203; number of prisoners and cost of incarceration, 200–201

Washington, D.C.: adolescent population by ethnicity, 99, 99 (table); crime's decline in, 169; heroin market in, 13–14; methadone program in, 165, 168–69

water pipes, 193

welfare state, growth of, 107

White Fence (gang), 79

White House conference on drug abuse (1962), 98

Wilkerson, David, 173

Wilson, James Q., 226n.19

Wilson, William Julius, 204

"wine and welfare" subculture, 176

Women's House of Detention (New York City), 130–31

work and social discipline, 204

yellow jackets (barbiturates), 77

ACKNOWLEDGMENTS

No scholar flies solo, even in a discipline in which one usually works alone. There are many colleagues, friends, students, and family members who deserve mention for their contributions to this project: Michael Katz has long been a supportive friend, his critique of the manuscript was invaluable, and his graduate student seminar offered helpful criticism of an earlier draft of Chapter 7. Howard Gillette, a friend, fellow urbanist, and pioneering explorer of the landscapes of postindustrial cities, also read the manuscript and helped me sharpen the argument. The field of drug history has several stellar scholars with whom I have shared the dais upon occasion and who have been very helpful in their criticism of my work: David Courtwright is the dean of drug scholars and generously welcomes newcomers to the field, and I have also benefited enormously from conversations with Caroline Acker, Nancy Campbell, Ric Curtis, John McWilliams, Joe Spillane, and Rhonda Williams. Bruce Johnson provided me with research leads and allowed me to copy Edward Preble's papers, the originals of which eventually perished in the collapse of the World Trade Center, and Bernard Lander gave me copies of his own research materials from the 1960s.

Alex Fleck has read several chapters as we consumed our drug of choice (caffeine), and Susan Porter, Bruce Lenthall, and Janet Tighe all read portions of the manuscript. Bert Hansen has offered sage advice on the use of images, Camilo Vergara graciously agreed to allow me to use two of his photographs, Roz Bernstein gave me permission to use a Cal Bernstein photograph, Roxann Livingston gave me permission to publish an Earl Theisen photograph, and David Toccafondi modified the map supplied by the New York Police Department that appears in Chapter 7. David Smith gave permission to use the tables in Chapter 8.

Owen Gutfreund invited me to present a paper at the Columbia University Seminar on the City, Tim Gilfoyle brought me to the Chicago Historical

Society to present my work to a group of fellow urbanists, and Mike Wallace invited me to join the CUNY Gotham Center's seminar on the city. I also had the opportunity to discuss my work in one of the Gotham Center's public programs. There are several historians of New York who have been supportive of my work, especially Josh Freeman, Steve Petrus, and Rob Snyder. The "crime gang" of the Social Science History Association, especially Jeffrey Adler, Ellen Dwyer, Marybeth Emmerichs, Mark Haller, Petula Iu, Joanne Klein, Bill Miller, the late Eric Monkkonen, Randy Roth, Pieter Spierenburg, and David Wolcott, have heard about this project for years, and I have appreciated their comments and appetite for beer.

I have enjoyed the support of the New York Academy of Medicine's Klemperer Fellowship for a summer's work in their public health collection and library, and Edward Mormon provided access to materials and opportunities for conversation as well as an early audience for some of my ideas about the history of heroin. The Gilder Lehrman Foundation supported a summer's work at the Columbia University Rare Books and Archives as well as in the oral history collection. David Courtwright and Herman Joseph gave me access to the oral histories they collected as part of the "Addicts Who Survived" collection at Columbia. I would also like to express my appreciation to the University Seminar at Columbia University for their help in publication. I presented a version of Chapter 2 to the University Seminar, the City.

No historian would survive without the generosity and assistance of librarians and archivists. In addition to the institutions noted above, I owe a debt of gratitude to the University of Pennsylvania interlibrary loan office, especially Lee Pugh; the Vanderbilt University Television News Archives; the Fales Library at New York University; the Burke Library at the Union Theological Seminary; the New York City Municipal Archives; the Chicago Historical Society; the Bentley Historical Library at the University of Michigan; the National Archives, especially Fred Romansky; the Drug Enforcement Agency library, especially Rose Russo; and the Prints and Photographs Division of the Library of Congress. Carlo Corea and Karen Kruse Thomas provided invaluable research help at special collections at Stanford University and the Social Welfare History Archives at the University of Minnesota, respectively. Jill Jonnes graciously donated her research materials on the Bronx to Special Collections at Lehman College and on the history of drug use to the National Library of Medicine and to the National Security Archives at the George Washington University Gelman Library. Bob Lockhart at Penn Press has heard me give several papers, has been unflagging in his enthusiasm for this project, and offered suggestions for the final draft. I appreciate both his friendship and his wisdom as an editor.

Reading the *New York Times* can become tedious, especially on microfilm and online, and what is now beginning to feel like a generation of University of Pennsylvania undergraduates shared in that work as well as other research tasks: Ben Berman, Sarah Bertozzi, Peter Bloom, Anthony Inguaggiato, Mark Kocivar-Norbury, Jennifer Lai, Adam Levin, Justin Lubell, Jessica Oliff, Rob Pringle, and James Yoo deserve special thanks. Greg Berger did an honors thesis on Richard Nixon's drug policies that I found very helpful, while Anthony Inguaggiato conducted a superb study of drug use and sales in Philadelphia.

Alex and Ben Schneider have grown to adulthood with my studies of deviance—what Alex once dubbed my "trilogy of darkness"—and they have even admitted upon occasion that they've found my work interesting. Their irreverent humor is the best antidote to academic pretension, and they continue to lighten up every aspect of my life.

My greatest debt is to my wife, Janet Golden, to whom this book is dedicated, and who read countless drafts of every chapter. For nearly three decades we have been partners in everything.